A Little Journey In The World

By Charles Dudley Warner

I

We were talking about the want of diversity in American life, the lack of salient characters. It was not at a club. It was a spontaneous talk of people who happened to be together, and who had fallen into an uncompelled habit of happening to be together. There might have been a club for the study of the Want of Diversity in American Life. The members would have been obliged to set apart a stated time for it, to attend as a duty, and to be in a mood to discuss this topic at a set hour in the future. They would have mortgaged another precious portion of the little time left us for individual life. It is a suggestive thought that at a given hour all over the United States innumerable clubs might be considering the Want of Diversity in American Life. Only in this way, according to our present methods, could one expect to accomplish anything in regard to this foreign-felt want. It seems illogical that we could produce diversity by all doing the same thing at the same time, but we know the value of congregate effort. It seems to superficial observers that all Americans are born busy. It is not so. They are born with a fear of not being busy; and if they are intelligent and in circumstances of leisure, they have such a sense of their responsibility that they hasten to allot all their time into portions, and leave no hour unprovided for. This is conscientiousness in women, and not restlessness. There is a day for music, a day for painting, a day for the display of tea-gowns, a day for Dante, a day for the Greek drama, a day for the Dumb Animals' Aid Society, a day for the Society for the Propagation of Indians, and so on. When the year is over, the amount that has been accomplished by this incessant activity can hardly be estimated. Individually it may not be much. But consider where Chaucer would be but for the work of the Chaucer clubs, and what an effect upon the universal progress of things is produced by the associate concentration upon the poet of so many minds.

A cynic says that clubs and circles are for the accumulation of superficial information and unloading it on others, without much individual absorption in anybody. This, like all cynicism, contains only a half-truth, and simply means that the general diffusion of half-digested information does not raise the general level of intelligence, which can only be raised to any purpose by thorough self-culture, by assimilation, digestion, meditation. The busy bee is a favorite simile with us, and we are apt to overlook the fact that the least important part of his example is buzzing around. If the hive simply got together and buzzed, or even brought unrefined treacle from some cyclopaedia, let us say, of treacle, there would be no honey added to the general store.

It occurred to some one in this talk at last to deny that there was this tiresome monotony in American life. And this put a new face on the discussion. Why should there be, with every race under the heavens represented here, and each one struggling to assert itself, and no homogeneity as yet established even between the people of the oldest States? The theory is that democracy levels, and that the anxious pursuit of a common object, money, tends to uniformity, and that facility of communication spreads all over the land the same fashion in dress; and repeats everywhere the same style of house, and that the public schools give all the children in the United States the same superficial smartness. And there is a more serious notion, that in a society without classes there is a sort of tyranny of public opinion which crushes out the play of individual peculiarities, without which human intercourse is uninteresting. It is true that a democracy is intolerant of variations from the general level, and that a new society allows less latitude in eccentricities to its members than an old society.

But with all these allowances, it is also admitted that the difficulty the American novelist has is in hitting upon what is universally accepted as characteristic of American life, so various are the types in regions widely separated from each other, such different points of view are had even in conventionalities, and conscience operates so variously on moral problems in one community and another. It is as impossible for one section to impose upon another its rules of taste and propriety in conduct and taste is often as strong to determine conduct as principle as it is to make its literature acceptable to the other. If in the land of the sun and the jasmine and the alligator and the fig, the literature of New England seems passionless and timid in face of the ruling emotions of life, ought we not to thank Heaven for the diversity of temperament as well as of climate which will in the long-run save us from that sameness into which we are supposed to be drifting?

When I think of this vast country with any attention to local developments I am more impressed with the unlikenesses than with the resemblances. And besides this, if one had the ability to draw to the life a single individual in the most homogeneous community, the product would be sufficiently startling. We cannot flatter ourselves, therefore, that under equal laws and opportunities we have rubbed out the saliencies of human nature. At a distance the mass of the Russian people seem as monotonous as their steppes and their commune villages, but the Russian novelists find characters in this mass perfectly individualized, and, indeed, give us the impression that all Russians are irregular polygons. Perhaps if our novelists looked at individuals as intently, they might give the world the impression that social life here is as unpleasant as it appears in the novels to be in Russia.

This is partly the substance of what was said one winter evening before the wood fire in the library of a house in Brandon, one of the lesser New England cities. Like hundreds of residences of its kind, it stood in the suburbs, amid forest-trees, commanding a view of city spires and towers on the one hand, and on the other of a broken country of clustering trees and cottages, rising towards a range of hills which showed purple and warm against the pale straw-color of the winter sunsets. The charm of the situation was that the house was one of many comfortable dwellings, each isolated, and yet near enough together to form a neighborhood; that is to say, a body of neighbors who respected each other's privacy, and yet flowed together, on occasion, without the least conventionality. And a real neighborhood, as our modern life is arranged, is becoming more and more rare.

I am not sure that the talkers in this conversation expressed their real, final sentiments, or that they should be held accountable for what they said. Nothing so surely kills the freedom of talk as to have some matter-of-fact person instantly bring you to book for some impulsive remark flashed out on the instant, instead of playing with it and tossing it about in a way that shall expose its absurdity or show its value. Freedom is lost with too much responsibility and seriousness, and the truth is more likely to be struck out in a lively play of assertion and retort than when all the words and sentiments are weighed. A person very likely cannot tell what he does think till his thoughts are exposed to the air, and it is the bright fallacies and impulsive, rash ventures in conversation that are often most fruitful to talker and listeners. The talk is always tame if no one dares anything. I have seen the most promising paradox come to grief by a simple "Do you think so?" Nobody, I sometimes think, should be held accountable for anything said in private conversation, the vivacity of which is in a tentative play about the subject. And this is a sufficient reason why one should repudiate any private conversation reported in the newspapers. It is bad enough to be held fast forever to what one writes and prints, but to shackle a man with all his flashing utterances, which may be put into his mouth by some imp in the air, is intolerable slavery. A man had better be silent if he can only say today what he will stand by tomorrow, or if he may not launch into the general talk the whim and fancy of the moment. Racy, entertaining talk is only exposed thought, and no one would hold a man responsible for the thronging thoughts that contradict and displace each other in his mind. Probably no one ever actually makes up his mind until he either acts or puts out his conclusion beyond his recall. Why should one be debarred the privilege of pitching his crude ideas into a conversation where they may have a chance of being precipitated?

I remember that Morgan said in this talk that there was too much diversity. "Almost every church has trouble with it the different social conditions."

An Englishman who was present pricked-up his ears at this, as if he expected to obtain a note on the character of Dissenters. "I thought all the churches here were organized on social affinities?" he inquired.

"Oh, no; it is a good deal a matter of vicinage. When there is a real-estate extension, a necessary part of the plan is to build a church in the centre of it, in order to "

"I declare, Page," said Mrs. Morgan, "you'll give Mr. Lyon a totally erroneous notion. Of course there must be a church convenient to the worshipers in every district."

"That is just what I was saying, my dear: As the settlement is not drawn together on religious grounds, but perhaps by purely worldly motives, the elements that meet in the church are apt to be socially incongruous, such as cannot always be fused even by a church-kitchen and a church-parlor."

"Then it isn't the peculiarity of the church that has attracted to it worshipers who would naturally come together, but the church is a neighborhood necessity?" still further inquired Mr. Lyon.

"All is," I ventured to put in, "that churches grow up like schoolhouses, where they are wanted."

"I beg your pardon," said Mr. Morgan; "I'm talking about the kind of want that creates them. If it's the same that builds a music hall, or a gymnasium, or a railway waiting-room, I've nothing more to say."

"Is it your American idea, then, that a church ought to be formed only of people socially agreeable together?" asked the Englishman.

"I have no American idea. I am only commenting on facts; but one of them is that it is the most difficult thing in the world to reconcile religious association with the real or artificial claims of social life."

"I don't think you try much," said Mrs. Morgan, who carried along her traditional religious observance with grateful admiration of her husband.

Mr. Page Morgan had inherited money, and a certain advantageous position for observing life and criticising it, humorously sometimes, and without any serious intention of disturbing it. He had added to his fair fortune by marrying the daintily reared daughter of a cotton-spinner, and he had enough to do in attending meetings of directors and looking out for his investments to keep him from the operation of the State law regarding vagrants, and give greater social weight to his opinions than if he had been compelled to work for his maintenance. The Page Morgans had been a good deal abroad, and were none the worse Americans for having come in contact with the knowledge that there are other peoples who are reasonably prosperous and happy without any of our advantages.

"It seems to me," said Mr. Lyon, who was always in the conversational attitude of wanting to know, "that you Americans are disturbed by the notion that religion ought to produce social equality."

Mr. Lyon had the air of conveying the impression that this question was settled in England, and that America was interesting on account of numerous experiments of this sort. This state of mind was not offensive to his interlocutors, because they were accustomed to it in transatlantic visitors. Indeed, there was nothing whatever offensive, and little defensive, in Mr. John Lyon. What we liked in him, I think, was his simple acceptance of a position that required neither explanation nor apology a social condition that banished a sense of his own personality, and left him perfectly free to be absolutely truthful. Though an eldest son and next in succession to an earldom, he was still young. Fresh from Oxford and South Africa and Australia and British Columbia he had come to study the States with a view of perfecting himself for his duties as a legislator for the world when he should be called to the House of Peers. He did not treat himself like an earl, whatever consciousness he may have had that his prospective rank made it safe for him to flirt with the various forms of equality abroad in this generation.

"I don't know what Christianity is expected to produce," Mr. Morgan replied, in a meditative way; "but I have an idea that the early Christians in their assemblies all knew each other, having met elsewhere in social intercourse, or, if they were not acquainted, they lost sight of distinctions in one paramount interest. But then I don't suppose they were exactly civilized."

"Were the Pilgrims and the Puritans?" asked Mrs. Fletcher, who now joined the talk, in which she had been a most animated and stimulating listener, her deep gray eyes dancing with intellectual pleasure.

"I should not like to answer 'no' to a descendant of the Mayflower. Yes, they were highly civilized. And if we had adhered to their methods, we should have avoided a good deal of confusion. The meeting-house, you remember, had a committee for seating people according to their quality. They were very shrewd, but it had not occurred to them to give the best pews to the sitters able to pay the most money for them. They escaped the perplexity of reconciling the mercantile and the religious ideas."

"At any rate," said Mrs. Fletcher, "they got all sorts of people inside the same meeting-house."

"Yes, and made them feel they were all sorts; but in those, days they were not much disturbed by that feeling."

"Do you mean to say," asked Mr. Lyon, "that in this country you have churches for the rich and other churches for the poor?"

"Not at all. We have in the cities rich churches and poor churches, with prices of pews according to the means of each sort, and the rich are always glad to have the poor come, and if they do not give them the best seats, they equalize it by taking up a collection for them."

"Mr. Lyon," Mrs. Morgan interrupted, "you are getting a travesty of the whole thing. I don't believe there is elsewhere in the world such a spirit of Christian charity as in our churches of all sects."

"There is no doubt about the charity; but that doesn't seem to make the social machine run any more smoothly in the church associations. I'm not sure but we shall have to go back to the old idea of considering the churches places of worship, and not opportunities for sewing-societies, and the cultivation of social equality."

"I found the idea in Rome," said Mr. Lyon, "that the United States is now the most promising field for the spread and permanence of the Roman Catholic faith."

"How is that?" Mr. Fletcher asked, with a smile of Puritan incredulity.

"A high functionary at the Propaganda gave as a reason that the United States is the most democratic country and the Roman Catholic is the most democratic religion, having this one notion that all men, high or low, are equally sinners and equally in need of one thing only. And I must say that in this country I don't find the question of social equality interfering much with the work in their churches."

"That is because they are not trying to make this world any better, but only to prepare for another," said Mrs. Fletcher.

"Now, we think that the nearer we approach the kingdom-of-heaven idea on earth, the better off we shall be hereafter. Is that a modern idea?"

"It is an idea that is giving us a great deal of trouble. We've got into such a sophisticated state that it seems easier to take care of the future than of the present."

"And it isn't a very bad doctrine that if you take care of the present, the future will take care of itself," rejoined Mrs. Fletcher.

"Yes, I know," insisted Mr. Morgan; "it's the modern notion of accumulation and compensation take care of the pennies and the pounds will take care of themselves the gospel of Benjamin Franklin."

"Ah," I said, looking up at the entrance of a newcomer, "you are just in time, Margaret, to give the coup de grace, for it is evident by Mr. Morgan's reference, in his Bunker Hill position, to Franklin, that he is getting out of powder."

The girl stood a moment, her slight figure framed in the doorway, while the company rose to greet her, with a half-hesitating, half-inquiring look in her bright face which I had seen in it a thousand times.

II

I remember that it came upon me with a sort of surprise at the moment that we had never thought or spoken much of Margaret Debree as beautiful. We were so accustomed to her; we had known her so long, we had known her always. We had never analyzed our admiration of her. She had so many qualities that are better than beauty that we had not credited her with the more obvious attraction. And perhaps she had just become visibly beautiful. It may be that there is an instant in a girl's life corresponding to what the Puritans called conversion in the soul, when the physical qualities, long maturing, suddenly glow in an effect which we call beauty. It cannot be that women do not have a consciousness of it, perhaps of the instant of its advent. I remember when I was a child that I used to think that a stick of peppermint candy must burn with a consciousness of its own deliciousness.

Margaret was just turned twenty. As she paused there in the doorway her physical perfection flashed upon me for the first time. Of course I do not mean perfection, for perfection has no promise in it, rather the sad note of limit, and presently recession. In the rounded, exquisite lines of her figure there was the promise of that ineffable fullness and delicacy of womanhood which all the world raves about and destroys and mourns. It is not fulfilled always in the most beautiful, and perhaps never except to the woman who loves passionately, and believes she is loved with a devotion that exalts her body and soul above every other human being.

It is certain that Margaret's beauty was not classic. Her features were irregular even to piquancy. The chin had strength; the mouth was sensitive and not too small; the shapely nose with thin nostrils had an assertive quality that contradicted the impression of humility in the eyes when downcast; the large gray eyes were uncommonly soft and clear, an appearance of alternate tenderness and brilliancy as they were veiled or uncovered by the long lashes. They were gently commanding eyes, and no doubt her most effective point. Her abundant hair, brown with a touch of red in it in some lights, fell over her broad forehead in the fashion of the time. She had a way of carrying her head, of throwing it back at times, that was not exactly imperious, and conveyed the impression of spirit rather than of mere vivacity. These details seem to me all inadequate and misleading, for the attraction of the face that made it interesting is still undefined. I hesitate to say that there was a dimple near the corner of her mouth that revealed itself when she smiled lest this shall seem mere prettiness, but it may have been the keynote of her face. I only knew there was something about it that won the heart, as a too conscious or assertive beauty never does. She may have been plain, and I may have seen the loveliness of her nature, which I knew well, in features that gave less sign of it to strangers. Yet I noticed that Mr. Lyon gave her a quick second glance, and his manner was instantly that of deference, or at least attention, which he had shown to no other lady in the room. And the whimsical idea came into my mind we are all so warped by international possibilities to observe whether she did not walk like a countess (that is, as a countess ought to walk) as she advanced to shake hands with my wife. It is so easy to turn life into a comedy!

Margaret's great-grandmother no, it was her great-great-grandmother, but we have kept the Revolutionary period so warm lately that it seems near was a Newport belle, who married an officer in the suite of Rochambeau what time the French defenders of liberty conquered the women of Rhode Island. After the war was over, our officer resigned his love of glory for the heart of one of the loveliest women and the care of the best plantation on the Island. I have seen a miniature of her, which her lover wore at Yorktown, and which he always swore that Washington coveted a miniature painted by a wandering artist of the day, which entirely justifies the French officer in his abandonment of the trade of a soldier. Such is man in his best estate. A charming face can make him campaign and fight and slay like a demon, can make a coward of him, can fill him with ambition to win the world, and can tame him into the domesticity of a drawing-room cat. There is this noble capacity in man to respond to the divinest thing visible to him in this world. Etienne Debree became, I believe, a very good citizen of the republic, and in '93 used occasionally to shake his head with satisfaction to find that it was still on his shoulders. I am not sure that he ever visited Mount Vernon, but after Washington's death Debree's intimacy with our first President became a more and more important part of his life and conversation. There is a pleasant tradition that Lafayette, when he was here in 1784, embraced the young bride in the French manner, and that this salute was valued as a sort of heirloom in the family.

I always thought that Margaret inherited her New England conscience from her great-great-grandmother, and a certain esprit or gayety that is, a sub-gayety which was never frivolity from her French ancestor. Her father and mother had died when she was ten years old, and she had been reared by a maiden aunt, with whom she still lived. The combined fortunes of both required economy, and after Margaret had passed her school course she added to their resources by teaching in a public school. I remember that she taught history, following, I suppose, the American notion that any one can teach history who has a text-book, just as he or she can teach literature with the same help. But it happened that Margaret was a better teacher than many, because she had not learned history in school, but in her father's well-selected library.

There was a little stir at Margaret's entrance; Mr. Lyon was introduced to her, and my wife, with that subtle feeling for effect which women have, slightly changed the lights. Perhaps Margaret's complexion or her black dress made this readjustment necessary to the harmony of the room. Perhaps she felt the presence of a different temperament in the little circle.

I never can tell exactly what it is that guides her in regard to the influence of light and color upon the intercourse of people, upon their conversation, making it take one cast or another. Men are susceptible to these influences, but it is women alone who understand how to produce them. And a woman who has not this subtle feeling always lacks charm, however intellectual she may be; I always think of her as sitting in the glare of disenchanting sunlight as indifferent to the exposure as a man would be. I know in a general way that a sunset light induces one kind of talk and noonday light another, and I have learned that talk always brightens up with the addition of a fresh crackling stick to the fire. I shouldn't have known how to change the lights for Margaret, although I think I had as distinct an impression of her personality as had my wife. There was nothing disturbing in it; indeed, I never saw her otherwise than serene, even when her voice betrayed strong emotion. The quality that impressed me most, however, was her sincerity, coupled with intellectual courage and clearness that had almost the effect of brilliancy, though I never thought of her as a brilliant woman.

"What mischief have you been attempting, Mr. Morgan?" asked Margaret, as she took a chair near him. "Were you trying to make Mr. Lyon comfortable by dragging in Bunker Hill?"

"No; that was Mr. Fairchild, in his capacity as host."

"Oh, I'm sure you needn't mind me," said Mr. Lyon, good-humoredly. "I landed in Boston, and the first thing I went to see was the Monument. It struck me as so odd, you know, that the Americans should begin life by celebrating their first defeat."

"That is our way," replied Margaret, quickly. "We have started on a new basis over here; we win by losing. He who loses his life shall find it. If the red slayer thinks he slays he is mistaken. You know the Southerners say that they surrendered at last simply because they got tired of beating the North."

"How odd!"

"Miss Debree simply means," I exclaimed, "that we have inherited from the English an inability to know when we are whipped."

"But we were not fighting the battle of Bunker Hill, or fighting about it, which is more serious, Miss Debree. What I wanted to ask you was whether you think the domestication of religion will affect its power in the regulation of conduct."

"Domestication? You are too deep for me, Mr. Morgan. I don't any more understand you than I comprehend the writers who write about the feminization of literature."

"Well, taking the mystery out of it, the predominant element of worship, making the churches sort of good-will charitable associations for the spread of sociability and good-feeling."

"You mean making Christianity practical?"

"Partially that. It is a part of the general problem of what women are going to make of the world, now they have got hold of it, or are getting hold of it, and are discontented with being women, or with being treated as women, and are bringing their emotions into all the avocations of life."

"They cannot make it any worse than it has been."

"I'm not sure of that. Robustness is needed in churches as much as in government. I don't know how much the cause of religion is advanced by these church clubs of Christian Endeavor if that is the name, associations of young boys and girls who go about visiting other like clubs in a sufficiently hilarious manner. I suppose it's the spirit of the age. I'm just wondering whether the world is getting to think more of having a good time than it is of salvation."

"And you think woman's influence for you cannot mean anything else is somehow taking the vigor out of affairs, making even the church a soft, purring affair, reducing us all to what I suppose you would call a mush of domesticity."

"Or femininity."

"Well, the world has been brutal enough; it had better try a little femininity now."

"I hope it will not be more cruel to women."

"That is not an argument; that is a stab. I fancy you are altogether skeptical about woman. Do you believe in her education?"

"Up to a certain point, or rather, I should say, after a certain point."

"That's it," spoke up my wife, shading her eyes from the fire with a fan. "I begin to have my doubts about education as a panacea. I've noticed that girls with only a smattering and most of them in the nature of things can go, no further are more liable to temptations."

"That is because 'education' is mistaken for the giving of information without training, as we are finding out in England," said Mr. Lyon.

"Or that it is dangerous to awaken the imagination without a heavy ballast of principle," said Mr. Morgan.

"That is a beautiful sentiment," Margaret exclaimed, throwing back her head, with a flash from her eyes. "That ought to shut out women entirely. Only I cannot see how teaching women what men know is going to give them any less principle than men have. It has seemed to me a long while that the time has come for treating women like human beings, and giving them the responsibility of their position."

"And what do you want, Margaret?" I asked.

"I don't know exactly what I do want," she answered, sinking back in her chair, sincerity coming to modify her enthusiasm. "I don't want to go to Congress, or be a sheriff, or a lawyer, or a locomotive engineer. I want the freedom of my own being, to be interested in everything in the world, to feel its life as men do. You don't know what it is to have an inferior person condescend to you simply because he is a man."

"Yet you wish to be treated as a woman?" queried Mr. Morgan.

"Of course. Do you think I want to banish romance out of the world?"

"You are right, my dear," said my wife. "The only thing that makes society any better than an industrial ant-hill is the love between women and men, blind and destructive as it often is."

"Well," said Mrs. Morgan, rising to go, "having got back to first principles "

"You think it is best to take your husband home before he denies even them," Mr. Morgan added.

When the others had gone, Margaret sat by the fire, musing, as if no one else were in the room. The Englishman, still alert and eager for information, regarded her with growing interest. It came into my mind as odd that, being such an uninteresting people as we are, the English should be so curious about us. After an interval, Mr. Lyon said:

"I beg your pardon, Miss Debree, but would you mind telling me whether the movement of Women's Rights is gaining in America?"

"I'm sure I don't know, Mr. Lyon," Margaret replied, after a pause, with a look of weariness. "I'm tired of all the talk about it. I wish men and women, every soul of them, would try to make the most of themselves, and see what would come of that."

"But in some places they vote about schools, and you have conventions "

"Did you ever attend any kind of convention yourself, Mr. Lyon?"

"I? No. Why?"

"Oh, nothing. Neither did I. But you have a right to, you know. I should like to ask you one question, Mr. Lyon," the girl, continued, rising.

"Should be most obliged."

"Why is it that so few English women marry Americans?"

"I I never thought of that," he stammered, reddening. "Perhaps perhaps it's because of American women."

"Thank you," said Margaret, with a little courtesy. "It's very nice of you to say that. I can begin to see now why so many American women marry Englishmen."

The Englishman blushed still more, and Margaret said good-night.

It was quite evident the next day that Margaret had made an impression on our visitor, and that he was struggling with some new idea.

"Did you say, Mrs. Fairchild," he asked my wife, "that Miss Debree is a teacher? It seems very odd."

"No; I said she taught in one of our schools. I don't think she is exactly a teacher."

"Not intending always to teach?"

"I don't suppose she has any definite intentions, but I never think of her as a teacher."

"She's so bright, and and interesting, don't you think? So American?"

"Yes; Miss Debree is one of the exceptions."

"Oh, I didn't mean that all American women were as clever as Miss Debree."

"Thank you," said my wife. And Mr. Lyon looked as if he couldn't see why she should thank him.

The cottage in which Margaret lived with her aunt, Miss Forsythe, was not far from our house. In summer it was very pretty, with its vine-shaded veranda across the front; and even in winter, with the inevitable raggedness of deciduous vines, it had an air of refinement, a promise which the cheerful interior more than fulfilled. Margaret's parting word to my wife the night before had been that she thought her aunt would like to see the "chrysalis earl," and as Mr. Lyon had expressed a desire to see something more of what he called the "gentry" of New England, my wife ended their afternoon walk at Miss Forsythe's.

It was one of the winter days which are rare in New England, but of which there had been a succession all through the Christmas holidays. Snow had not yet come, all the earth was brown and frozen, whichever way you looked the interlacing branches and twigs of the trees made a delicate lace-work, the sky was gray-blue, and the low-sailing sun had just enough heat to evoke moisture from the frosty ground and suffuse the atmosphere into softness, in which all the landscape became poetic. The phenomenon known as "red sunsets" was faintly repeated in the greenish crimson glow along the violet hills, in which Venus burned like a jewel.

There was a fire smoldering on the hearth in the room they entered, which seemed to be sitting-room, library, parlor, all in one; the old table of oak, too substantial for ornament, was strewn with late periodicals and pamphlets English, American, and French and with books which lay unarranged as they were thrown down from recent reading. In the centre was a bunch of red roses in a pale-blue Granada jug. Miss Forsythe rose from a seat in the western window, with a book in her hand, to greet her callers. She was slender, like Margaret, but taller, with soft brown eyes and hair streaked with gray, which, sweeping plainly aside from her forehead in a fashion then antiquated, contrasted finely with the flush of pink in her cheeks. This flush did not suggest youth, but rather ripeness, the tone that comes with the lines made in the face by gentle acceptance of the inevitable in life. In her quiet and self-possessed manner there was a little note of graceful timidity, not perhaps noticeable in itself, but in contrast with that unmistakable air of confidence which a woman married always has, and which in the unrefined becomes assertive, an exaggerated notion of her importance, of the value added to her opinions by the act of marriage. You can see it in her air the moment she walks away from the altar, keeping step to Mendelssohn's tune. Jack Sharpley says that she always seems to be saying, "Well, I've done it once for all." This assumption of the married must be one of the hardest things for single women to bear in their self-congratulating sisters.

I have no doubt that Georgiana Forsythe was a charming girl, spirited and handsome; for the beauty of her years, almost pathetic in its dignity and self-renunciation, could not have followed mere prettiness or a commonplace experience. What that had been I never inquired, but it had not soured her. She was not communicative nor confidential, I fancy, with any one, but she was always friendly and sympathetic to the trouble of others, and helpful in an undemonstrative way. If she herself had a secret feeling that her life was a failure, it never impressed her friends so, it was so even, and full of good offices and quiet enjoyment. Heaven only knows, however, the pathos of this apparently undisturbed life. For did a woman ever live who would not give all the years of tasteless serenity, for one year, for one month, for one hour, of the uncalculating delirium of love poured out upon a man who returned it? It may be better for the world that there are these women to whom life has still some mysteries, who are capable of illusions and the sweet sentimentality that grows out of a romance unrealized.

Although the recent books were on Miss Forsythe's table, her tastes and culture were of the past age. She admired Emerson and Tennyson. One may keep current with the news of the world without changing his principles. I imagine that Miss Forsythe read without injury to herself the passionate and the pantheistic novels of the young women who have come forward in these days of emancipation to teach their grandmothers a new basis of morality, and to render meaningless all the consoling epitaphs on the mossy New England gravestones. She read Emerson for his sweet spirit, for his belief in love and friendship, her simple Congregationalist faith remaining undisturbed by his philosophy, from which she took only a habit of toleration.

"Miss Debree has gone to church," she said, in answer to Mr. Lyon's glance around the room.

"To vespers?"

"I believe they call it that. Our evening meetings, you know, only begin at early candlelight."

"And you do not belong to the Church?"

"Oh, yes, to the ancient aristocratic church of colonial times," she replied, with a little smile of amusement. "My niece has stepped off Plymouth Rock."

"And was your religion founded on Plymouth Rock?"

"My niece says so when I rally her deserting the faith of her fathers," replied Miss Forsythe, laughing at the working of the Episcopalian mind.

"I should like to understand about that; I mean about the position of Dissenters in America."

"I'm afraid I could not help you, Mr. Lyon. I fancy an Englishman would have to be born again, as the phrase used to be, to comprehend that."

While Mr. Lyon was still unsatisfied on this point, he found the conversation shifted to the other side. Perhaps it was a new experience to him that women should lead and not follow in conversation. At any rate, it was an experience that put him at his ease. Miss Forsythe was a great admirer of Gladstone and of General Gordon, and she expressed her admiration with a knowledge that showed she had read the English newspapers.

"Yet I confess I don't comprehend Gladstone's conduct with regard to Egypt and Gordon's relief," she said.

"Perhaps," interposed my wife, "it would have been better for Gordon if he had trusted Providence more and Gladstone less."

"I suppose it was Gladstone's humanity that made him hesitate."

"To bombard Alexandria?" asked Mr. Lyon, with a look of asperity.

"That was a mistake to be expected of a Tory, but not of Mr. Gladstone, who seems always seeking the broadest principles of justice in his statesmanship."

"Yes, we regard Mr. Gladstone as a very great man, Miss Forsythe. He is broad enough. You know we consider him a rhetorical phenomenon. Unfortunately he always 'muffs' anything he touches."

"I suspected," Miss Forsythe replied, after a moment, "that party spirit ran as high in England as it does with us, and is as personal."

Mr. Lyon disclaimed any personal feeling, and the talk drifted into a comparison of English and American politics, mainly with reference to the social factor in English politics, which is so little an element here.

In the midst of the talk Margaret came in. The brisk walk in the rosy twilight had heightened her color, and given her a glowing expression which her face had not the night before, and a tenderness and softness, an unworldliness, brought from the quiet hour in the church.

"My lady comes at last,

Timid and stepping fast,

And hastening hither,

Her modest eyes downcast."

She greeted the stranger with a Puritan undemonstrativeness, and as if not exactly aware of his presence.

"I should like to have gone to vespers if I had known," said Mr. Lyon, after an embarrassing pause.

"Yes?" asked the girl, still abstractedly. "The world seems in a vesper mood," she added, looking out the west windows at the red sky and the evening star.

In truth Nature herself at the moment suggested that talk was an impertinence. The callers rose to go, with an exchange of neighborhood friendliness and invitations.

"I had no idea," said Mr. Lyon, as they walked homeward, "what the New World was like."

III

Mr. Lyon's invitation was for a week. Before the end of the week I was called to New York to consult Mr. Henderson in regard to a railway investment in the West, which was turning out more permanent than profitable. Rodney Henderson the name later became very familiar to the public in connection with a certain Congressional investigation was a graduate of my own college, a New Hampshire boy, a lawyer by profession, who practiced, as so many American lawyers do, in Wall Street, in political combinations, in Washington, in railways. He was already known as a rising man.

When I returned Mr. Lyon was still at our house. I understood that my wife had persuaded him to extend his visit a proposal he was little reluctant to fall in with, so interested had he become in studying social life in America. I could well comprehend this, for we are all making a "study" of something in this age, simple enjoyment being considered an unworthy motive. I was glad to see that the young Englishman was improving himself, broadening his knowledge of life, and not wasting the golden hours of youth. Experience is what we all need, and though love or love-making cannot be called a novelty, there is something quite fresh about the study of it in the modern spirit.

Mr. Lyon had made himself very agreeable to the little circle, not less by his inquiring spirit than by his unaffected manners, by a kind of simplicity which women recognize as unconscious, the result of an inherited habit of not thinking about one's position. In excess it may be very disagreeable, but when it is combined with genuine good-nature and no self-assertion, it is attractive. And although American women like a man who is aggressive towards the world and combative, there is the delight of novelty in one who has leisure to be agreeable, leisure for them, and who seems to their imagination to have a larger range in life than those who are driven by business one able to offer the peace and security of something attained.

There had been several little neighborhood entertainments, dinners at the Morgans' and at Mrs. Fletcher's, and an evening cup of tea at Miss Forsythe's. In fact Margaret and Mr. Lyon had been thrown much together. He had accompanied her to vespers, and they had taken a wintry walk or two together before the snow came. My wife had not managed it she assured me of that; but she had not felt authorized to interfere; and she had visited the public library and looked into the British Peerage. Men were so suspicious. Margaret was quite able to take care of herself. I admitted that, but I suggested that the Englishman was a stranger in a strange land, that he was far from home, and had perhaps a weakened sense of those powerful social influences which must, after all, control him in the end. The only response to this was, "I think, dear, you'd better wrap him up in cotton and send him back to his family."

Among her other activities Margaret was interested in a mission school in the city, to which she devoted an occasional evening and Sunday afternoons. This was a new surprise for Mr. Lyon. Was this also a part of the restlessness of American life? At Mrs. Howe's german the other evening the girl had seemed wholly absorbed in dress, and the gayety of the serious formality of the occasion, feeling the responsibility of it scarcely less than the "leader." Yet her mind was evidently much occupied with the "condition of women," and she taught in a public school. He could not at all make it out. Was she any more serious about the german than about the mission school? It seemed odd at her age to take life so seriously. And was she serious in all her various occupations, or only experimenting? There was a certain mocking humor in the girl that puzzled the Englishman still more.

"I have not seen much of your life," he said one night to Mr. Morgan; "but aren't most American women a little restless, seeking an occupation?"

"Perhaps they have that appearance; but about the same number find it, as formerly, in marriage."

"But I mean, you know, do they look to marriage as an end so much?"

"I don't know that they ever did look to marriage as anything but a means."

"I can tell you, Mr. Lyon," my wife interrupted, "you will get no information out of Mr. Morgan; he is a scoffer."

"Not at all, I do assure you," Morgan replied. "I am just a humble observer. I see that there is a change going on, but I cannot comprehend it. When I was young, girls used to go in for society; they danced their feet off from seventeen to twenty-one. I never heard anything about any occupation; they had their swing and their fling, and their flirtations; they appeared to be skimming off of those impressionable, joyous years the cream of life."

"And you think that fitted them for the seriousness of life?" asked his wife.

"Well, I am under the impression that very good women came out of that society. I got one out of that dancing crowd who has been serious enough for me."

"And little enough you have profited by it," said Mrs. Morgan.

"I'm content. But probably I'm old-fashioned. There is quite another spirit now. Girls out of pinafores must begin seriously to consider some calling. All their flirtation from seventeen to twenty-one is with some occupation. All their dancing days they must go to college, or in some way lay the foundation for a useful life. I suppose it's all right. No doubt we shall have a much higher style of women in the future than we ever had in the past."

"You allow nothing," said Mrs. Fletcher, "for the necessity of earning a living in these days of competition. Women never will come to their proper position in the world, even as companions of men, which you regard as their highest office, until they have the ability to be self-supporting."

"Oh, I admitted the fact of the independence of women a long time ago. Every one does that before he comes to middle life. About the shifting all round of this burden of earning a living, I am not so sure. It does not appear yet to make competition any less; perhaps competition would disappear if everybody did earn his own living and no more. I wonder, by-the-way, if the girls, the young women, of the class we seem to be discussing ever do earn as much as would pay the wages of the servants who are hired to do the housework in their places?"

"That is a most ignoble suggestion," I could not help saying, "when you know that the object in modern life is the cultivation of the mind, the elevation of women, and men also, in intellectual life."

"I suppose so. I should like to have asked Abigail Adams's opinion on the way to do it."

"One would think," I said, "that you didn't know that the spinning-jenny and the stocking-knitter had been invented. Given these, the women's college was a matter of course."

"Oh, I'm a believer in all kinds of machinery anything to save labor. Only, I have faith that neither the jenny nor the college will change human nature, nor take the romance out of life."

"So have I," said my wife. "I've heard two things affirmed: that women who receive a scientific or professional education lose their faith, become usually agnostics, having lost sensitiveness to the mysteries of life."

"And you think, therefore, that they should not have a scientific education?"

"No, unless all scientific prying into things is a mistake. Women may be more likely at first to be upset than men, but they will recover their balance when the novelty is worn off. No amount of science will entirely change their emotional nature; and besides, with all our science, I don't see that the supernatural has any less hold on this generation than on the former."

"Yes, and you might say the world was never before so credulous as it is now. But what was the other thing?"

"Why, that co-education is likely to diminish marriages among the co-educated. Daily familiarity in the classroom at the most impressionable age, revelation of all the intellectual weaknesses and petulances, absorption of mental routine on an equality, tend to destroy the sense of romance and mystery that are the most powerful attractions between the sexes. It is a sort of disenchanting familiarity that rubs off the bloom."

"Have you any statistics on the subject?"

"No. I fancy it is only a notion of some old fogy who thinks education in any form is dangerous for women."

"Yes, and I fancy that co-education will have about as much effect on life generally as that solemn meeting of a society of intelligent and fashionable women recently in one of our great cities, who met to discuss the advisability of limiting population."

"Great Scott!" I exclaimed, "this is an interesting age."

I was less anxious about the vagaries of it when I saw the very old-fashioned way in which the international drama was going on in our neighborhood. Mr. Lyon was increasingly interested in Margaret's mission work. Nor was there much affectation in this. Philanthropy, anxiety about the working-classes, is nowhere more serious or in the fashion than it is in London. Mr. Lyon, wherever he had been, had made a special study of the various aid and relief societies, especially of the work for young waifs and strays.

One Sunday afternoon they were returning from the Bloom Street Mission. Snow covered the ground, the sky was leaden, and the air had a penetrating chill in it far more disagreeable than extreme cold.

"We also," Mr. Lyon was saying, in continuation of a conversation, "are making a great effort for the common people."

"But we haven't any common people here," replied Margaret, quickly. "That bright boy you noticed in my class, who was a terror six months ago, will no doubt be in the City Council in a few years, and likely enough mayor."

"Oh, I know your theory. It practically comes to the same thing, whatever you call it. I couldn't see that the work in New York differed much from that in London. We who have leisure ought to do something for the working-classes."

"I sometimes doubt if it is not all a mistake most of our charitable work. The thing is to get people to do something for themselves."

"But you cannot do away with distinctions?"

"I suppose not, so long as so many people are born vicious, or incompetent, or lazy. But, Mr. Lyon, how much good do you suppose condescending charity does?" asked Margaret, firing up in a way the girl had at times. "I mean the sort that makes the distinctions more evident. The very fact that you have leisure to meddle in their affairs may be an annoyance to the folks you try to help by the little palliatives of charity. What effect upon a wretched city neighborhood do you suppose is produced by the advent in it of a stylish carriage and a lady in silk, or even the coming of a well-dressed, prosperous woman in a horse-car, however gentle and unassuming she may be in this distribution of sympathy and bounty? Isn't the feeling of inequality intensified? And the degrading part of it may be that so many are willing to accept this sort of bounty. And your men of leisure, your club men, sitting in the windows and seeing the world go by as a spectacle-men who never did an hour's necessary work in their lives what effect do you suppose the sight of them has upon men out of work, perhaps by their own fault, owing to the same disposition to be idle that the men in the club windows have?"

"And do you think it would be any better if all were poor alike?"

"I think it would be better if there were no idle people. I'm half ashamed that I have leisure to go every time I go to that mission. And I'm almost sorry, Mr. Lyon, that I took you there. The boys knew you were English. One of them asked me if you were a 'lord' or a 'juke' or something. I cannot tell how they will take it. They may resent the spying into their world of an 'English juke,' and they may take it in the light of a show."

Mr. Lyon laughed. And then, perhaps after a little reflection upon the possibility that the nobility was becoming a show in this world, he said:

"I begin to think I'm very unfortunate, Miss Debree. You seem to remind me that I am in a position in which I can do very little to help the world along."

"Not at all. You can do very much."

"But how, when whatever I attempt is considered a condescension? What can I do?"

"Pardon me," and Margaret turned her eyes frankly upon him. "You can be a good earl when your time comes."

Their way lay through the little city park. It is a pretty place in summer a varied surface, well planted with forest and ornamental trees, intersected by a winding stream. The little river was full now, and ice had formed on it, with small openings here and there, where the dark water, hurrying along as if in fear of arrest, had a more chilling aspect than the icy cover. The ground was white with snow, and all the trees were bare except for a few frozen oak-leaves here and there, which shivered in the wind and somehow added to the desolation. Leaden clouds covered the sky, and only in the west was there a gleam of the departing winter day.

Upon the elevated bank of the stream, opposite to the road by which they approached, they saw a group of people perhaps twenty-drawn closely together, either in the sympathy of segregation from an unfeeling world, or for protection from the keen wind. On the hither bank, and leaning on the rails of the drive, had collected a motley crowd of spectators, men, women, and boys, who exhibited some impatience and much curiosity, decorous for the most part, but emphasized by occasional jocose remarks in an undertone. A serious ceremony was evidently in progress. The separate group had not a prosperous air. The women were thinly clad for such a day. Conspicuous in the little assembly was a tall, elderly man in a shabby long coat and a broad felt hat, from under which his white hair fell upon his shoulders. He might be a prophet in Israel come out to testify to an unbelieving world, and the little group around him, shaken like reeds in the wind, had the appearance of martyrs to a cause. The light of another world shone in their thin, patient faces. Come, they seemed to say to the worldlings on the opposite bank come and see what happiness it is to serve the Lord. As they waited, a faint tune was started, a quavering hymn, whose feeble notes the wind blew away of first, but which grew stronger.

Before the first stanza was finished a carriage appeared in the rear of the group. From it descended a middle-aged man and a stout woman, and they together helped a young girl to alight. She was clad all in white. For a moment her thin, delicate figure shrank from the cutting wind. Timid, nervous, she glanced an instant at the crowd and the dark icy stream; but it was only a protest of the poor body; the face had the rapt, exultant look of joyous sacrifice.

The tall man advanced to meet her, and led her into the midst of the group.

For a few moments there was prayer, inaudible at a distance. Then the tall man, taking the girl by the hand, advanced down the slope to the stream. His hat was laid aside, his venerable locks streamed in the breeze, his eyes were turned to heaven; the girl walked as in a vision, without a tremor, her wide-opened eyes fixed upon invisible things. As they moved on, the group behind set up a joyful hymn in a kind of mournful chant, in which the tall man joined with a strident voice. Fitfully the words came on the wind, in an almost heart-breaking wail:

"Beyond the smiling and the weeping I shall be soon;

Beyond the waking and the sleeping,

Beyond the sowing and the reaping, I shall be soon."

They were near the water now, and the tall man's voice sounded out loud and clear:

"Lord, tarry not, but come!"

They were entering the stream where there was an opening clear of ice; the footing was not very secure, and the tall man ceased singing, but the little band sang on:

"Beyond the blooming and the fading I shall be soon."

The girl grew paler and shuddered. The tall man sustained her with an attitude of infinite sympathy, and seemed to speak words of encouragement. They were in the mid-stream; the cold flood surged about their waists. The group sang on:

"Beyond the shining and the shading,

Beyond the hoping and the dreading, I shall be soon."

The strong, tender arms of the tall man gently lowered the white form under the cruel water; he staggered a moment in the swift stream, recovered himself, raised her, white as death, and the voices of the wailing tune came:

"Love, rest, and home

Sweet hope! Lord, tarry not, but come!"

And the tall man, as he struggled to the shore with his almost insensible burden, could be heard above the other voices and the wind and the rush of the waters:

"Lord, tarry not, but come!"

The girl was hurried into the carriage, and the group quickly dispersed. "Well, I'll be " The tender-hearted little wife of the rough man in the crowd who began that sentence did not permit him to finish it. "That'll be a case for a doctor right away," remarked a well-known practitioner who had been looking on.

Margaret and Mr. Lyon walked home in silence. "I can't talk about it," she said. "It's such a pitiful world."

IV

In the evening, at our house, Margaret described the scene in the park.

"It's dreadful," was the comment of Miss Forsythe. "The authorities ought not to permit such a thing."

"It seemed to me as heroic as pitiful, aunt. I fear I should be incapable of making such a testimony."

"But it was so unnecessary."

"How do we know what is necessary to any poor soul? What impressed me most strongly was that there is in the world still this longing to suffer physically and endure public scorn for a belief."

"It may have been a disappointment to the little band," said Mr. Morgan, "that there was no demonstration from the spectators, that there was no loud jeering, that no snowballs were thrown by the boys."

"They could hardly expect that," said I; "the world has become so tolerant that it doesn't care."

"I rather think," Margaret replied, "that the spectators for a moment came under the spell of the hour, and were awed by something supernatural in the endurance of that frail girl."

"No doubt," said my wife, after a little pause. "I believe that there is as much sense of mystery in the world as ever, and as much of what we call faith, only it shows itself eccentrically. Breaking away from traditions and not going to church have not destroyed the need in the minds of the mass of people for something outside themselves."

"Did I tell you," interposed Morgan "it is almost in the line of your thought of a girl I met the other day on the train? I happened to be her seat-mate in the car-thin face, slight little figure a commonplace girl, whom I took at first to be not more than twenty, but from the lines about her large eyes she was probably nearer forty. She had in her lap a book, which she conned from time to time, and seemed to be committing verses to memory as she looked out the window. At last I ventured to ask what literature it was that interested her so much, when she turned and frankly entered into conversation. It was a little Advent song-book. She liked to read it on the train, and hum over the tunes. Yes, she was a good deal on the cars; early every morning she rode thirty miles to her work, and thirty miles back every evening. Her work was that of clerk and copyist in a freight office, and she earned nine dollars a week, on which she supported herself and her mother. It was hard work, but she did not mind it much. Her mother was quite feeble. She was an Adventist. 'And you?' I asked. 'Oh, yes; I am. I've been an Adventist twenty years, and I've been perfectly happy ever since I joined perfectly,' she added, turning her plain face, now radiant, towards me. 'Are you one?' she asked, presently. 'Not an immediate Adventist,' I was obliged to confess. 'I thought you might be, there are so many now, more and more.' I learned that in our little city there were two Advent societies; there had been a split on account of some difference in the meaning of original sin. 'And you are not discouraged by the repeated failure of the predictions of the end of the world?' I asked. 'No. Why should we be? We don't fix any certain day now, but all the signs show that it is very near. We are all free to think as we like. Most of our members now think it will be next year.' 'I hope not!' I exclaimed. 'Why?' she asked, turning to me with a look of surprise. 'Are you afraid?' I evaded by saying that I supposed the good had nothing to fear. 'Then you must be an Adventist, you have so much sympathy.' 'I shouldn't like to have the world come to an end next year, because there are so many interesting problems, and I want to see how they will be worked out.' 'How can you want to put it off' and there was for the first time a little note of fanaticism in her voice 'when there is so much poverty and hard work? It is such a hard world, and so much suffering and sin. And it could all be ended in a moment. How can you want it to go on?' The train approached the station, and she rose to say good-by. 'You will see the truth some day,' she said, and went away as cheerful as if the world was actually destroyed. She was the happiest woman I have seen in a long time."

"Yes," I said, "it is an age of both faith and credulity."

"And nothing marks it more," Morgan added, "than the popular expectation among the scientific and the ignorant of something to come out of the dimly understood relation of body and mind. It is like the expectation of the possibilities of electricity."

"I was going on to say," I continued, "that wherever I walk in the city of a Sunday afternoon, I am struck with the number of little meetings going on, of the faithful and the unfaithful, Adventists, socialists, spiritualists, culturists, Sons and Daughters of Edom; from all the open windows of the tall buildings come notes of praying, of exhortation, the melancholy wail of the inspiring Sankey tunes, total abstinence melodies, over-the-river melodies, songs of entreaty, and songs of praise. There is so much going on outside of the regular churches!"

"But the churches are well attended," suggested my wife.

"Yes, fairly, at least once a day, and if there is sensational preaching, twice. But there is nothing that will so pack the biggest hall in the city as the announcement of inspirational preaching by some young woman who speaks at random on a text given her when she steps upon the platform. There is something in her rhapsody, even when it is incoherent, that appeals to a prevailing spirit.'"

"How much of it is curiosity?" Morgan asked. "Isn't the hall just as jammed when the clever attorney of Nothingism, Ham Saversoul, jokes about the mysteries of this life and the next?"

"Very likely. People like the emotional and the amusing. All the same, they are credulous, and entertain doubt and belief on the slightest evidence."

"Isn't it natural," spoke up Mr. Lyon, who had hitherto been silent, "that you should drift into this condition without an established church?"

"Perhaps it's natural," Morgan retorted, "that people dissatisfied with an established religion should drift over here. Great Britain, you know, is a famous recruiting-ground for our socialistic experiments."

"Ah, well," said my wife, "men will have something. If what is established repels to the extent of getting itself disestablished, and all churches should be broken up, society would somehow precipitate itself again spiritually. I heard the other day that Boston, getting a little weary of the Vedas, was beginning to take up the New Testament."

"Yes," said Morgan, "since Tolstoi mentioned it."

After a little the talk drifted into psychic research, and got lost in stories of "appearances" and "long-distance" communications. It appeared to me that intelligent people accepted this sort of story as true on evidence on which they wouldn't risk five dollars if it were a question of money. Even scientists swallow tales of prehistoric bones on testimony they would reject if it involved the title to a piece of real estate.

Mr. Lyon still lingered in the lap of a New England winter as if it had been Capua. He was anxious to visit Washington and study the politics of the country, and see the sort of society produced in the freedom of a republic, where there was no court to give the tone and there were no class lines to determine position. He was restless under this sense of duty. The future legislator for the British Empire must understand the Constitution of its great rival, and thus be able to appreciate the social currents that have so much to do with political action.

In fact he had another reason for uneasiness. His mother had written him, asking why he stayed so long in an unimportant city, he who had been so active a traveler hitherto. Knowledge of the capitals was what he needed. Agreeable people he could find at home, if his only object was to pass the time. What could he reply? Could he say that he had become very much interested in studying a schoolteacher a very charming school-teacher? He could see the vision raised in the minds of his mother and of the earl and of his elder sister as they should read this precious confession a vision of a schoolma'am, of an American girl, and an American girl without any money at that, moving in the little orbit of Chisholm House. The thing was absurd. And yet why was it absurd? What was English politics, what was Chisholm House, what was everybody in England compared to this noble girl? Nay, what would the world be without her? He grew hot in thinking of it, indignant at his relations and the whole artificial framework of things.

The situation was almost humiliating. He began, to doubt the stability of his own position. Hitherto he had met no obstacle: whatever he had desired he had obtained. He was a sensible fellow, and knew the world was not made for him; but it certainly had yielded to him in everything. Why did he doubt now? That he did doubt showed him the intensity of his interest in Margaret. For love is humble, and undervalues self in contrast with that which it desires. At this touchstone rank, fortune, all that go with them, seemed poor. What were all these to a woman's soul? But there were women enough, women enough in England, women more beautiful than Margaret, doubtless as amiable and intellectual. Yet now there was for him only one woman in the world. And Margaret showed no sign. Was he about to make a fool of himself? If she should reject him he would seem a fool to himself. If she accepted him he would seem a fool to the whole circle that made his world at home. The situation was intolerable. He would end it by going.

But he did not go. If he went today he could not see her tomorrow. To a lover anything can be borne if he knows that he shall see her tomorrow. In short, he could not go so long as there was any doubt about her disposition towards him.

And a man is still reduced to this in the latter part of the nineteenth century, notwithstanding all our science, all our analysis of the passion, all our wise jabber about the failure of marriage, all our commonsense about the relation of the sexes. Love is still a personal question, not to be reasoned about or in any way disposed of except in the old way. Maidens dream about it; diplomats yield to it; stolid men are upset by it; the aged become young, the young grave, under its influence; the student loses his appetite God bless him! I like to hear the young fellows at the club rattle on bravely, indifferent to the whole thing skeptical, in fact, about it. And then to see them, one after another, stricken down, and looking a little sheepish and not saying much, and by-and-by radiant. You would think they owned the world. Heaven, I think, shows us no finer sarcasm than one of these young skeptics as a meek family man.

Margaret and Mr. Lyon were much together.

And their talk, as always happens when two persons find themselves much together, became more and more personal. It is only in books that dialogues are abstract and impersonal. The Englishman told her about his family, about the set in which he moved and he had the English frankness in setting it out unreservedly about the life he led at Oxford, about his travels, and so on to what he meant to do in the world. Margaret in return had little to tell, her own life had been so simple not much except the maidenly reserves, the discontents with herself, which interested him more than anything else; and of the future she would not speak at all. How can a woman, without being misunderstood? All this talk had a certain danger in it, for sympathy is unavoidable between two persons who look ever so little into each other's hearts and compare tastes and desires.

"I cannot quite understand your social life over here," Mr. Lyon was saying one day. "You seem to make distinctions, but I cannot see exactly for what."

"Perhaps they make themselves. Your social orders seem able to resist Darwin's theory, but in a republic natural selection has a better chance."

"I was told by a Bohemian on the steamer coming over that money in America takes the place of rank in England."

"That isn't quite true."

"And I was told in Boston by an acquaintance of very old family and little fortune that 'blood' is considered here as much as anywhere."

"You see, Mr. Lyon, how difficult it is to get correct information about us. I think we worship wealth a good deal, and we worship family a good deal, but if any one presumes too much upon either, he is likely to come to grief. I don't understand it very well myself."

"Then it is not money that determines social position in America?"

"Not altogether; but more now than formerly. I suppose the distinction is this: family will take a person everywhere, money will take him almost everywhere; but money is always at this disadvantage it takes more and more of it to gain position. And then you will find that it is a good deal a matter of locality. For instance, in Virginia and Kentucky family is still very powerful, stronger than any distinction in letters or politics or success in business; and there is a certain diminishing number of people in New York, Philadelphia, Boston, who cultivate a good deal of exclusiveness on account of descent."

"But I am told that this sort of aristocracy is succumbing to the new plutocracy."

"Well, it is more and more difficult to maintain a position without money. Mr. Morgan says that it is a disheartening thing to be an aristocrat without luxury; he declares that he cannot tell whether the Knickerbockers of New York or the plutocrats are more uneasy just now. The one is hungry for social position, and is morose if he cannot buy it; and when the other is seduced by luxury and yields, he finds that his distinction is gone. For in his heart the newly rich only respects the rich. A story went about of one of the Bonanza princes who had built his palace in the city, and was sending out invitations to his first entertainment. Somebody suggested doubts to him about the response. 'Oh,' he said, 'the beggars will be glad enough to come!'"

"I suppose, Mr. Lyon," said Margaret, demurely, "that this sort of thing is unknown in England?"

"Oh, I couldn't say that money is not run after there to some extent."

"I saw a picture in Punch of an auction, intended as an awful satire on American women. It struck me that it might have two interpretations."

"Yes, Punch is as friendly to America as it is to the English aristocracy."

"Well, I was only thinking that it is just an exchange of commodities. People will always give what they have for what they want. The Western man changes his pork in New York for pictures. I suppose that what do you call it? the balance of trade is against us, and we have to send over cash and beauty."

"I didn't know that Miss Debree was so much of a political economist."

"We got that out of books in school. Another thing we learned is that England wants raw material; I thought I might as well say it, for it wouldn't be polite for you."

"Oh, I'm capable of saying anything, if provoked. But we have got away from the point. As far as I can see, all sorts of people intermarry, and I don't see how you can discriminate socially where the lines are."

Mr. Lyon saw the moment that he had made it that this was a suggestion little likely to help him. And Margaret's reply showed that he had lost ground.

"Oh, we do not try to discriminate except as to foreigners. There is a popular notion that Americans had better marry at home."

"Then the best way for a foreigner to break your exclusiveness is to be naturalized." Mr. Lyon tried to adopt her tone, and added, "Would you like to see me an American citizen?"

"I don't believe you could be, except for a little while; you are too British."

"But the two nations are practically the same; that is, individuals of the nations are. Don't you think so?"

"Yes, if one of them gives up all the habits and prejudices of a lifetime and of a whole social condition to the other."

"And which would have to yield?"

"Oh, the man, of course. It has always been so. My great-great-grandfather was a Frenchman, but he became, I have always heard, the most docile American republican."

"Do you think he would have been the one to give in if they had gone to France?"

"Perhaps not. And then the marriage would have been unhappy. Did you never take notice that a woman's happiness, and consequently the happiness of marriage, depends upon a woman's having her own way in all social matters? Before our war all the men who married down South took the Southern view, and all the Southern women who married up North held their own, and sensibly controlled the sympathies of their husbands."

"And how was it with the Northern women who married South, as you say?"

"Well, it must be confessed that a good many of them adapted themselves, in appearance at least. Women can do that, and never let anyone see they are not happy and not doing it from choice."

"And don't you think American women adapt themselves happily to English life?"

"Doubtless some; I doubt if many do; but women do not confess mistakes of that kind. Woman's happiness depends so much upon the continuation of the surroundings and sympathies in which she is bred. There are always exceptions. Do you know, Mr. Lyon, it seems to me that some people do not belong in the country where they were born. We have men who ought to have been born in England, and who only find themselves really they go there. There are who are ambitious, and court a career different from any that a republic can give them. They are not satisfied here. Whether they are happy there I do not know; so few trees, when at all grown, will bear transplanting."

"Then you think international marriages are a mistake?"

"Oh, I don't theorize on subjects I am ignorant of."

"You give me very cold comfort."

"I didn't know," said Margaret, with a laugh that was too genuine to be consoling, "that you were traveling for comfort; I thought it was for information."

"And I am getting a great deal," said Mr. Lyon, rather ruefully. "I'm trying to find out where. I ought to have been born."

"I'm not sure," Margaret said, half seriously, "but you would have been a very good American."

This was not much of an admission, after all, but it was the most that Margaret had ever made, and Mr. Lyon tried to get some encouragement out of it. But he felt, as any man would feel, that this beating about the bush, this talk of nationality and all that, was nonsense; that if a woman loved a man she wouldn't care where he was born; that all the world would be as nothing to him; that all conditions and obstacles society and family could raise would melt away in the glow of a real passion. And he wondered for a moment if American girls were not "calculating" a word to which he had learned over here to attach a new and comical meaning.

V

The afternoon after this conversation Miss Forsythe was sitting reading in her favorite window-seat when Mr. Lyon was announced. Margaret was at her school. There was nothing un usual in this afternoon call; Mr. Lyon's visits had become frequent and informal; but Miss Forsythe had a nervous presentiment that something important was to happen, that showed itself in her greeting, and which was perhaps caught from a certain new diffidence in his manner.

Perhaps the maiden lady preserves more than any other this sensitiveness, inborn in women, to the approach of the critical moment in the affairs of the heart. The day may some time be past when she is sensitive for herself philosophers say otherwise but she is easily put in a flutter by the affair of another. Perhaps this is because the negative (as we say in these days) which takes impressions retains all its delicacy from the fact that none of them have ever been developed, and perhaps it is a wise provision of nature that age in a heart unsatisfied should awaken lively apprehensive curiosity and sympathy about the manifestation of the tender passion in others. It certainly is a note of the kindliness and charity of the maiden mind that its sympathies are so apt to be most strongly excited in the success of the wooer. This interest may be quite separable from the common feminine desire to make a match whenever there is the least chance of it. Miss Forsythe was not a match-maker, but Margaret herself would not have been more embarrassed than she was at the beginning of this interview.

When Mr. Lyon was seated she made the book she had in her hand the excuse for beginning a talk about the confidence young novelists seem to have in their ability to upset the Christian religion by a fictitious representation of life, but her visitor was too preoccupied to join in it. He rose and stood leaning his arm upon the mantel-piece, and looking into the fire, and said, abruptly, at last:

"I called to see you, Miss Forsythe, to to consult you about your niece."

"About her career?" asked Miss Forsythe, with a nervous consciousness of falsehood.

"Yes, about her career; that is, in a way," turning towards her with a little smile.

"Yes?"

"You must have seen my interest in her. You must have known why I stayed on and on. But it was, it is, all so uncertain. I wanted to ask your permission to speak my mind to her."

"Are you quite sure you know your own mind?" asked Miss Forsythe, defensively.

"Sure sure; I have never had the feeling for any other woman I have for her."

"Margaret is a noble girl; she is very independent," suggested Miss Forsythe, still avoiding the point.

"I know. I don't ask you her feeling." Mr. Lyon was standing quietly looking down into the coals. "She is the only woman in the world to me. I love her. Are you against me?" he asked, suddenly looking up, with a flush in his face.

"Oh, no! no!" exclaimed Miss Forsythe, with another access of timidity. "I shouldn't take the responsibility of being against you, or or otherwise. It is very manly in you to come to me, and I am sure I we all wish nothing but your own happiness. And so far as I am concerned "

"Then I have your permission?" he asked, eagerly.

"My permission, Mr. Lyon? why, it is so new to me, I scarcely realized that I had any permission," she said, with a little attempt at pleasantry. "But as her aunt and guardian, as one may say personally I should have the greatest satisfaction to know that Margaret's destiny was in the hands of one we all esteem and know as we do you."

"Thank you, thank you," said Mr. Lyon, coming forward and seizing her hand.

"But you must let me say, let me suggest, that there are a great many things to be thought of. There is such a difference in education, in all the habits of your lives, in all your relations. Margaret would never be happy in a position where less was accorded to her than she had all her life. Nor would her pride let her take such a position."

"But as my wife "

"Yes, I know that is sufficient in your mind. Have you consulted your mother, Mr. Lyon?"

"Not yet."

"And have you written to any one at home about my niece?"

"Not yet."

"And does it seem a little difficult to do so?" This was a probe that went even deeper than the questioner knew. Mr. Lyon hesitated, seeing again as in a vision the astonishment of his family. He was conscious of an attempt at self-deception when he replied:

"Not difficult, not at all difficult, but I thought I would wait till I had something definite to say."

"Margaret is, of course, perfectly free to act for herself. She has a very ardent nature, but at the same time a great deal of what we call common sense. Though her heart might be very much engaged, she would hesitate to put herself in any society which thought itself superior to her. You see I speak with great frankness."

It was a new position for Mr. Lyon to find his prospective rank seemingly an obstacle to anything he desired. For a moment the whimsicality of it interrupted the current of his feeling. He thought of the probable comments of the men of his London club upon the drift his conversation was taking with a New England spinster about his fitness to marry a school-teacher. With a smile that was summoned to hide his annoyance, he said, "I don't see how I can defend myself, Miss Forsythe."

"Oh," she replied, with an answering smile that recognized his view of the humor of the situation, "I was not thinking of you, Mr. Lyon, but of the family and the society that my niece might enter, to which rank is of the first importance."

"I am simply John Lyon, Miss Forsythe. I may never be anything else. But if it were otherwise, I did not suppose that Americans objected to rank."

It was an unfortunate speech, felt to be so the instant it was uttered. Miss Forsythe's pride was touched, and the remark was not softened to her by the air of half banter with which the sentence concluded. She said, with a little stillness and formality: "I fear, Mr. Lyon, that your sarcasm is too well merited. But there are Americans who make a distinction between rank and blood. Perhaps it is very undemocratic, but there is nowhere else more pride of family, of honorable descent, than here. We think very much of what we call good blood. And you will pardon me for saying that we are accustomed to speak of some persons and families abroad which have the highest rank as being thoroughly bad blood. If I am not mistaken, you also recognize the historic fact of ignoble blood in the owners of noble titles. I only mean, Mr. Lyon," she added, with a softening of manner, "that all Americans do not think that rank covers a multitude of sins."

"Yes, I think I get your American point of view. But to return to myself, if you will allow me; if I am so fortunate as to win Miss Debree's love, I have no fear that she would not win the hearts of all my family. Do you think that my my prospective position would be an objection to her?"

"Not your position, no; if her heart were engaged. But expatriation, involving a surrender of all the habits and traditions and associations of a lifetime and of one's kindred, is a serious affair. One would need to be very much in love" and Miss Forsythe blushed a little as she said it "to make such a surrender."

"I know. I am sure I love her too much to wish to bring any change in her life that would ever cause her unhappiness."

"I am glad to feel sure of that."

"And so I have your permission?"

"Most sincerely," said Miss Forsythe, rising and giving him her hand. "I could wish nothing better for Margaret than union with a man like you. But whatever I wish, you two have your destiny in your own hands." Her tone was wholly frank and cordial, but there was a wistful look in her face, as of one who knew how roughly life handles all youthful enthusiasms.

When John Lyon walked away from her door his feelings were very much mixed. At one instant his pride rebelled against the attitude he had just assumed. But this was only a flash, which he put away as unbecoming a man towards a true woman. The next thought was one of unselfish consideration for Margaret herself. He would not subject her to any chance of social mortifications. He would wait. He would return home and test his love by renewing his lifelong associations, and by the reception his family would give to his proposal. And the next moment he saw Margaret as she had become to him, as she must always be to him. Should he risk the loss of her by timidity? What were all these paltry considerations to his love?

Was there ever a young man who could see any reasons against the possession of the woman he loved? Was there ever any love worth the name that could be controlled by calculations of expediency? I have no doubt that John Lyon went through the usual process which is called weighing a thing in the mind. It is generally an amusing process, and it is consoling to the conscience. The mind has little to do with it except to furnish the platform on which the scales are set up. A humorist says that he must have a great deal of mind, it takes him so long to make it up. There is the same apparent deliberation where love is concerned. Everything "contra" is carefully placed in one scale of the balance, and it is always satisfactory and convincing to see how quickly it kicks the beam when love is placed in the other scale. The lightest love in the world, under a law as invariable as gravitation, is heavier than any other known consideration. It is perhaps doing injustice to Mr. Lyon not to dwell upon this struggle in his mind, and to say that in all honesty he may not have known that the result of it was predetermined. But interesting and commendable as are these processes of the mind, I confess that I should have respected him less if the result had not been predetermined. And this does not in any way take from him the merit of a restless night and a tasteless breakfast.

Philosophizers on this topic say that a man ought always to be able to tell by a woman's demeanor towards him whether she is favorably inclined, and that he need run no risk. Little signs, the eyes alone, draw people together, and make formal language superfluous. This theory is abundantly sustained by examples, and we might rest on it if all women knew their own minds, and if, on the other hand, they could always tell whether a man was serious before he made a definite avowal. There is another notion, fortunately not yet extinct, that the manliest thing a man can do is to take his life in his hand, pay the woman he loves the highest tribute in his power by offering her his heart and name, and giving her the definite word that may be the touchstone to reveal to herself her own feeling. In our conventional life women must move behind a mask in a world of uncertainties. What wonder that many of them learn in their defensive position to play a game, and sometimes experiment upon the honest natures of their admirers! But even this does not absolve the chivalrous man from the duty of frankness and explicitness. Life seems ideal in that far country where the handsome youth stops his carriage at the gate of the vineyard, and says to the laughing girl carrying a basket of grapes on her head, "My pretty maid, will you marry me?" And the pretty maid, dropping a courtesy, says, "Thank you, sir; I am already bespoken," or "Thank you; I will consider of it when I know you better."

Not for a moment, I suppose, is a woman ever ignorant of a man's admiration of her, however uncertain she may be of his intentions, and it was with an unusual flutter of the heart that Margaret received Mr. Lyon that afternoon. If she had doubts, they were dissipated by a certain constraint in his manner, and the importance he seemed to be attaching to his departure, and she was warned to go within her defenses. Even the most complaisant women like at least the appearance of a siege.

"I'm off tomorrow," he said, "for Washington. You know you recommended it as necessary to my American education."

"Yes. We send Representatives and strangers there to be educated. I have never been there myself."

"And do you not wish to go?"

"Very much. All Americans want to go to Washington. It is the great social opportunity; everybody there is in society. You will be able to see there, Mr. Lyon, how a republican democracy manages social life.

"Do you mean to say there are no distinctions?"

"Oh, no; there are plenty of official distinctions, and a code that is very curious and complicated, I believe. But still society is open."

"It must be pardon me a good deal like a mob."

"Well, our mobs of that sort are said to be very well behaved. Mr. Morgan says that Washington is the only capital in the world where the principle of natural selection applies to society; that it is there shown for the first time that society is able to take care of itself in the free play of democratic opportunities."

"It must be very interesting to see that."

"I hope you will find it so. The resident diplomats, I have heard, say that they find society there more agreeable than at any other capital at least those who have the qualities to make themselves agreeable independent of their rank."

"Is there nothing like a court? I cannot see who sets the mode."

"Officially there may be something like a court, but it can be only temporary, for the personnel of it is dissolved every four years. And society, always forming and reforming, as the voters of the republic dictate, is almost independent of the Government, and has nothing of the social caste of Berlin or London."

"You make quite an ideal picture."

"Oh, I dare say it is not at all ideal; only it is rather fluid, and interesting, to see how society, without caste and subject to such constant change, can still be what is called 'society.' And I am told that while it is all open in a certain way, it nevertheless selects itself into agreeable groups, much as society does elsewhere. Yes, you ought to see what a democracy can do in this way."

"But I am told that money makes your aristocracy here."

"Very likely rich people think they are an aristocracy. You see, Mr. Lyon, I don't know much about the great world. Mrs. Fletcher, whose late husband was once a Representative in Washington, says that life is not nearly so simple there as it used to be, and that rich men in the Government, vying with rich men who have built fine houses and who live there permanently without any Government position, have introduced an element of expense and display that interferes very much with the natural selection of which Mr. Morgan speaks. But you will see. We are all right sorry to have you leave us," Margaret added, turning towards him with frank, unclouded eyes.

"It is very good in you to say so. I have spent here the most delightful days of my life."

"Oh, that is charming flattery. You will make us all very conceited."

"Don't mock me, Miss Debree. I hoped I had awakened something more valuable to me than conceit," Lyon said, with a smile.

"You have, I assure you: gratitude. You have opened quite another world to us. Reading about foreign life does not give one at all the same impression of it that seeing one who is a part of it does."

"And don't you want to see that life for yourself? I hope some time "

"Of course," Margaret said, interrupting; "all Americans expect to go to Europe. I have a friend who says she should be mortified if she reached heaven and there had to confess that she never had seen Europe. It is one of the things that is expected of a person. Though you know now that the embarrassing question that everybody has to answer is, 'Have you been to Alaska?' Have you been to Alaska, Mr. Lyon?"

This icy suggestion seemed very inopportune to Lyon. He rose and walked a step or two, and stood by the fire facing her. He confessed, looking down, that he had not been in Alaska, and he had no desire to go there. "In fact, Miss Debree," he said, with effort at speaking lightly, "I fear I am not in a geographical mood today. I came to say good-by, and and "

"Shall I call my aunt?" said Margaret, rising also.

"No, I beg; I had something to say that concerns us; that is, that concerns myself. I couldn't go away without knowing from you that is, without telling you "

The color rose in Margaret's cheek, and she made a movement of embarrassment, and said, with haste: "Some other time; I beg you will not say I trust that I have done nothing that "

"Nothing, nothing," he went on quickly; "nothing except to be yourself; to be the one woman" he would not heed her hand raised in a gesture of protest; he stood nearer her now, his face flushed and his eyes eager with determination "the one woman I care for. Margaret, Miss Debree, I love you!"

Her hand that rested on the table trembled, and the hot blood rushed to her face, flooding her in an agony of shame, pleasure, embarrassment, and anger that her face should contradict the want of tenderness in her eyes. In an instant self-possession came back to her mind, but not strength to her body, and she sank into the chair, and looking up, with only pity in her eyes, said, "I am sorry."

Lyon stopped; his heart seemed to stand still; the blood left his face; for an instant the sunshine left the world. It was a terrible blow, the worst a man can receive a bludgeon on the head is nothing to it. He half turned, he looked again for an instant at the form that was more to him than all the world besides, unable to face the dreadful loss, and recovering speech, falteringly said, "Is that all?"

"That is all, Mr. Lyon," Margaret answered, not looking up, and in a voice that was perfectly steady.

He turned to go mechanically, and passed to the door in a sort of daze, forgetful of all conventionality; but habit is strong, and he turned almost immediately back from the passage. Margaret was still sitting, with no recognition of his departure.

"I beg you will make my excuses, and say good-by to Miss Forsythe. I had mentioned it to her. I thought perhaps she had told you, perhaps I should like to know if it is anything about difference in in nationality, about family, or "

"No, no," said Margaret; "this could never be anything but a personal question with me. I "

"But you said, 'some other time:' Might I ever expect "

"No, no; there is no other time; do not go on. It can only be painful."

And then, with a forced cheerfulness: "You will no doubt thank me some day. Your life must be so different from mine. And you must not doubt my esteem, my appreciation," (her sense of justice forced this from her), "my good wishes. Good-by." She gave him her hand. He held it for a second, and then was gone.

She heard his footstep, rapid and receding. So he had really gone! She was not sorry no. If she could have loved him! She sank back in her chair.

No, she could not love him. The man to command her heart must be of another type. But the greatest experience in a woman's life had come to her here, just now, in this commonplace room. A man had said he loved her. A thousand times as a girl she had dreamed of that, hardly confessing it to herself, and thought of such a scene, and feared it. And a man had said that he loved her.

Her eyes grew tenderer and her face burned at the thought. Was it with pleasure? Yes, and with womanly pain. What an awful thing it was! Why couldn't he have seen? A man had said he loved her. Perhaps it was not in her to love any one. Perhaps she should live on and on like her aunt Forsythe. Well, it was over; and Margaret roused herself as her aunt entered the room.

"Has Mr. Lyon been here?"

"Yes; he has just gone. He was so sorry not to see you and say good-by. He left ever so many messages for you."

"And" (Margaret was moving as if to go) "did he say nothing nothing to you?"

"Oh yes, he said a great deal," answered this accomplished hypocrite, looking frankly in her aunt's eyes. "He said how delightful his visit had been, and how sorry he was to go."

"And nothing else, Margaret?"

"Oh yes; he said he was going to Washington." And the girl was gone from the room.

VI

Margaret hastened to her chamber. Was the air oppressive? She opened the window and sat down by it. A soft south wind was blowing, eating away the remaining patches of snow; the sky was full of fleecy clouds. Where do these days come from in January? Why should nature be in a melting mood? Margaret instinctively would have preferred a wild storm, violence, anything but this elemental languor. Her emotion was incredible to herself.

It was only an incident. It had all happened in a moment, and it was over. But it was the first of the kind in a woman's life. The thrilling, mysterious word had been dropped into a woman's heart. Hereafter she would be changed. She never again would be as she was before. Would her heart be hardened or softened by the experience? She did not love him; that was clear. She had done right; that was clear. But he had said he loved her. Unwittingly she was following him in her thought. She had rejected plain John Lyon, amiable, intelligent, unselfish, kindly, deferential. She had rejected also the Earl of Chisholm, a conspicuous position, an honorable family, luxury, a great opportunity in life. It came to the girl in a flash. She moved nervously in her chair. She put down the thought as unworthy of her. But she had entertained it for a moment. In that second, ambition had entered the girl's soul. She had a glimpse of her own nature that seemed new to her. Was this, then, the meaning of her restlessness, of her charitable activities, of her unconfessed dreams of some career? Ambition had entered her soul in a definite form. She expelled it. It would come again in some form or other. She was indignant at herself as she thought of it. How odd it was! Her privacy had been invaded. The even tenor of her life had been broken. Henceforth would she be less or more sensitive to the suggestion of love, to the allurements of ambition? Margaret tried, in accordance with her nature, to be sincere with herself.

After all, what nonsense it was! Nothing really had happened. A stranger of a few weeks before had declared himself. She did not love him; he was no more to her than any other man. It was a common occurrence. Her judgment accorded with her feeling in what she had done. How was she to know that she had made a mistake, if mistake it was? How was she to know that this hour was a crisis in her life? Surely the little tumult would pass; surely the little whisper of worldliness could not disturb her ideals. But all the power of exclusion in her mind could not exclude the returning thought of what might have been if she had loved him. Alas! in that moment was born in her heart something that would make the idea of love less simple than it had been in her mind. She was heart-free, but her nature was too deep not to be profoundly affected by this experience.

Looking back upon this afternoon in the light of after-years, she probably could not feel no one could say that she had done wrong. How was she to tell? Why is it that to do the right thing is often to make the mistake of a life? Nothing could have been nobler than for Margaret indignantly to put aside a temptation that her heart told her was unworthy. And yet if she had yielded to it?

I ought to ask pardon, perhaps, for dwelling upon a thing so slight as the entrance of a thought in a woman's life. For as to Margaret, she seemed unchanged. She made no sign that anything unusual had occurred. We only knew that Mr. Lyon went away less cheerful than he usually was, that he said nothing of returning in response to our invitations, and that he seemed to anticipate nothing but the fulfillment of a duty in his visit to Washington.

What had happened was regarded as only an episode. In fact, however, I doubt if there are any episodes in our lives, any asides, that do not permanently affect our entire career. Are not the episodes, the casual thoughts, the fortuitous, unplanned meetings, the brief and maybe at the moment unnoted events, those which exercise the most influence on our destiny? To all observation the career of Lyon, and not of Margaret, was most affected by their interview. But often the implanting of an idea in the mind is more potent than the frustration of a plan or the gratification of a desire, so hidden are the causes that make character.

For some time I saw little of Margaret. Affairs in which I was not alone or chiefly concerned took me from home. One of the most curious and interesting places in the world is a Chamber in the business heart of New York if that scene of struggle and passion can be said to have a heart situated midway where the currents of eagerness to acquire the money of other people, not to make it, ceaselessly meet and dash against each other. If we could suppose there was a web covering this region, spun by the most alert and busy of men to catch those less alert and more productive, here in this Chamber would sit the ingenious spiders. But the analogy fails, for spiders do not prey upon each other. Scientists say that the human system has two nerve-centres one in the brain, to which and from which are telegraphed all movements depending upon the will, and another in the small of the back, the centre of the involuntary operations of respiration, digestion, and so on. It may be fanciful to suppose that in the national system Washington is the one nervous centre and New York the other. And yet it does sometimes seem that the nerves and ganglions in the small of the back in the commercial metropolis act automatically and without any visible intervention of intelligence. For all that, their operations may be as essential as the other, in which the will-power sometimes gets into a deadlock, and sometimes telegraphs the most eccentric and incomprehensible orders. Puzzled by these contradictions, some philosophers have said that there may be somewhere outside of these two material centres another power that keeps affairs moving along with some steadiness.

This noble Chamber has a large irregular area of floor space, is very high, and has running round three sides a narrow elevated gallery, from which spectators can look down upon the throng below. Upon a raised dais at one side sits the presiding genius of the place, who rules very much as Jupiter was supposed to govern the earthly swarms, by letting things run and occasionally launching a thunderbolt. High up on one side, in an Olympian seclusion, away from the noise and the strife, sits a Board, calm as fate, and panoplied in the responsibility of chance, whose function seems to be that of switch-shifters in their windowed cubby at a network of railway intersections to prevent collisions.

At both ends of the floor and along one side are narrow railed-off spaces full of clerks figuring at desks, of telegraph operators clicking their machines, of messenger-boys arriving and departing in haste, of unprivileged operators nervously watching the scene and waiting the chance of a word with some one on the floor; through noiseless swinging doors men are entering and departing every moment men in a hurry, men with anxious faces, conscious that the fate of the country is in their hands. On the floor itself are five hundred, perhaps a thousand, men, gathered for the most part in small groups about little stands upon the summit of which is a rallying legend, talking, laughing, screaming, good-natured, indifferent, excited, running hither and thither in response to changing figures in the checker-board squares on the great wall opposite calm, cynical one moment, the next violently agitated, shouting, gesticulating, rushing together, shaking their fists in a tumult of passion which presently subsides.

The swarms ebb and flow about these little stands bees, not bringing any honey, but attracted to the hive where it is rumored most honey is to be had. By habit some always stand or sit about a particular hive, waiting for the show of comb. By-and-by there is a stir; the crowd thickens; one beardless youth shouts out the figure "one-half"; another howls, "three-eighths." The first one nods. It is done. The electric wire running up the stand quivers and takes the figure, passes it to all the other wires, transmits it to every office and hotel in the city, to all the "tickers" in ten thousand chambers and "bucketshops" and offices in the republic. Suddenly on the bulletin-boards in New Orleans, Chicago, San Francisco, Podunk, Liverpool, appear the mysterious "three-eighths," electrifying the watchers of these boards, who begin to jabber and gesticulate and "transact business." It is wonderful.

What induced the beardless young man to make this "investment" in "three-eighths" who can tell? Perhaps he had heard, as he came into the room, that the Secretary of the Treasury was going to make a call of Fives; perhaps he had heard that Bismarck had said that the French blood was too thin and needed a little more iron; perhaps he had heard that a norther in Texas had killed a herd of cattle, or that two grasshoppers had been seen in the neighborhood of Fargo, or that Jay Hawker had been observed that morning hurrying to his brokers with a scowl on his face and his hat pulled over his eyes. The young man sold what he did not have, and the other young man bought what he will never get.

This is business of the higher and almost immaterial sort, and has an element of faith in it, and, as one may say, belief in the unseen, whence it is characterized by an expression "dealing in futures." It is not gambling, for there are no "chips" used, and there is no roulette-table in sight, and there are no piles of money or piles of anything else. It is not a lottery, for there is no wheel at which impartial men preside to insure honest drawings, and there are no predestined blanks and prizes, and the man who buys and the man who sells can do something, either in the newspapers or elsewhere, to affect the worth of the investment, whereas in a lottery everything depends upon the turn of the blind wheel. It is not necessary, however, to attempt a defense of the Chamber. It is one of the recognized ways of becoming important and powerful in this world. The privilege of the floor a seat, as it is called in this temple of the god Chance to be Rich is worth more than a seat in the Cabinet. It is not only true that a fortune may be made here in a day or lost here in a day, but that a nod and a wink here enable people all over the land to ruin others or ruin themselves with celerity. The relation of the Chamber to the business of the country is therefore evident. If an earthquake should suddenly sink this temple and all its votaries into the bowels of the earth, with all its nervousness and all its electricity, it is appalling to think what would become of the business of the country.

Not far from this vast Chamber, where great financial operations are conducted on the highest principles of honor, and with the strictest regard to the Marquis of Dusenbury's rules, there is another less pretentious Chamber, known as "open," a sort of overflow meeting. Those who have not quite left hope behind can go in here. Here are the tickers communicating with the Chamber, tended by lads, who transfer the figures to big blackboards on the wall. In front of these boards sit, from morning to night, rows, perhaps relays, of men intently or listlessly watching the figures. Many of them, who seldom make a sign, come here from habit; they have nowhere else to go. Some of them were once lords in the great Chamber, who have been, as the phrase is, "cleaned out." There is a gray-bearded veteran in seedy clothes, with sunken fiery eyes, who was once many times a millionaire, was a power in the Board, followed by reporters, had a palace in the Avenue, and drove to his office with coachman and footman in livery, and his wife headed the list of charities. Now he spends his old age watching this blackboard, and considers it a good day that brings him five dollars and his car-fare. At one end of the low-ceiled apartment are busy clerks behind a counter, alert and cheerful. If one should go through a side door and down a passage he might encounter the smell of rum. Smart young men, clad in the choicest raiment from the misfit counters, with greed stamped on their astute faces, bustle about, watch the blackboards, and make investments with each other. Middle-aged men in slouch hats lounge around with hungry eyes. The place is feverish rather than exciting. A tall fellow, whose gait and clothes proclaim him English, with a hard face and lack-lustre eyes, saunters about; his friends at home suppose he is making his fortune in America. A dapper young gentleman, quite in the mode, and with the quick air of prosperity, rapidly enters the room and confers with a clerk at the counter. He has the run of the Chamber, and is from the great house of Flamm and Slamm. Perhaps he is taking a "flier" on his own account, perhaps he represents his house in a side transaction; there are so many ways open to enterprising young men in the city; at any rate, his entrance is regarded as significant: This is not a hospital for the broken down and "cleaned out" of the Chamber, but it is a place of business, which is created and fed by the incessant "ticker." How men existed or did any business at all before the advent of the "ticker" is a wonder.

But the Chamber, the creator of low-pressure and high-pressure, the inspirer of the "ticker," is the great generator of business. Here I found Henderson in the morning hour, and he came up to me on the call of a messenger. He approached, nonchalant and smiling as usual. "Do you see that man," he said, as we stood a moment looking down, "sitting there on a side bench big body, small head, hair grayish, long beard parted apparently taking no interest in anything?

"That's Flink, who made the corner in O. B. one of the longest-headed operators in the Chamber. He is about the only man who dare try a hold with Jay Hawker. And for some reason or another, though they have apparent tussles, Hawker rather favors him. Five years ago he could just raise money enough to get into the Chamber. Now he is reckoned at anywhere from five to ten millions. I was at his home the other night. Everybody was there. I had a queer feeling, in all the magnificence, that the sheriff might be in there in ten days. Yet he may own a good slice of the island in ten years. His wife, whom I complimented, and who thanked me for coming, said she had invited none but the reshershy."

"He looks like a rascal," I ventured to remark.

"Oh, that is not a word used in the Chamber. He is called a 'daisy.' I was put into his pew in church the other Sunday, and the preacher described him and his methods so exactly that I didn't dare look at him. When we came out he whispered, 'That was rather hard on Slack; he must have felt it.' These men rather like that sort of preaching."

"I don't come here often," Henderson resumed, as we walked away. "The market is flat today. There promised to be a little flurry in L. and P., and I looked in for a customer."

We walked to his down-town club to lunch. Everybody, I noticed, seemed to know Henderson, and his presence was hailed with a cordial smile, a good-humored nod, or a hearty grasp of the hand. I never knew a more prepossessing man; his bonhomie was infectious. Though his demeanor was perfectly quiet and modest, he carried the air of good-fellowship. He was entirely frank, cordial, and had that sort of sincerity which one can afford to have who does not take life too seriously. Tall at least six feet-with a well-shaped head set on square shoulders, brown hair inclined to curl, large blue eyes which could be merry or exceedingly grave, I thought him a picture of manly beauty. Good-natured, clever, prosperous, and not yet thirty. What a dower!

After we had disposed of our little matter of business, which I confess was not exactly satisfactory to me, although when I was told that "the first bondholders will be obliged to come in," he added that "of course we shall take care of our friends," we went to his bachelor quarters uptown. "I want you to see," he said, "how a hermit lives."

The apartments were not my idea of a hermitage except in the city. A charming library, spacious, but so full as to be cozy, with an open fire; chamber, dressing-room, and bathroom connecting, furnished with everything that a luxurious habit could suggest and good taste would not refuse, made a retreat that could almost reconcile a sinner to solitude. There were a few good paintings, many rare engravings, on the walls, a notable absence, even in the sleeping-room, of photographs of actresses and professional beauties, but here and there souvenirs of travel and evidences that the gentler sex had contributed the skill of their slender fingers to the cheerfulness of the bachelor's home. Scattered about were the daily and monthly products of the press, the newest sensations, the things talked about at dinners, but the walls for the most part were lined with books that are recognized as the proper possessions of the lover of books, and most of them in exquisite bindings. Less care, I thought, had been given in the collection to "sets" of "standards" than to those that are rare, or for some reason, either from distinguished ownership or autograph notes, have a peculiar value.

In this atmosphere, when we were prepared to take our ease, the talk was no longer of stocks, or railways, or schemes, but of books. Whether or not Henderson loved literature I did not then make up my mind, but he had a passion for books, especially for rare and first editions; and the delight with which he exhibited his library, the manner in which he handled the books that he took down one after the other, the sparkle in his eyes over a "find" or a bargain, gave me a side of his character quite different from that I should have gained by seeing him "in the street" only. He had that genuine respect and affection for a "book" which has become almost traditional in these days of cheap and flimsy publications, a taste held by scholars and collectors, and quite beyond the popular comprehension. The respect for a book is essential to the dignity and consideration of the place of literature in the world, and when books are treated with no more regard than the newspaper, it is a sign that literature is losing its power. Even the collector, who may read little and care more for the externals than for the soul of his favorites, by the honor he pays them, by the solicitude he expends upon their preservation without spot, by the lavishness of expense upon binding, contributes much to the dignity of that art which preserves for the race the continuity of its thought and development. If Henderson loved books merely as a collector whose taste for luxury and expense takes this direction, his indulgence could not but have a certain refining influence. I could not see that he cultivated any decided specialty, but he had many rare copies which had cost fabulous prices, the possession of which gives a reputation to any owner. "My shelves of Americana," he said, "are nothing like Goodloe's, who has a lot of scarce things that I am hoping to get hold of some day. But there's a little thing" (it was a small coffee-colored tract of six leaves, upon which the binder of the city had exercised his utmost skill) "which Goodloe offered me five hundred dollars for the other day. I picked it up in a New Hampshire garret." Not the least interesting part of the collection was first editions of American authors a person's value to a collector is often in proportion to his obscurity and what most delighted him among them were certain thin volumes of poetry, which the authors since becoming famous had gone to a good deal of time and expense to suppress. The world seems to experience a lively pleasure in holding a man to his early follies. There were many examples of superb binding, especially of exquisite tooling on hog-skin covers the appreciation of which has lately greatly revived. The recent rage for bindings has been a sore trouble to students and collectors in special lines, raising the prices of books far beyond their intrinsic value. I had a charming afternoon in Henderson's library, an enjoyment not much lessened at the time by experiencing in it, with him, rather a sense of luxury than of learning. It is true, one might pass an hour altogether different in the garret of a student, and come away with quite other impressions of the pageant of life.

At five o'clock his stylish trap was sent around from the boarding stable, and we drove in the Park till twilight. Henderson handling the reins, and making a part of that daily display which is too heterogeneous to have distinction, reverted quite naturally to the tone of worldliness and tolerant cynicism which had characterized his conversation in the morning. If the Park and the moving assemblage had not the air of distinction, it had that of expense, which is quite as attractive to many. Here, as downtown, my companion seemed to know and be known by everybody, returning the familiar salutes of brokers and club men, receiving gracious bows from stout matrons, smiles and nods from pretty women, and more formal recognition from stately and stiff elderly men, who sat bolt-upright beside their wives and tried to look like millionaires. For every passerby Henderson had a quick word of characterization sufficiently amusing, and about many a story which illuminated the social life of the day. It was wonderful how many of this chance company had little "histories" comic, tragic, pitiful, interesting enough for the pages of a novel.

"There is a young lady" Henderson touched his hat, and I caught a glimpse of golden hair and a flash of dark eyes out of a mass of furs "who has no history: the world is all before her."

"Who is that?"

"The daughter of old Eschelle Carmen Eschelle the banker and politician, you remember; had a diplomatic position abroad, and the girl was educated in Europe. She is very clever. She and her mother have more money than they ought to know what to do with."

"That was the celebrated Jay Hawker" (a moment after), "in the modest coupe not much display about him."

"Is he recognized by respectable people?"

"Recognized?" Henderson laughed. "He's a power. There are plenty of people who live by trying to guess what he is going to do. Hawker isn't such a bad fellow. Other people have used the means he used to get rich and haven't succeeded. They are not held up to point a moral. The trouble is that Hawker succeeded. Of course, it's a game. He plays as fair as anybody."

"Yes," Henderson resumed, walking his horses in sight of the obelisk, which suggested the long continuance of the human race, "it is the same old game, and it is very interesting to those who are in it. Outsiders think it is all greed. In the Chamber it is a good deal the love of the game, to watch each other, to find out a man's plans, to circumvent him, to thwart him, to start a scheme and manipulate it, to catch somebody, to escape somebody; it is a perpetual excitement."

"The machine in the Chamber appears to run very smoothly," I said. "Oh, that is a public register and indicator. The system back of it is comprehensive, and appears to be complicated, but it is really very simple. Spend an hour some day in the office of Flamm and Slamm, and you will see a part of the system. There are, always a number of men watching the blackboard, figures on which are changed every minute by the attendants. Telegrams are constantly arriving from every part of the Union, from all over the continent, from all the centres in Europe, which are read by some one connected with the firm, and then displayed for the guidance of the watchers of the blackboard. Upon this news one or another says, 'I think I'll buy,' or 'I think I'll sell,' so and so. His order is transmitted instantly to the Chamber. In two minutes the result comes back and appears upon the blackboard."

"But where does the news come from?"

"From the men whose special business it is to pick it up or make it. They are inside of politics, of the railways, of the weather bureau, everywhere. The other day in Chicago I sat some time in a broker's office with others watching the market, and dropped into conversation with a bright young fellow, at whose right hand, across the rail, was a telegraph operator at the end of a private wire. Soon a man came in quietly, and whispered in the ear of my neighbor and went out. The young fellow instantly wrote a despatch and handed it to the operator, and turning to me, said, 'Now watch the blackboard.'

"In an incredibly short space of time a fall in a leading railway showed on the blackboard. 'What was it?' I asked. 'Why, that man was the general freight manager of the A. B. road. He told me that they were to cut rates. I sent it to New York by a private wire.' I learned by further conversation that my young gentleman was a Manufacturer of News, and that such was his address and intelligence that though he was not a member of the broker's firm, he made ten thousand a year in the business. Soon another man came in, whispered his news, and went away. Another despatch another responsive change in the figures. 'That,' explained my companion, 'was a man connected with the weather bureau. He told me that there would be a heavy frost tonight in the Northwest.'"

"Do they sell the weather?" I asked, very much amused.

"Yes, twice; once over a private wire, and then to the public, after the value of it has been squeezed out, in the shape of predictions. Oh, the weather bureau is worth all the money it costs, for business purposes. It is a great auxiliary."

Dining that evening with Henderson at his club, I had further opportunity to study a representative man. He was of a good New Hampshire family, exceedingly respectable without being distinguished. Over the chimney-place in the old farmhouse hung a rusty Queen Anne that had been at the taking of Louisburg. His grandfather shouldered a musket at Bunker Hill; his father, the youngest son, had been a judge as well as a farmer, and noted for his shrewdness and reticence. Rodney, inheriting the thrift of his ancestors, had pushed out from his home, adapting this thrift to the modern methods of turning it to account. He had brought also to the city the stamina of three generations of plain living a splendid capital, by which the city is constantly reinforced, and which one generation does not exhaust, except by the aid of extreme dissipation. With sound health, good ability, and fair education, he had the cheerful temperament which makes friends, and does not allow their misfortunes to injure his career. Generous by impulse, he would rather do a favor than not, and yet he would be likely to let nothing interfere with any object he had in view for himself. Inheriting a conventional respect for religion and morality, he was not so bigoted as to rebuke the gayety of a convivial company, nor so intractable as to make him an uncomfortable associate in any scheme, according to the modern notions of business, that promised profit. His engaging manner made him popular, and his good-natured adroitness made him successful. If his early experience of life caused him to be cynical, he was not bitterly so; his cynicism was of the tolerant sort that does not condemn the world and withdraw from it, but courts it and makes the most of it, lowering his private opinion of men in proportion as he is successful in the game he plays with them. At this period I could see that he had determined to be successful, and that he had not determined to be unscrupulous. He would only drift with the tide that made for fortune. He enjoyed the world a sufficient reason why the world should like him. His business morality was gauged by what other people do in similar circumstances. In short, he was a product of the period since the civil war closed, that great upheaval of patriotic feeling and sacrifice, which ended in so much expansion and so many opportunities. If he had remained in New Hampshire he would probably have been a successful politician, successful not only in keeping in place, but in teaching younger aspirants that serving the country is a very good way to the attainment of luxury and the consideration that money brings. But having chosen the law as a stepping-stone to the lobby, to speculation, and the manipulation of chances, he had a poor opinion of politics and of politicians. His success thus far, though considerable, had not been sufficient to create for him powerful enemies, so that he may be said to be admired by all and feared by none. In the general opinion he was a downright good fellow and amazingly clever.

VII

In youth, as at the opera, everything seems possible. Surely it is not necessary to choose between love and riches. One may have both, and the one all the more easily for having attained the other. It must be a fiction of the moralists who construct the dramas that the god of love and the god of money each claims an undivided allegiance. It was in some wholly legendary, perhaps spiritual, world that it was necessary to renounce love to gain the Rhine gold. The boxes at the Metropolitan did not believe this. The spectators of the boxes could believe it still less. For was not beauty there seen shining in jewels that have a market value, and did not love visibly preside over the union, and make it known that his sweetest favors go with a prosperous world? And yet, is the charm of life somewhat depending upon a sense of its fleetingness, of its phantasmagorial character, a note of coming disaster, maybe, in the midst of its most seductive pageantry, in the whirl and glitter and hurry of it? Is there some subtle sense of exquisite satisfaction in snatching the sweet moments of life out of the very delirium of it, that must soon end in an awakening to bankruptcy of the affections, and the dreadful loss of illusions? Else why do we take pleasure a pleasure so deep that it touches the heart like melancholy in the common drama of the opera? How gay and joyous is the beginning! Mirth, hilarity, entrancing sound, brilliant color, the note of a trumpet calling to heroism, the beseeching of the concordant strings, and the soft flute inviting to pleasure; scenes placid, pastoral, innocent; light-hearted love, the dance on the green, the stately pageant in the sunlit streets, the court, the ball, the mad splendor of life. And then love becomes passion, and passion thwarted hurries on to sin, and sin lifts to the heights of the immortal, sweetly smiling gods, and plunges to the depths of despair. In vain the orchestra, the inevitable accompaniment of life, warns and pleads and admonishes; calm has gone, and gayety has gone; there is no sweetness now but in the wildness of surrender and of sacrifice. How sad are the remembered strains that aforetime were incentives to love and promises of happiness! Gloom settles upon the scene; Mephisto, the only radiant one, flits across it, and mocks the poor broken-hearted girl clinging to the church door. There is a dungeon, the chanting of the procession of tonsured priests, the passing-bell. Seldom appears the golden bridge over which the baffled and tired pass into Valhalla.

Do we like this because it is life, or because there is a certain satisfaction in seeing the tragedy which impends over all, pervades the atmosphere, as it were, and adds something of zest to the mildest enjoyment? Should we go away from the mimic stage any, better and stronger if the drama began in the dungeon and ended on the greensward, with innocent love and resplendent beauty in possession of the Rhine gold?

How simple, after all, was the created world on the stage to the real world in the auditorium, with its thousand complexities and dramatic situations, and if the little knot of players of parts for an hour could have had leisure to be spectators of the audience, what a deeper revelation of life would they not have seen! For the world has never assembled such an epitome of itself, in its passion for pleasure and its passion for display, as in the modern opera, with its ranks and tiers of votaries from the pit to the dome. I fancy that even Margaret, whose love for music was genuine, was almost as much fascinated by the greater spectacle as by the less.

It was a crowded night, for the opera was one that appealed to the senses and stimulated them to activity, and left the mind free to pursue its own schemes; in a word, orchestra and the scenes formed a sort of accompaniment and interpreter to the private dramas in the boxes. The opera was made for society, and not society for the opera. We occupied a box in the second tier the Morgans, Margaret, and my wife. Morgan said that the glasses were raised to us from the parquet and leveled at us from the loges because we were a country party, but he well enough knew whose fresh beauty and enthusiastic young face it was that drew the fire when the curtain fell on the first act, and there was for a moment a little lull in the hum of conversation.

"I had heard," Morgan was saying, "that the opera was not acclimated in New York; but it is nearly so. The audience do not jabber so loud nor so incessantly as at San Carlo, and they do not hum the airs with the singers "

"Perhaps," said my wife, "that is because they do not know the airs."

"But they are getting on in cultivation, and learning how to assert the social side of the opera, which is not to be seriously interfered with by the music on the stage."

"But the music, the scenery, were never before so good," I replied to these cynical observations.

"That is true. And the social side has risen with it. Do you know what an impudent thing the managers did the other night in protesting against the raising of the lights by which the house was made brilliant and the cheap illusions of the stage were destroyed? They wanted to make the house positively gloomy for the sake of a little artificial moonlight on the painted towers and the canvas lakes."

As the world goes, the scene was brilliant, of course with republican simplicity. The imagination was helped by no titled names any more than the eye was by the insignia of rank, but there was a certain glow of feeling, as the glass swept the circle, to know that there were ten millions in this box, and twenty in the next, and fifty in the next, attested well enough by the flash of jewels and the splendor of attire, and one might indulge a genuine pride in the prosperity of the republic. As for beauty, the world, surely, in this later time, had flowered here flowered with something of Aspasia's grace and something of the haughty coldness of Agrippina. And yet it was American. Here and there in the boxes was a thoroughbred portrait by Copley the long shapely neck, the sloping shoulders, the drooping eyelids, even to the gown in which the great-grandmother danced with the French officers.

"Who is that lovely creature?" asked Margaret, indicating a box opposite.

I did not know. There were two ladies, and behind them I had no difficulty in making out Henderson and Margaret evidently had not seen him Mr. Lyon. Almost at the same moment Henderson recognized me, and signaled for me to come to his box. As I rose to do so, Mrs. Morgan exclaimed: "Why, there is Mr. Lyon! Do tell him we are here." I saw Margaret's color rise, but she did not speak.

I was presented to Mrs. Eschelle and her daughter; in the latter I recognized the beauty who had flashed by us in the Park. The elder lady inclined to stoutness, and her too youthful apparel could not mislead one as to the length of her pilgrimage in this world, nor soften the hard lines of her worldly face-lines acquired, one could see, by a social struggle, and not drawn there by an innate patrician insolence.

"We are glad to see a friend of Mr. Henderson's," she said, "and of Mr. Lyon's also. Mr. Lyon has told us much of your charming country home. Who is that pretty girl in your box, Mr. Fairchild?"

Miss Eschelle had her glass pointed at Margaret as I gave the desired information.

"How innocent!" she murmured. "And she's quite in the style isn't she, Mr. Lyon?" she asked, turning about, her sweet mobile face quite the picture of what she was describing. "We are all innocent in these days."

"It is a very good style," I said.

"Isn't it becoming?" asked the girl, making her dark eyes at once merry and demure.

Mr. Lyon was looking intently at the opposite box, and a slight shade came over his fine face. "Ah, I see!"

"I beg your pardon, Miss Eschelle," he said, after a second, "I hardly know which to admire most, the beauty, or the wit, or the innocence of the American women."

"There is nothing so confusing, though, as the country innocence," the girl said, with the most natural air; "it never knows where to stop."

"You are too absurd, Carmen," her mother interposed; "as if the town girl did!"

"Well, mamma, there is authority for saying that there is a time for everything, only one must be in the fashion, you know."

Mr. Lyon looked a little dubious at this turn of the talk; Mr. Henderson was as evidently amused at the girl's acting. I said I was glad to see that goodness was in fashion.

"Oh, it often is. You know we were promised a knowledge of good as well as evil. It depends upon the point of view. I fancy, now, that Mr. Henderson tolerates the good that is the reason we get on so well together; and Mr. Lyon tolerates the evil that's the reason he likes New York. I have almost promised him that I will have a mission school."

The girl looked quite capable of it, or of any other form of devotion. Notwithstanding her persistent banter, she had a most inviting innocence of manner, almost an ingenuousness, that well became her exquisite beauty. And but for a tentative daring in her talk, as if the gentle creature were experimenting as to how far one could safely go, her innocence might have seemed that of ignorance.

It came out in the talk that Mr. Lyon had been in Washington for a week, and would return there later on.

"We had a claim on him," said Mrs. Eschelle, "for his kindness to us in London, and we are trying to convince him that New York is the real capital."

"Unfortunately," added Miss Eschelle, looking up in Mr. Lyon's face, "he visited Brandon first, and you seem to have bewitched him with your simple country ways. I can get him to talk of nothing else."

"You mean to say," Mr. Lyon replied, with the air of retorting, "that you have asked me about nothing else."

"Oh, you know we felt a little responsible for you; and there is no place so dangerous as the country. Now here you are protected we put all the wickedness on the stage, and learn to recognize and shun it."

"It may be wicked," said her mother, "but it is dull. Don't you find it so, Mr. Henderson? I am passionately fond of Wagner, but it is too noisy for anything tonight."

"I notice, dear," the dutiful daughter replied for all of us, "that you have to raise your voice. But there is the ballet. Let us all listen now."

Mr. Lyon excused himself from going with me, saying that he would call at our hotel, and I took Henderson. "I shall count the minutes you are going to lose," the girl said as we went out-to our box. The lobbies in the interact were thronged with men for the most part the young speculators of the Chamber turned into loungers in the foyer knowing, alert, attitudinizing in the extreme of the mode, unable even in this hour to give beauty the preference to business, well knowing, perhaps, that beauty itself in these days has a fine eye for business.

I liked Henderson better in our box than in his own. Was it because the atmosphere was more natural and genuine? Or was it Margaret's transparent nature, her sincere enjoyment of the scene, her evident pleasure in the music, the color, the gayety of the house, that made him drop the slight cynical air of the world which had fitted him so admirably a moment before? He already knew my wife and the Morgans, and, after the greetings were made, he took a seat by Margaret, quite content while the act was going on to watch its progress in the play of her responsive features. How quickly she felt, how the frown followed the smile, how, she seemed to weigh and try to apprehend the meaning of what went on how her every sense enjoyed life!

"It is absurd," she said, turning her bright face to him when the curtain dropped, "to be so interested in fictitious trouble."

"I'm not so sure that it is," he replied, in her own tone; "the opera is a sort of pulpit, and not seldom preaches an awful sermon more plainly than the preacher dares to make it."

"But not in nomine Dei."

"No. But who can say what is most effective? I often wonder, as I watch the congregations coming from the churches on the Avenue, if they are any more solemnized than the audiences that pour out of this house. I confess that I cannot shake off 'Lohengrin' in a good while after I hear it."

"And so you think the theatres have a moral influence?"

"Honestly" and I heard his good-natured laugh "I couldn't swear to that. But then we don't know what New York might be without them."

"I don't know," said Margaret, reflectively, "that my own good impulses, such as I have, are excited by anything I see on the stage; perhaps I am more tolerant, and maybe toleration is not good. I wonder if I should grow worldly, seeing more of it?"

"Perhaps it is not the stage so much as the house," Henderson replied, beginning to read the girl's mind.

"Yes, it would be different if one came alone and saw the play, unconscious of the house, as if it were a picture. I think it is the house that disturbs one, makes one restless and discontented."

"I never analyzed my emotions," said Henderson, "but when I was a boy and came to the theatre I well remember that it made me ambitious; every sort of thing seemed possible of attainment in the excitement of the crowded house, the music, the lights, the easy successes on the stage; nothing else is more stimulating to a lad; nothing else makes the world more attractive."

"And does it continue to have the same effect, Mr. Henderson?"

"Hardly," and he smiled; "the illusion goes, and the stage is about as real as the house usually less interesting. It can hardly compete with the comedy in the boxes."

"Perhaps it is lack of experience, but I like the play for itself."

"Oh yes; desire for the dramatic is natural. People will have it somehow. In the country village where there are no theatres the people make dramas out of each other's lives; the most trivial incidents are magnified and talked about dramatized, in short."

"You mean gossiped about?"

"Well, you may call it gossip nothing can be concealed; everybody knows about everybody else; there is no privacy; everything is used to create that illusory spectacle which the stage tries to give. I think that in the country village a good theatre would be a wholesome influence, satisfy a natural appetite indicated by the inquisition into the affairs of neighbors, and by the petty scandal."

"We are on the way to it," said Mr. Morgan, who sat behind them; "we have theatricals in the church parlors, which may grow into a nineteenth century substitute for the miracle-plays. You mustn't, Margaret, let Mr. Henderson prejudice you against the country."

"No," said the latter, quickly; "I was only trying to defend the city. We country people always do that. We must base our theatrical life on something in nature."

"What is the difference, Mr. Henderson," asked Margaret, "between the gossip in the boxes and the country gossip you spoke of?"

"In toleration mainly, and lack of exact knowledge. It is here rather cynical persiflage, not concentrated public opinion."

"I don't follow you," said Morgan. "It seems to me that in the city you've got gossip plus the stage."

"That is to say, we have the world."

"I don't like to believe that," said Margaret, seriously "your definition of the world."

"You make me see that it was a poor jest," he said, rising to go. "By-the-way, we have a friend of yours in our box tonight a young Englishman."

"Oh, Mr. Lyon. We were all delighted with him. Such a transparent, genuine nature!"

"Tell him," said my wife, "that we should be happy to see him at our hotel."

When Henderson came back to his box Carmen did not look up, but she said, indifferently: "What, so soon? But your absence has made one person thoroughly miserable. Mr. Lyon has not taken his eyes off you. I never saw such an international attachment."

"What more could I do for Miss Eschelle than to leave her in such company?"

"I beg your pardon," said Lyon. "Miss Eschelle must believe that I thoroughly appreciate Mr. Henderson's self-sacrifice. If I occasionally looked over where he was, I assure you it was in pity."

"You are both altogether too self-sacrificing," the beauty replied, turning to Henderson a look that was sweetly forgiving. "They who sin much shall be forgiven much, you know."

"That leaves me," Mr. Lyon answered, with a laugh, "as you say over here, out in the cold, for I have passed a too happy evening to feel like a transgressor."

"The sins of omission are the worst sort," she retorted.

"You see what you must do to be forgiven," Henderson said to Lyon, with that good-natured smile that was so potent to smooth away sharpness.

"I fear I can never do enough to qualify myself." And he also laughed.

"You never will," Carmen answered, but she accompanied the doubt with a witching smile that denied it.

"What is all this about forgiveness?" asked Mrs. Eschelle, turning to them from regarding the stage.

"Oh, we were having an experience meeting behind your back, mamma, only Mr. Henderson won't tell his experience."

"Miss Eschelle is in such a forgiving humor tonight that she absolves before any one has a chance to confess," he replied.

"Don't you think I am always so, Mr. Lyon?"

Mr. Lyon bowed. "I think that an opera-box with Miss Eschelle is the easiest confessional in the world."

"That's something like a compliment. You see" (to Henderson) "how much you Americans have to learn."

"Will you be my teacher?"

"Or your pupil," the girl said, in a low voice, standing near him as she rose.

The play was over. In the robing and descending through the corridors there were the usual chatter, meaning looks, confidential asides. It is always at the last moment, in the hurry, as in a postscript, that woman says what she means, or what for the moment she wishes to be thought to mean. In the crowd on the main stairway the two parties saw each other at a distance, but without speaking.

"Is it true that Lyon is 'epris' there?" Carmen whispered to Henderson when she had scanned and thoroughly inventoried Margaret.

"You know as much as I do."

"Well, you did stay a long time," she said, in a lower tone.

As Margaret's party waited for their carriage she saw Mrs. Eschelle and her daughter enter a shining coach, with footman and coachman in livery. Henderson stood raising his hat. A little white hand was shaken to him from the window, and a sweet, innocent face leaned forward a face with dark, eyes and golden hair, lit up with a radiant smile. That face for the moment was New York to Margaret, and New York seemed a vain show.

Carmen threw herself back in her seat as if weary. Mrs. Eschelle sat bolt-upright.

"What in the world, child, made you go on so tonight?"

"I don't know."

"What made you snub Mr. Lyon so often?"

"Did I? He won't mind much. Didn't you see, mother, that he was distrait the moment he espied that girl? I'm not going to waste my time. I know the signs. No fisheries imbroglio for me, thank you."

"Fish? Who said anything about fish?"

"Oh, the international business. Ask Mr. Henderson to explain it. The English want to fish in our waters, I believe. I think Mr. Lyon has had a nibble from a fresh-water fish. Perhaps it's the other way, and he's hooked. There be fishers of men, you know, mother."

"You are a strange child, Carmen. I hope you will be civil to both of them." And they rode on in silence.

VIII

In real life the opera or the theatre is only the prologue to the evening. Our little party supped at Delgardo's. The play then begins. New York is quite awake by that time, and ready to amuse itself. After the public duty, the public attitudinizing, after assisting at the artificial comedy and tragedy which imitate life under a mask, and suggest without satisfying, comes the actual experience. My gentle girl God bless your sweet face and pure heart! who looked down from the sky-parlor at the Metropolitan upon the legendary splendor of the stage, and the alluring beauty and wealth of the boxes, and went home to create in dreams the dearest romance in a maiden's life, you did not know that for many the romance of the night just began when the curtain fell.

The streets were as light as day. At no other hour were the pavements so thronged, was there such a crush of carriages, such a blockade of cars, such running, and shouting, greetings and decorous laughter, such a swirl of pleasurable excitement. Never were the fashionable cafes and restaurants so crowded and brilliant. It is not a carnival time; it is just the flow and ebb of a night's pleasure, an electric night which has all of the morning except its peace, a night of the gayest opportunity and unlimited possibility.

At each little table was a drama in progress, light or serious all the more serious for being light at the moment and unconsidered. Morgan, who was so well informed in the gossip of society and so little involved in it some men have this faculty, which makes them much more entertaining than the daily newspaper knew the histories of half the people in the room. There were an Italian marquis and his wife supping together like lovers, so strong is the force of habit that makes this public life necessary even when the domestic life is established. There is a man who shot himself rather seriously on the doorsteps of the beauty who rejected him, and in a year married the handsome and more wealthy woman who sits opposite him in that convivial party. There is a Russian princess, a fair woman with cool observant eyes, making herself agreeable to a mixed company in three languages. In this brilliant light is it not wonderful how dazzlingly beautiful the women are brunettes in yellow and diamonds, blondes in elaborately simple toilets, with only a bunch of roses for ornament, in the flush of the midnight hour, in a radiant glow that even the excitement and the lifted glass cannot heighten? That pretty girl yonder is she wife or widow? slight and fresh and fair, they say has an ambition to extend her notoriety by going upon the stage; the young lady with her, who does not seem to fear a public place, may be helping her on the road. The two young gentlemen, their attendants, have the air of taking life more seriously than the girls, but regard with respectful interest the mounting vivacity of their companions, which rises and sparkles like the bubbles in the slender glasses which they raise to their lips with the dainty grace of practice. The staid family parties who are supping at adjoining tables notice this group with curiosity, and express their opinion by elevated eyebrows.

Margaret leaned back in her chair and regarded the whole in a musing' frame of mind. I think she apprehended nothing of it except the light, the color, the beauty, the movement of gayety. For her the notes of the orchestra sounded through it all the voices of the singers, the hum of the house; it was all a spectacle and a play. Why should she not enjoy it? There was something in the nature of the girl that responded to this form of pleasure the legitimate pleasure the senses take in being gratified. "It is so different," she said to me, "from the pleasure one has in an evening by the fire. Do you know, even Mr. Morgan seems worldly here."

It was a deeper matter than she thought, this about worldliness, which had been raised in Margaret's mind. Have we all double natures, and do we simply conform to whatever surrounds us? Is there any difference in kind between the country worldliness and the city worldliness? I do not suppose that Margaret formulated any of these ideas in words. Her knowledge of the city had hitherto been superficial. It was a place for shopping, for a day in a picture exhibition, for an evening in the theatre, no more a part of her existence than a novel or a book of travels: of the life of the town she knew nothing. That night in her room she became aware for the first time of another world, restless, fascinating, striving, full of opportunities. What must London be?

If we could only note the first coming into the mind of a thought that changes life and re-forms character supposing that every act and every new departure has this subtle beginning we might be less the sport of circumstances than we seem to be. Unnoted, the desire so swiftly follows the thought and juggles with the will.

The next day Mr. Henderson left his card and a basket of roses. Mr. Lyon called. It was a constrained visit. Margaret was cordially civil, and I fancied that Mr. Lyon would have been more content if she had been less so. If he were a lover, there was little to please him in the exchange of the commonplaces of the day.

"Yes," he was saying to my wife, "perhaps I shall have to change my mind about the simplicity of your American life. It is much the same in New York and London. It is only a question of more or less sophistication."

"Mr. Henderson tells us," said my wife, "that you knew the Eschelles in London."

"Yes. Miss Eschelle almost had a career there last season."

"Why almost?"

"Well you will pardon me one needs for success in these days to be not only very clever, but equally daring. It is every day more difficult to make a sensation."

"I thought her, across the house," Margaret said, "very pretty and attractive. I did not know you were so satirical, Mr. Lyon. Do you mean that one must be more daring, as you call it, in London than in New York?"

"I hope it will not hurt your national pride, Miss Debree, if I say that there is always the greater competition in the larger market."

"Oh, my pride," Margaret answered, "does not lie in that direction."

"And to do her justice, I don't think Miss Eschelle's does, either. She appears to be more interested now in New York than in London."

He laughed as he said this, and Margaret laughed also, and then stopped suddenly, thinking of the roses that came that morning. Could she be comparing the Londoner with the handsome American who sat by her side at the opera last night? She was half annoyed with herself at the thought.

"And are not you also interested in New York, Mr. Lyon?" my wife asked.

"Yes, moderately so, if you will permit me to say it." It was an effort on his part to keep up the conversation, Margaret was so wholly unresponsive; and afterwards, knowing how affairs stood with them, I could understand his well-bred misery. The hardest thing in the world is to suffer decorously and make no sign in the midst of a society which insists on stoicism, no matter how badly one is hurt. The Society for First Aid to the Injured hardens its heart in these cases. "I have never seen another place," he continued, "where the women are so busy in improving themselves. Societies, clubs, parlor lectures, readings, recitations, musicales, classes it fatigues one to keep in sight of them. Every afternoon, every evening, something. I doubt if men are capable of such incessant energy, Mrs. Fairchild."

"And you find they have no time to be agreeable?"

"Quite the contrary. There is nothing they are not interesting in, nothing about which they cannot talk, and talk intensely. They absorb everything, and have the gift of acquiring intelligence without, as one of them told me, having to waste time in reading. Yes, it is a most interesting city."

The coming in of Mr. Morgan gave another turn to the talk. He had been to see a rural American play, an exhibition of country life and character, constructed in absolute disregard of any traditions of the stage.

"I don't suppose," Mr. Morgan said, "a foreigner would understand it; it would be impossible in Paris, incomprehensible in London."

"Yes, I saw it," said Mr. Lyon, thus appealed to. "It was very odd, and seemed to amuse the audience immensely. I suppose one must be familiar with American farm life to see the points of it. I confess that while I sat there, in an audience so keenly in sympathy with the play almost a part of it, one might say I doubted if I understood your people as well as I thought I did when I had been here a week only. Perhaps this is the beginning of an American drama."

"Some people say that it is."

"But it is so local!"

"Anything that is true must be true to local conditions, to begin with. The only question is, is it true to human nature? What puzzled me in this American play was its raising the old question of nature and art. You've seen Coquelin? Well, that is acting, as artificial as a sonnet, the perfection of training, skill in an art. You never doubt that he is performing in a play for the entertainment of an audience. You have the same enjoyment of it that you have of a picture a picture, I mean, full of character and sentiment, not a photograph. But I don't think of Denman Thompson as an actor trained to perfection in a dramatic school, but as a New Hampshire farmer. I don't admire his skill; I admire him. There is plenty that is artificial, vulgarly conventional, in his play, plenty of imitation of the rustic that shows it is imitation, but he is the natural man. If he is a stage illusion, he does not seem so to me." "Probably to an American audience only he does not," Mr. Lyon remarked.

"Well, that is getting to be a tolerably large audience."

"I doubt if you will change the laws of art," said Mr. Lyon, rising to go.

"We shall hope to see you again at our house," my wife said.

"You are very good. I should like it; but my time is running out."

"If you cannot come, you may leave your adieus with Miss Debree, who is staying some time in the city," my wife said, evidently to Margaret's annoyance. But she could do no less than give him her city address, though the information was not accompanied by any invitation in her manner.

Margaret was to stay some time with two maiden ladies, old friends of her mother, the Misses Arbuser. The Arbusers were people of consequence in their day, with a certain social prestige; in fact, the excellent ladies were two generations removed from successful mercantile life, which in the remote prospective took on an old-family solidity. Nowhere else in the city could Margaret have come closer in contact with a certain phase of New York life in which women are the chief actors a phase which may be a transition, and may be only a craze. It is not so much a condescension of society to literature as it is a discovery that literature and art, in the persons of those who produce both, may be sources of amusement, or perhaps, to be just, of the enlargement of the horizon and the improvement of the mind. The society mind was never before so hospitable to new ideas and new sensations. Charities, boards of managers, missions, hospitals, news-rooms, and lodging-houses for the illiterate and the homeless these are not sufficient, even with balls, dancing classes, and teas, for the superfluous energies of this restless, improving generation; there must be also radical clubs, reading classes, study classes, ethical, historical, scientific, literary lectures, the reading of papers by ladies of distinction and gentlemen of special attainments an unremitting pursuit of culture and information. Curiosity is awake. The extreme of social refinement and a mild Bohemianism almost touch. It passes beyond the affectation of knowing persons who write books and write for the press, artists in paint and artists in music. "You cannot be sure in the most exclusive circle" it was Carmen Eschelle who said this "that you will not meet an author or even a journalist." Not all the women, however, adore letters or affect enthusiasm at drawing-room lectures; there are some bright and cynical ones who do not, who write papers themselves, and have an air of being behind the scenes.

Margaret had thought that she was fully occupied in the country, with her teaching, her reading, her literature and historical clubs, but she had never known before what it was to be busy and not have time for anything, always in pursuit of some new thing, and getting a fragment here and there; life was a good deal like reading the dictionary and remembering none of the words. And it was all so cosmopolitan and all-embracingly sympathetic. One day it was a paper by a Servian countess on the social life of the Servians, absorbingly interesting both in itself and because it was a countess who read it; and this was followed by the singing of an Icelandic tenor and a Swedish soprano, and a recital on the violin by a slight, red-haired, middle-aged woman from London. All the talents seem to be afloat and at the service of the strenuous ones who are cultivating themselves.

The first function at which Margaret assisted in the long drawing-rooms of the Arbusers was a serious one one that combined the charm of culture with the temptations of benevolence. The rooms were crowded with the fashion of the town, with a sprinkling of clergymen and of thin philanthropic gentlemen in advanced years. It was a four-o'clock, and the assembly had the cheerfulness of a reception, only that the display of toilets was felt to be sanctified by a purpose. The performance opened with a tremendous prelude on the piano by Herr Bloomgarten, who had been Liszt's favorite pupil; indeed, it was whispered that Liszt had said that, old as he was, he never heard Bloomgarten without learning something. There was a good deal of subdued conversation while the pianist was in his extreme agony of execution, and a hush of extreme admiration it was divine, divine, ravishing when he had finished. The speaker was a learned female pundit from India, and her object was to interest the women of America in the condition of their unfortunate Hindoo sisters. It appeared that thousands and tens of thousands of them were doomed to early and lifelong widowhood, owing to the operation of cruel caste laws, which condemned even girls betrothed to deceased Brahmins to perpetual celibacy. This fate could only be alleviated by the education and elevation of women. And money was needed for schools, especially for medical schools, which would break down the walls of prejudice and enfranchise the sex. The appeal was so charmingly made that every one was moved by it, especially the maiden ladies present, who might be supposed to enter into the feelings of their dusky sisters beyond the seas. The speaker said, with a touch of humor that always intensifies a serious discourse, that she had been told that in one of the New England States there was a superfluity of unmarried women; but this was an entirely different affair; it was a matter of choice with these highly educated and accomplished women. And the day had come when woman could make her choice! At this there was a great clapping of hands. It was one thing to be free to lead a life of single self-culture, and quite another to be compelled to lead a single fife without self-culture. The address was a great success, and much enthusiasm spread abroad for the cause of the unmarried women of India.

In the audience were Mrs. Eschelle and her daughter. Margaret and Carmen were made acquainted, and were drawn together by curiosity, and perhaps by a secret feeling of repulsion. Carmen was all candor and sweetness, and absorbingly interested in the women of India, she said. With Margaret's permission she would come and see her, for she believed they had common friends.

It would seem that there could not be much sympathy between natures so opposed, persons who looked at life from such different points of view, but undeniably Carmen had a certain attraction for Margaret. The New Englander, whose climate is at once his enemy and his tonic, always longs for the tropics, which to him are a region of romance, as Italy is to the German. In his nature, also, there is something easily awakened to the allurements of a sensuous existence, and to a desire for a freer experience of life than custom has allowed him. Carmen, who showed to Margaret only her best side she would have been wise to exhibit no other to Henderson, but women of her nature are apt to cheapen themselves with men seemed an embodiment of that graceful gayety and fascinating worldliness which make the world agreeable.

One morning, a few days after the Indian function, Margaret was alone in her own cozy sitting-room. Nothing was wanting that luxury could suggest to make it in harmony with a beautiful woman, nothing that did not flatter and please, or nurse, perhaps, a personal sense of beauty, and impart that glow of satisfaction which comes when the senses are adroitly ministered to. Margaret had been in a mood that morning to pay extreme attention to her toilet. The result was the perfection of simplicity, of freshness, of maiden purity, enhanced by the touch of art. As she surveyed herself in the pier-glass, and noted the refined lines of the morning-gown which draped but did not conceal the more exquisite lines of her figure, and adjusted a rose in her bosom, she did not feel like a Puritan, and, although she may not have noted the fact, she did not look like one. It was not a look of vanity that she threw into the mirror, or of special self-consciousness; in her toilet she had obeyed only her instinct (that infallible guide in a woman of refinement), and if she was conscious of any emotion, it was of the stirring within her of the deepest womanly nature.

In fact, she was restless. She flung herself into an easy-chair before the fire, and took up a novel. It was a novel with a religious problem. In vain she tried to be interested in it. At home she would have absorbed it eagerly; they would have discussed it; the doubts and suggestions in it would have assumed the deepest personal importance. It might have made an era in her thoughtful country life. Here it did not so appeal to her; it seemed unreal and shadowy in a life that had so much more of action than of reflection in it. It was a life fascinating and exciting, and profoundly unsatisfactory. Yet, after all, it was more really life than that placid vegetation in the country. She felt that in the whirl of only a few days of it operas, receptions, teas, readings, dances, dinners, where everybody sparkled with a bewildering brilliancy, and yet from which one brought away nothing but a sense of strain; such gallantry, such compliments, such an easy tossing about of every topic under heaven; such an air of knowing everything, and not caring about anything very much; so much mutual admiration and personal satisfaction! She liked it, and perhaps was restless because she liked it. To be admired, to be deferred to was there any harm in that? Only, if one suffers admiration today, it becomes a necessity tomorrow. She began to feel the influence of that life which will not let one stand still for a moment. If it is not the opera, it is a charity; if it is not a lover, it is some endowed cot in a hospital. There must be something going on every day, every hour.

Yes, she was restless, and could not read. She thought of Mr. Henderson. He had called formally. She had seen him, here and there, again and again. He had sought her out in all companies; his face had broken into a smile when he met her; he had talked with her lightly, gayly; she remembered the sound of his voice; she had learned to know his figure in a room among a hundred; and she blushed as she remembered that she had once or twice followed him with her eyes in a throng. He was, to be sure, nothing to her; but he was friendly; he was certainly entertaining; he was a part, somehow, of this easy-flowing life.

Miss Eschelle was announced. Margaret begged that she would come upstairs without ceremony. The mutual taking-in of the pretty street costume and the pretty morning toilet was the work of a moment the photographer has invented no machine that equals a woman's eyes for such a purpose.

"How delightful it is! how altogether charming!" and Margaret felt that she was included with the room in this admiration. "I told mamma that I was coming to see you this morning, even if I missed the Nestors' luncheon. I like to please myself sometimes. Mamma says I'm frivolous, but do you know" the girls were comfortably seated by the fire, and Carmen turned her sweet face and candid eyes to her companion "I get dreadfully tired of all this going round and round. No, I don't even go to the Indigent Mothers' Home; it's part of the same thing, but I haven't any gift that way. Ah, you were reading that novel."

"Yes; I was trying to read it; I intend to read it."

"Oh, we have had it! It's a little past now, but it has been all the rage. Everybody has read it; that is, I don't know that anybody has read it, but everybody has been talking about it. Of course somebody must have read it, to set the thing agoing. And it has been discussed to death. I sometimes feel as if I had changed my religion half a dozen times in a fortnight. But I haven't heard anything about it for a week. We have taken up the Hindoo widows now, you know." And the girl laughed, as if she knew she were talking nonsense.

"And you do not read much in the city?" Margaret asked, with an answering smile.

"Yes; in the summer. That is, some do. There is a reading set. I don't know that they read much, but there is a reading set. You know, Miss Debree, that when a book is published really published, as Mr. Henderson says you don't need to read it. Somehow it gets into the air and becomes common property.

Everybody hears the whole thing. You can talk about it from a notice. Of course there are some novels that one must read in order to understand human nature. Do you read French?"

"Yes; but not many French novels; I cannot."

"Nor can I," said Carmen, with a sincere face. "They are too realistic for me." She was at the moment running over in her mind a "situation" in a paper-covered novel turned down on her nightstand. "Mr. Henderson says that everybody condemns the French novels, and that people praise the novels they don't read."

"You know Mr. Henderson very well?"

"Yes; we've known him a long time. He is the only man I'm afraid of."

"Afraid of?"

"Well, you know he is a sort of Club man; that style of man provokes your curiosity, for you never can tell how much such men know. It makes you a little uneasy."

Carmen was looking into the fire, as if abstractedly reflecting upon the nature of men in general, but she did not fail to notice a slight expression of pain on Margaret's face.

"But there is your Mr. Lyon "

Margaret laughed. "You do me too much honor. I think you discovered him first."

"Well, our Mr. Lyon." Carmen was still looking into the fire. "He is such a good young man!"

Margaret did not exactly fancy this sort of commendation, and she replied, with somewhat the tone of defending him, "We all have the highest regard for Mr. Lyon."

"Yes, and he is quite gone on Brandon, I assure you. He intends to do a great deal of good in the world. I think he spends half his time in New York studying, he calls it, our charitable institutions. Mamma reproaches me that I don't take more interest in philanthropy. That is her worldly side. Everybody has a worldly side. I'm as worldly as I can be" this with a look of innocence that denied the self-accusation "but I haven't any call to marry into Exeter Hall and that sort of thing. That is what she means dear mamma. Are you High-Church or evangelical?" she asked, after a moment, turning to Margaret?

Margaret explained that she was neither.

"Well, I am High-Church, and Mr. Lyon is evangelical-Church evangelical. There couldn't be any happiness, you know, without harmony in religious belief."

"I should think not," said Margaret, now quite recovering herself. "It must be a matter of great anxiety to you here."

Carmen was quick to note the change of tone, and her face beamed with merriment as she rose.

"What nonsense I've been talking! I did not intend to go into such deep things. You must not mind what I said about Mr. (a little pause to read Margaret's face) Mr. Lyon. We esteem him as much as you do. How charming you are looking this morning! I wish I had your secret of not letting this life tell on one." And she was gone in a shower of compliments and smiles and caressing ways. She had found out what she came to find out. Mr. Henderson needs watching, she said to herself.

The interview, as Margaret thought it over, was amusing, but it did not raise her spirits. Was everybody worldly and shallow? Was this the sort of woman whom Mr. Henderson fancied? Was Mr. Henderson the sort of man to whom such a woman would be attracted?

IX

It was a dinner party in one of the up-town houses palaces that begin to repeat in size, spaciousness of apartments, and decoration the splendor of the Medicean merchant princes. It is the penalty that we pay for the freedom of republican opportunity that some must be very rich. This is the logical outcome of the open chance for everybody to be rich and it is the surest way to distinction. In a free country the course must be run, and it is by the accumulation of great wealth that one can get beyond anxiety, and be at liberty to indulge in republican simplicity.

Margaret and Miss Arbuser were ushered in through a double row of servants in livery shortclothes and stockings in decorous vacuity an array necessary to bring into relief the naturalness and simplicity of the entertainers. Vulgarity, one can see, consists in making one's self a part of the display of wealth: the thing to be attained is personal simplicity on a background of the richest ostentation. It is difficult to attain this, and theory says that it takes three generations for a man to separate himself thus from his display. It was the tattle of the town that the first owner of the pictures in the gallery of the Stott mansion used to tell the prices to his visitors; the third owner is quite beyond remembering them. He might mention, laughingly, that the ornamented shovel in the great fireplace in the library was decorated by Vavani it was his wife's fancy. But he did not say that the ceiling in the music-room was painted by Pontifex Lodge, or that six Italian artists had worked four years making the Corean room, every inch of it exquisite as an intaglio indeed, the reporters had made the town familiar with the costly facts.

The present occupants understood quite well the value of a background: the house swarmed with servants retainers, one might say. Margaret, who was fresh from her history class, recalled the days of Elizabeth, when a man's importance was gauged by the retinue of servitors and men and women in waiting. And this is, after all, a better test of wealth than a mere accumulation of things and cost of decoration; for though men and women do not cost so much originally as good pictures that is, good men and women everybody knows that it needs more revenue to maintain them. Though the dinner party was not large, there was to be a dance afterwards, and for every guest was provided a special attendant.

The dinner was served in the state dining-room, to which Mr. Henderson had the honor of conducting Margaret. Here prevailed also the same studied simplicity. The seats were for sixteen. The table went to the extremity of elegant plainness, no crowding, no confusion of colors under the soft lights; if there was ostentation anywhere, it was in the dazzling fineness of the expanse of table-linen, not in the few rare flowers, or the crystal, or the plate, which was of solid gold, simply modest. The eye is pleased by this chastity pure whiteness, the glow of yellow, the slight touch of sensuous warmth in the rose. The dinner was in keeping, short, noiselessly served under the eye of the maitre d'hotel, few courses, few wines; no anxiety on the part of the host and hostess perhaps just a little consciousness that everything was simple and elegant, a little consciousness of the background; but another generation will remove that.

If to Margaret's country apprehension the conversation was not quite up to the level of the dinner and the house what except that of a circle of wits, who would be out of place there, could be? the presence of Mr. Henderson, who devoted himself to her, made the lack unnoticed. The talk ran, as usual, on the opera, Wagner, a Christmas party at Lenox, at Tuxedo, somebody's engagement, some lucky hit in the Exchange, the irritating personalities of the newspapers, the last English season, the marriage of the Duchess of

Bolinbroke, a confidential disclosure of who would be in the Cabinet and who would have missions, a jocular remark across the table about a "corner" (it is impossible absolutely here, as well as at a literary dinner, to sink the shop), the Sunday opening of galleries anything to pass the hour, the ladies contributing most of the vivacity and persiflage.

"I saw you, Mr. Henderson" it was Mrs. Laflamme raising her voice "the other night in a box with a very pretty woman."

"Yes Miss Eschelle."

"I don't know them. We used to hear of them in Naples, Venice, various places; they were in Europe some time; I believe. She was said to be very entertaining and enterprising."

"Well, I suppose they have seen something of the world. The other lady was her mother. And the man with us that might interest you more, Mrs. Laflamme, was Mr. Lyon, who will be the Earl of Chisholm."

"Ah! Then I suppose she has money?"

"I never saw any painful evidence of poverty. But I don't think Mr. Lyon is fortune-hunting. He seems to be after information and goodness."

Margaret flushed a little, but apparently Henderson did not notice it. Then she said (after Mrs. Laflamme had dropped the subject with the remark that he had come to the right place), "Miss Eschelle called on me yesterday."

"And was, no doubt, agreeable."

"She was, as Mrs. Laflamme says, entertaining. She quoted you a good deal."

"Quoted me? For what?"

"As one would a book, as a familiar authority."

"I suppose I ought to be flattered, if you will excuse the street expression, to have my stock quotable. Perhaps you couldn't tell whether Miss Eschelle was a bull or a bear in this case?"

"I don't clearly know what that is. She didn't offer me any," said Margaret, in a tone of carrying on the figure without any personal meaning.

"Well, she is a bit of an operator. A good many women here amuse themselves a little in stocks."

"It doesn't seem to me very feminine."

"No? But women generally like to' take risks and chances. In countries where lotteries are established they always buy tickets."

"Ah! then they only risk what they have. I think women are more prudent and conservative than men."

"No doubt. They are conservatives usually. But when they do go in for radical measures and risks, they leave us quite behind." Mr. Henderson did not care to extend the conversation in this direction, and he asked, abruptly, "Are you finding New York agreeable, Miss Debree?"

"Yes. Yes and no. One has no time to one's self. Do you understand why it is, Mr. Henderson, that one can enjoy the whole day and then be thoroughly dissatisfied with it?"

"Perfectly; when the excitement is over."

"And then I don't seem to be myself here. I have a feeling of having lost myself."

"Because the world is so big?"

"Not that. Do you know, the world seems much smaller here than at home."

"And the city appears narrow and provincial?"

"I cannot quite explain it. The interests of life don't seem so large the questions, I mean, what is going on in Europe, the literature, the reforms, the politics. I get a wider view when I stand off at home. I suppose it is more concentrated here. And, oh dear, I'm so stupid! Everybody is so alert in little things, so quick to turn a compliment, and say a bright thing. While I am getting ready to say what I really think about Browning, for instance, he is disposed of in a sentence."

"That is because you try to say what you really think."

"If one don't, what's the use of talk?"

"Oh, to pass the time."

Margaret looked up to see if Henderson was serious. There was a smile of amusement on his face, but not at all offensive, because the woman saw that it was a look of interest also.

"Then I sha'n't be serious any more," she said, as there was a movement to quit the table.

"That lays the responsibility on me of being serious," he replied, in the same light tone.

Later they were wandering through the picture-gallery together. A gallery of modern pictures appeals for the most part to the senses represents the pomps, the color, the allurements of life. It struck Henderson forcibly that this gallery, which he knew well, appeared very different looking at it with Miss Debree from what it would if he had been looking at it with Miss Eschelle. There were some pictures that he hurried past, some technical excellences only used for sensuous effects that he did not call attention to as he might have done with another. Curiously enough, he found himself seeking sentiment, purity. If the drawing was bad, Margaret knew it; if a false note was struck, she saw it. But she was not educated up to a good many of the suggestions of the gallery. Henderson perceived this, and his manner to her became more deferential and protective. It was a manner to which every true woman responds, and Margaret was happy, more herself, and talked with a freedom and gayety, a spice of satire, and a note of reality that made her every moment more attractive to her companion. In her, animation the charm of her unworn beauty blazed upon him with a direct personal appeal. He hardly cared to conceal his frank admiration. She, on her part, was thinking, what could Miss Eschelle mean by saying that she was afraid of him?

"Does the world seem any larger here, Miss Debree?" he asked, as they had lingeringly made the circuit of the room and passed out through the tropical conservatory to join the rest of the company.

"Yes away from people."

"Then it is not numbers, I am glad to know, that make a world."

She did not reply. But when he encountered her, robed for departure, at the foot of the stairway, she gave him her hand in good-night, and their eyes met for a moment.

I wonder if that was the time? Probably not. I fancy that when the right day came she confessed that the moment was when she first saw him enter their box at the opera.

Henderson walked down the avenue slowly, hearing the echo of his own steps in the deserted street. He was in no haste to reach home. It was such a delightful evening-snowing a little, and cold, but so exhilarating. He remembered just how she turned her head as she got into the carriage. She had touched his arm lightly once in the gallery to call his attention to a picture. Yes, the world was larger, larger, by one, and it would seem large her image came to him distinctly if she were the only one.

Henderson was under the spell of this evening when the next, in response to a note asking him to call for a moment on business, he was shown into the Eschelle drawing-room. It was dimly lighted, but familiarity with the place enabled him without difficulty to find his way down the long suite, rather overcrowded with luxurious furniture, statuary, and pictures on easels, to the little library at the far end glowing in a rosy light.

There, ensconced in a big chair, a book in her hand, one pretty foot on the fender, sat Carmen, in a grayish, vaporous toilet, which took a warm hue from the color of the spreading lamp-shades. On the carved table near was a litter of books and of nameless little articles, costly and coquettish, which assert femininity, even in a literary atmosphere. Over the fireplace hung a picture of spring a budding girl, smiling and winning, in a semi-transparent raiment, advancing with swift steps to bring in the season of flowers and of love. The hand that held the book rested upon the arm of the chair, a finger inserted in the place where she had been reading, her rounded white arm visible to the elbow, and Carmen was looking into the fire in the attitude of reflection upon a suggestive passage.

Women have so many forms of attraction, different women are attractive in so many different ways, moods are so changing, beauty is so undefinable, and has so many weapons. And yet men are called inconstant!

It was not until Henderson had time to take in the warmth of this domestic picture that Carmen rose.

"It is so good of you to come, with all your engagements. Mamma is excused with a headache, but she has left me power of attorney to ask questions about our little venture."

"I hope the attorney will not put me through a cross-examination."

"That depends upon how you have been behaving, Mr. Henderson. I'm not very cross yet. Now, sit there so that I can look at you and see how honest you are."

"Do you want me to put on my business or my evening expression?"

"Oh, the first, if you mean business."

"Well, your stocks are going up."

"That's nice. You are so lucky! Everything goes up with you. Do you know what they say of you.

"Nothing bad, I hope."

"That everything you touch turns to gold. That you will be one of the nabobs of New York in ten years."

"That's a startling destiny."

"Isn't it? I don't like it." The girl seemed very serious. "I'd like you to be distinguished. To be in the Cabinet. To be minister go to England. But one needs a great deal of money for that, to go as one ought to go. What a career is open to a man in this country if he has money!"

"But I don't care for politics."

"Who does? But position. You can afford that if you have money enough. Do you know, Mr. Henderson, I think you are dull."

"Thank you. I reckoned you'd find it out."

"The other night at the Nestor ball a lady no, I won't tell you who she is asked me if I knew who that man was across the room; such an air of distinction; might be the new British Minister. You know, I almost blushed when I said I did know him."

"Well?"

"You see what people expect of you. When a man looks distinguished and is clever, and knows how to please if he likes, he cannot help having a career, unless he is afraid to take the chances."

Henderson was not conscious of ever being wanting in this direction. The picture conjured up by the ingenious girl was not unfamiliar to his mind, and he understood quite well the relation to it that Carmen had in her mind; but he did not take the lead offered. Instead, he took refuge in the usual commonplace, and asked, "Wouldn't you like to have been a man?"

"Heaven forbid! I should be too wicked. It is responsibility enough to be a woman. I did not expect such a banality from you. Do you think, Mr. Henderson, we had better sell?"

"Sell what?"

"Our stocks. You are so occupied that I thought they might fall when you are up in the clouds somewhere."

"No, I shall not forget."

"Well, such things happen. I might forget you if it were not for the stocks."

"Then I shall keep the stocks, even if they fall."

"And we should both fall together. That would be some compensation. Not much. Going to smash with you would be something like going to church with Mr. Lyon. It might have a steadying effect."

"What has come over you tonight, Carmen?" Henderson asked, leaning forward with an expression of half amusement, half curiosity.

"I've been thinking doesn't that astonish you? about life. It is very serious. I got some new views talking with that Miss Debree from Brandon. Chiefly from what she didn't say. She is such a lovely girl, and just as unsophisticated well, as we are. I fear I shocked her by telling her your opinion of French novels."

"You didn't tell her that I approved of all the French novels you read?"

"Oh no! I didn't say you approved of any. It sort of came out that you knew about them. She is so downright and conscientious. I declare I felt virtuous shivers running all over me all the time I was with her. I'm conscientious myself. I want everybody to know the worst of me. I wish I could practice some concealment. But she rather discourages me. She would take the color out of a career. She somehow doesn't allow for color, I could see. Duty, duty that is the way she looks at life. She'd try to keep me up to it; no playing by the way. I liked her very much. I like people not to have too much toleration. She would be just the wife for some nice country rector."

"Perhaps I ought to tell her your plan for her? I dined with her last night at the Stotts'."

"Yes?" Carmen had been wondering if he would tell her of that. "Was it very dull?"

"Not very. There was music, distant enough not to interfere with conversation, and the gallery afterwards."

"It must have been very exhilarating. You talked about the Duchess of Bolinbroke, and the opera, and Prince Talleyrand, and the corner in wheat dear me, I know, so decorous! And you said Miss Debree was there?"

"I had the honor of taking her out."

"Mr. Henderson" the girl had risen to adjust the lamp-shade, and now stood behind his chair with her arm resting on it, so that he was obliged to turn his head backward to see her "Mr. Henderson, do you know you are getting to be a desperate flirt?" The laughing eyes looking into his said that was not such a desperate thing to do if he chose the right object.

"Who taught me?" He raised his left hand. She did not respond to the overture, except to snap the hand with her index-finger, and was back in her chair again, regarding him demurely.

"I think we shall go abroad soon." The little foot was on the fender again, and the face had the look of melancholy resolution.

"And leave Mr. Lyon without any protection here?" The remark was made in a tone of good-humored raillery, but for some reason it seemed to sting the girl.

"Pshaw!" she said. "How can you talk such nonsense? You," and she rose to her feet in indignation "you to advise an American girl to sell herself for a title the chance of a title. I'm ashamed of you!"

"Why, Carmen," he replied, flushing, "I advised nothing of the sort. I hadn't the least idea. I don't care a straw for Mr. Lyon."

"That's just it; you don't care," sinking into her seat, still unappeased. "I think I'll tell Mr. Lyon that he will have occupation enough to keep him in this country if he puts his money into that scheme you were talking over the other night."

Henderson was in turn annoyed. "You can tell him anything you like. I'm no more responsible for his speculations than for his domestic concerns."

"Now you are offended. It's not nice of you to put me in the wrong when you know how impulsive I am. I wish I didn't let my feelings run away with me." This said reflectively, and looking away from him. And then, turning towards him with wistful, pleading eyes: "Do you know, I sometimes wish I had never seen you. You have so much power to make a person very bad or very good."

"Come, come," said Henderson, rising, "we mustn't quarrel about an Englishman such old friends."

"Yes, we are very old friends." The girl rose also, and gave him her hand. "Perhaps that's the worst of it. If I should lose your esteem I should go into a convent." She dropped his hand, and snatching a bunch of violets from the table, fixed them in his button-hole, looking up in his face with vestal sweetness. "You are not offended?"

"Not a bit; not the least in the world," said Henderson, heartily, patting the hand that still lingered upon his lapel.

When he had gone, Carmen sank into her chair with a gesture of vexation, and there were hard lines in her sweet face. "What an insensible stick!" Then she ran up-stairs to her mother, who sat in her room reading one of the town-weeklies, into which some elderly ladies look for something to condemn.

"Well?"

"Such a stupid evening! He is just absorbed in that girl from Brandon. I told him we were going abroad."

"Going abroad! You are crazy, child. New York is forty times as amusing."

"And forty times as tiresome. I'm sick of it. Mamma, don't you think it would be only civil to ask Mr. Lyon to a quiet dinner before he goes?"

"Certainly. That is what I said the other day. I thought you "

"Yes, I was ill-natured then. But I want to please you. And we really ought to be civil."

One day is so like another in the city. Every day something new, and, the new the same thing over again. And always the expectation that it will be different tomorrow. Nothing is so tiresome as a kaleidoscope, though it never repeats itself.

Fortunately there are two pursuits that never pall making money and making love.

Henderson had a new object in life, though the new one did not sensibly divert him from the old; it rather threw a charming light over it, and made the possibilities of it more attractive. In all his schemes he found the thought of Margaret entering. Why should it not have been Carmen? he sometimes thought. She thoroughly understood him. She would never stand in the way of his most daring ambitions with any scruples. Her conscience would never nag his. She would be ambitious for a career for him. Would she care for him or the career? How clever she was! And affectionate? She would be if she had a heart.

He was not balancing the two. What man ever does, in fact? It was simply because Margaret had a heart that he loved her, that she seemed necessary to him. He was quite capable of making a match for his advancement, but he felt strong enough to make one for his own pleasure. And if there are men so worldly as not to be attracted to unworldliness in a woman, Henderson was not one of them. If his heart had not dictated, his brain would have told him the value of the sympathy of a good woman.

He was a very busy man, in the thick of the struggle for a great fortune. It did not occur to him to reflect whether she would approve all the methods he resorted to, but all the women he knew liked success, and the thought of her invigorated him. If she once loved him, she would approve what he did.

He saw much of her in those passing days days that went like a dream to one of them at least. He was a welcome guest at the Arbusers', but he saw little of Margaret alone. It did not matter. A chance look is a volume; a word is a library. They saw each other; they heard each other. And then passion grows almost as well in the absence as in the presence of the object. Imagination then has free play. A little separation sometimes will fan it into a flame.

The days went by, and Margaret's visit was over. I am obliged to say that the leave-taking was a gay one, as full of laughter as it was of hope. Brandon was such a little way off. Henderson often had business there. The Misses Arbuser said, "Of course." And Margaret said he must not forget that she lived there. Even when she bade her entertainers an affectionate good-by, she could not look very unhappy.

Spring was coming. That day in the cars there were few signs of it on the roadside to be seen, but the buds were swelling. And Margaret, neglecting the book which lay on her lap, and looking out the window, felt it in all her veins.

X

It is said that the world is created anew for every person who is in love. There is therefore this constant miracle of a new heavens and a new earth. It does not depend upon the seasons. The subtle force which is in every human being, more or less active, has this power, as if love were somehow a principle pervading nature itself, and capable of transforming it. Is this a divine gift? Can it be used more than once? Once spent, does the world to each succeeding experimenter in it become old and stale? We say the world is old. In one sense, the real sense to every person, it is no older than the lives lived in it at any given time. If it is always passing away, it is always being renewed. Every time a youth looks love in a maiden's eyes, and sees the timid appealing return of the universal passion, the world for those two is just as certainly created as it was on the first morning, in all its color, odor, song, freshness, promise. This is the central mystery of life.

Unconsciously to herself, Margaret had worked this miracle. Never before did the little town look so bright; never before was there exactly such a color on the hills-sentiment is so pale compared with love; never before did her home appear so sweet; never before was there such a fine ecstasy in the coming of spring.

For all this, home-coming, after the first excitement of arrival is over, is apt to be dull. The mind is so occupied with other emotions that the friends even seem a little commonplace and unresponsive, and the routine is tame. Out of such a whirl of new experiences to return and find that nothing has happened; that the old duties and responsibilities are waiting! Margaret had eagerly leaped from the carriage to throw herself into her aunt's arms-what a sweet welcome it is, that of kin! and yet almost before the greeting was over she felt alone. There was that in the affectionate calmness of Miss Forsythe that seemed to chill the glow and fever of passion in her new world. And she had nothing to tell. Everything had changed, and she must behave as if nothing had happened. She must take up her old life the interests of the neighborhood. Even the little circle of people she loved appeared distant from her at the moment; impossible it seemed to bring them into the rushing current of her life. Their joy in getting her back again she could not doubt, nor the personal affection with which she was welcomed. But was the New England atmosphere a little cold? What was the flavor she missed in it all? The next day a letter came. The excuse for it was the return of a fan which Mr. Henderson had carried off in his pocket from the opera. What a wonderful letter it was his handwriting, the first note from him! Miss Forsythe saw in it only politeness. For Margaret it outweighed the town of Brandon. It lay in her lap as she sat at her chamber window looking out over the landscape, which was beginning to be flushed with a pale green. There was a robin on the lawn, and a blackbird singing in the pine. "Go not, happy day," she said, with tears in her eyes. She took up the brief letter and read it again. Was he really hers, "truly"? And she answered the letter, swiftly and with no hesitation, but with a throbbing heart. It was a civil acknowledgment; that was all. Henderson might have lead it aloud in the Exchange. But what color, what charming turns of expression, what of herself, had the girl put into it, that gave him such a thrill of pleasure when he read it? What secret power has a woman to make a common phrase so glow with her very self?

Here was something in her life that was her own, a secret, a hope, and yet a tremulous anticipation to be guarded almost from herself. It colored everything; it was always, whatever she was doing or saying, present, like an air that one unconsciously hums for days after it has caught his fancy. Blessed be the capacity of being fond and foolish! If that letter was under her pillow at night, if this new revelation was last in her thought as she fell asleep, if it mingled with the song of the birds in the spring morning, as some great good pervading the world, is there anything distinguishing in such an experience that it should be dwelt on? And if there were questionings and little panics of doubt, did not these moments also reveal Margaret to herself more certainly than the hours of happy dreaming?

Questionings no doubt there were, and, later, serious questionings; for habit is almost as strong as love, and the old ways of life and of thought will reassert themselves in a thoughtful mind, and reason will insist on analyzing passion and even hope.

Gradually the home life and every-day interests began to assume their natural aspect and proportions. It was so sweet and sane, this home life, interesting and not feverish. There was time for reading, time for turning over things in the mind, time for those interchanges of feeling and of ideas, by the fireside; she was not required to be always on dress parade, in mind or person, always keyed up to make an impression or receive one; how much wider and sounder was Morgan's view of the world, allowing for his kindly cynicism, than that prevalent in the talk where she had lately been! How sincere and hearty and free ran the personal currents in this little neighborhood! In the very fact that the daily love and affection for her and interest in her were taken for granted she realized the difference between her position here and that among newer friends who showed more open admiration.

Little by little there was a readjustment. In comparison, the city life, with its intensity of action and feeling, began to appear distant, not so real, mixed, turbid, even frivolous. And was Henderson a vanishing part of this pageant? Was his figure less distinct as the days went by? It could not be affirmed. Love is such a little juggler, and likes, now and again, to pretend to be so reasonable and judicious. There were no more letters. If there had been a letter now and then, on any excuse, the nexus would have been more distinct: nothing feeds the flame exactly like a letter; it has intention, personality, secrecy. And the little excitement of it grows. Once a week gets to be twice a week, three times, four times, and then daily. And then a day without a letter is such a blank, and so full of fear! What can have happened? Is he ill? Has he changed? The opium habit is nothing to the letter habit-between lovers. Not that Margaret expected a letter. Indeed, reason told her that it had not gone so far as that. But she should see him. She felt sure of that. And the thought filled all the vacant places in her imagination of the future.

And yet she thought she was seeing him more clearly than when he was with her. Oh wise young woman! She fancied she was deliberating, looking at life with great prudence. It must be one's own fault if one makes a radical mistake in marriage. She was watching the married people about her with more interest-the Morgans, our own household, Mrs. Fletcher; and besides, her aunt, whose even and cheerful life lacked this experience. It is so wise to do this, to keep one's feelings in control, not to be too hasty! Everybody has these intervals of prudence. That is the reason there are so few mistakes.

I dare say that all these reflections and deliberations in the maidenly mind were almost unconscious to herself; certainly unacknowledged. It was her imagination that she was following, and scarcely a distinct reality or intention. She thought of Henderson, and he gave a certain personality, vivid maybe, to that dream of the future which we all in youth indulge; but she would have shrunk from owning this even to herself. We deceive ourselves as often as we deceive others. Margaret would have repudiated with some warmth any intimation that she had lost her heart, and was really predicting the practical possibilities of that loss, and she would have been quite honest with herself in thinking that she was still mistress of her own feeling. Later on she would know, and delight to confess, that her destiny was fixed at a certain hour, at a certain moment, in New York, for subsequent events would run back to that like links in a chain. And she would have been right and also wrong in that; for but for those subsequent events the first impression would have faded, and been taken little account of in her life. I am more and more convinced that men and women act more upon impulse and less upon deep reflection and self-examination than the analytic novelists would have us believe, duly weighing motives and balancing considerations; and that men and women know themselves much less thoroughly than they suppose they do. There is a great deal of exaggeration, I am convinced, about the inward struggles and self-conflicts. The reader may know that Margaret was hopelessly in love, because he knows everything; but that charming girl would have been shocked and wounded to the most indignant humiliation if she had fancied that her friends thought that. Nay, more, if Henderson had at this moment made by letter a proposal for her hand, her impulse would have been to repudiate the offer as unjustified by anything that had taken place, and she would no doubt have obeyed that impulse.

But something occurred, while she was in this mood, that did not shock her maidenly self-consciousness, nor throw her into antagonism, but which did bring her face to face with a possible reality. And this was simply the receipt of a letter from Henderson; not a love-letter far enough from that but one in which there was a certain tone and intention that the most inexperienced would recognize as possibly serious. Aside from the announcement in the letter, the very fact of writing it was significant, conveying an intimation that the reader might be interested in what concerned the writer. The letter was longer than it need have been, for one thing, as if the pen, once started on its errand, ran on con amore. The writer was coming to Brandon; business, to be sure, was the excuse; but why should it have been necessary to announce to her a business visit? There crept into the letter somehow a good deal about his daily life, linked, to be sure, with mention of places and people in which she had recently an interest. He had been in Washington, and there were slight sketches of well-known characters in Congress and in the Government; he had been in Chicago, and even as far as Denver, and there were little pictures of scenes that might amuse her. There was no special mystery about all this travel and hurrying from place to place, but it gave Margaret a sense of varied and large occupations that she did not understand. Through it all there was the personality that had been recently so much in her thoughts. He was coming. That was a very solid fact that she must meet. And she did not doubt that he was coming to see her, and soon. That was a definite and very different idea from the dim belief that he would come some time. He had signed himself hers "faithfully."

It was a letter that could not be answered like the other one; for it raised questions and prospects, and the thousand doubts that make one hesitate in any definite step; and, besides, she pleased herself to think that she did not know her own mind. He had not asked if he might come; he had said he was coming, and really there was no answer to that. Therefore she put it out of her mind-another curious mental process we have in dealing with a matter that is all the time the substratum of our existence. And she was actually serious; if she was reflective, she was conscious of being judicially reflective.

But in this period of calm and reflection it was impossible that a woman of Margaret's habits and temperament should not attempt to settle in her mind what that life was yonder of which she had a little taste; what was the career that Henderson had marked out for himself; what were his principles; what were the methods and reasons of his evident success. Endeavoring in her clear mind to separate the person, about whose personality she was so fondly foolish, from his schemes, which she so dimly comprehended, and applying to his somewhat hazy occupations her simple moral test, were the schemes quite legitimate? Perhaps she did not go so far as this; but what she read in the newspapers of moneymaking in these days made her secretly uneasy, and she found herself wishing that he were definitely practicing some profession, or engaged in some one solid occupation.

In the little parliament at our house, where everything, first and last, was overhauled and brought to judgment, without, it must be confessed, any visible effect on anything, one evening a common "incident" of the day started the conversation. It was an admiring account in a newspaper of a brilliant operation by which three or four men had suddenly become millionaires.

"I don't see," said my wife, "any mention in this account of the thousands who have been reduced to poverty by this operation."

"No," said Morgan; "that is not interesting."

"But it would be very interesting to me," Mrs. Fletcher remarked. "Is there any protection, Mr. Morgan, for people who have invested their little property?"

"Yes; the law."

"But suppose your money is all invested, say in a railway, and something goes wrong, where are you to get the money to pay for the law that will give you restitution? Is there anything in the State, or public opinion, or anywhere, that will protect your interests against clever swindling?"

"Not that I know of," Morgan admitted. "You take your chance when you let your money go out of your stocking. You see there are so many people who want it. You can put it in the ground."

"But if I own the ground I put it in, the voters who have no ground will tax it till there is nothing left for me."

"That is equality."

"But it isn't equality, for somebody gets very rich in railways or lands, while we lose our little all. Don't you think there ought to be a public official whose duty it is to enforce the law gratis which I cannot afford to enforce when I am wronged?"

"The difficulty is to discover whether you are wronged or only unfortunate. It needs a lawyer to find that out. And very likely if you are wronged, the wrongdoer has so cleverly gone round the law that it needs legislation to set you straight, and that needs a lobbyist, whom the lawyer must hire, or he must turn lobbyist himself. Now, a lawyer costs money, and a lobbyist is one of the most expensive of modern luxuries; but when you have a lawyer and lobbyist in one, you will find it economical to let him take your claim and all that can be made out of it, and not bother you any more about it. But there is no doubt about the law, as I said. You can get just as much law as you can pay for. It is like any other commodity."

"You mean to say," I asked, "that the lawyer takes what the operator leaves?"

"Not exactly. There is a great deal of unreasonable prejudice against lawyers. They must live. There is no nobler occupation than the application of the principle of justice in human affairs. The trouble is that public opinion sustains the operator in his smartness, and estimates the lawyer according to his adroitness. If we only evoked the aid of a lawyer in a just cause, the lawyers would have less to do.

"Usually and naturally the best talent goes with the biggest fees."

"It seems to me," said my wife, musing along, in her way, on parallel lines, "that there ought to be a limit to the amount of property one man can get into his absolute possession, to say nothing of the methods by which he gets it."

"That never yet could be set," Morgan replied. "It is impossible for any number of men to agree on it. I don't see any line between absolute freedom of acquisition, trusting to circumstances, misfortune, and death to knock things to pieces, and absolute slavery, which is communism."

"Do you believe, Mr. Morgan, that any vast fortune was ever honestly come by?"

"That is another question. Honesty is such a flexible word. If you mean a process the law cannot touch, yes. If you mean moral consideration for others, I doubt. But property accumulates by itself almost. Many a man who has got a start by an operation he would not like to have investigated, and which he tries to forget, goes on to be very rich, and has a daily feeling of being more and more honorable and respectable, using only means which all the world calls fair and shrewd."

"Mr. Morgan," suddenly asked Margaret, who had been all the time an uneasy listener to the turn the talk had taken, "what is railroad wrecking?"

"Oh, it is very simple, at least in some of its forms. The 'wreckers,' as they are called, fasten upon some railway that is prosperous, pays dividends, pays a liberal interest on its bonds, and has a surplus. They contrive to buy, no matter of what cost, a controlling interest in it, either in its stock or its management. Then they absorb its surplus; they let it run down so that it pays no dividends, and by-and-by cannot even pay its interest; then they squeeze the bondholders, who may be glad to accept anything that is offered out of the wreck, and perhaps then they throw the property into the hands of a receiver, or consolidate it with some other road at a value enormously greater than the cost to them in stealing it. Having in one way or another sucked it dry, they look round for another road."

"And all the people who first invested lose their money, or the most of it?"

"Naturally, the little fish get swallowed."

"It is infamous," said Margaret "infamous! And men go to work to do this, to get other people's property, in cool blood?"

"I don't know how cool, but it is in the way of business."

"What is the difference between that and getting possession of a bank and robbing it?" she asked, hot with indignation.

"Oh, one is an operation, and the other is embezzlement."

"It is a shame. How can people permit it? Suppose, Mrs. Fletcher, a wrecker should steal your money that way?"

"I was thinking of that."

I never saw Margaret more disturbed out of all proportion, I thought, to the cause; for we had talked a hundred times about such things.

"Do you think all men who are what you call operating around are like that?" she asked.

"Oh, no," I said. "Probably most men who are engaged in what is generally called speculation are doing what seems to them a perfectly legitimate business. It is a common way of making a fortune."

"You see, Margaret," Morgan explained, "when people in trade buy anything, they expect to sell it for more than they gave for it."

"It seems to me," Margaret replied, more calmly, "that a great deal of what you men call business is just trying to get other people's money, and doesn't help anybody or produce anything."

"Oh, that is keeping up the circulation, preventing stagnation."

"And that is the use of brokers in grain and stocks?"

"Partly. They are commonly the agents that others use to keep themselves from stagnation."

"I cannot see any good in it," Margaret persisted. "No one seems to have the things he buys or sells. I don't understand it."

"That is because you are a woman, if you will pardon me for saying it. Men don't need to have things in hand; business is done on faith and credit, and when a transaction is over, they settle up and pay the difference, without the trouble of transporting things back and forth."

"I know you are chaffing me, Mr. Morgan. But I should call that betting."

"Oh, there is a risk in everything you do. But you see it is really paying for a difference of knowledge or opinion."

"Would you buy stocks that way?"

"What way?"

"Why, agreeing to pay for your difference of opinion, as you call it, not really having any stock at all."

"I never did. But I have bought stocks and sold them pretty soon, if I could make anything by the sale. All merchants act on that principle."

"Well," said Margaret, dimly seeing the sophistry of this, "I don't understand business morality."

"Nobody does, Margaret. Most men go by the law. The Golden Rule seems to be suspended by a more than two-thirds vote."

It was by such inquiries, leading to many talks of this sort, that Margaret was groping in her mind for the solution of what might become to her a personal question. Consciously she did not doubt Henderson's integrity or his honor, but she was perplexed about the world of which she had recently had a glimpse, and it was impossible to separate him from it. Subjected to an absolutely new experience, stirred as her heart had never been before by any man a fact which at once irritated and pleased her she was following the law of her own nature, while she was still her own mistress, to ponder these things and to bring her reason to the guidance of her feeling. And it is probable that she did not at all know the strength of her feeling, or have any conception of the real power of love, and how little the head has to do with the great passion of life, the intensity of which the poets have never in the least exaggerated. If she thought of Mr. Lyon occasionally, of his white face and pitiful look of suffering that day, she could not, after all, make it real or permanently serious. Indeed, she was sure that no emotion could so master her. And yet she looked forward to Henderson's coming with a sort of nervous apprehension, amounting almost to dread.

XI

It was the susceptible time of the year for plants, for birds, for maids: all innocent natural impulses respond to the subtle influence of spring. One may well gauge his advance in selfishness, worldliness, and sin by his loss of this annual susceptibility, by the failure of this sweet appeal to touch his heart. One must be very far gone if some note of it does not for a moment bring back the tenderest recollections of the days of joyous innocence.

Even the city, with its mass of stone and brick, rectangles, straight lines, dust, noise, and fever of activity, is penetrated by this divine suggestion of the renewal of life. You can scarcely open a window without letting in a breath of it; the south wind, the twitter of a sparrow, the rustle of leaves in the squares, the smell of the earth and of some struggling plant in the area, the note of a distant hand-organ softened by distance, are begetting a longing for youth, for green fields, for love. As Carmen walked down the avenue with Mr. Lyon on a spring morning she almost made herself believe that an unworldly life with this simple-hearted gentleman when he should come into his title and estate would be more to her liking than the most brilliant success in place and power with Henderson. Unfortunately the spring influence also suggested the superior attractiveness of the only man who had ever taken her shallow fancy. And unfortunately the same note of nature suggested to Mr. Lyon the contrast of this artificial piece of loveliness with the domestic life of which he dreamed.

As for Margaret, she opened her heart to the spring without reserve. It was May. The soft maples had a purple tinge, the chestnuts showed color, the apple-trees were in bloom (all the air was full of their perfume), the blackbirds were chattering in convention in the tall oaks, the bright leaves and the flowering shrubs were alive with the twittering and singing of darting birds. The soft, fleecy clouds, hovering as over a world just created, seemed to make near and participant in the scene the delicate blue of the sky. Margaret I remember the morning was standing on her piazza, as I passed through the neighborhood drive, with a spray of apple-blossoms in her hand. For the moment she seemed to embody all the maiden purity of the scene, all its promise. I said, laughing:

"We shall have to have you painted as spring."

"But spring isn't painted at all," she replied, holding up the apple blossoms, and coming down the piazza with a dancing step.

"And so it won't last. We want something permanent," I was beginning to say, when a carriage passed, going to our house. "I think that must be Henderson."

"Ah!" she exclaimed. Her sunny face clouded at once, and she turned to go in as I hurried away.

It was Mr. Henderson, and there was at least pretense enough of business to occupy us, with Mr. Morgan, the greater part of the day. It was not till late in the afternoon that Henderson appeared to remember that Margaret was in the neighborhood, and spoke of his intention of calling. My wife pointed out the way to him across the grounds, and watched him leisurely walking among the trees till he was out of sight.

"What an agreeable man Mr. Henderson is!" she said, turning to me; "most companionable; and yet and yet, my dear, I'm glad he is not my husband. You suit me very well." There was an air of conviction about this remark, as if it were the result of deep reflection and comparison, and it was emphasized by the little possessory act of readjusting my necktie one of the most subtle of female flatteries.

"But who wanted him to be your husband?" I asked. "Married women have the oddest habit of going about the world picking out the men they would not like to have married. Do they need continually to justify themselves?"

"No; they congratulate themselves. You never can understand."

"I confess I cannot. My first thought about an attractive woman whose acquaintance I make is not that I am glad I did not marry her."

"I dare say not. You are all inconsistent, you men. But you are the least so of any man in the world, I do believe."

It would be difficult to say whether the spring morning seemed more or less glorious to Margaret when she went indoors, but its serenity was gone.

It was like the premonition in nature of a change. She put the apple blossoms in water and placed the jug on the table, turning it about half a dozen times, moving her head from side to side to get the effect. When it was exactly right, she said to her aunt, who sat sewing in the bay-window, in a perfectly indifferent tone, "Mr. Fairchild just passed here, and said that Mr. Henderson had come."

"Ah!" Her aunt did not lift her eyes from her work, or appear to attach the least importance to this tremendous piece of news. Margaret was annoyed at what seemed to her an assumed indifference. Her nerves were quivering with the knowledge that he had arrived, that he was in the next house, that he might be here any moment the man who had entered into her whole life and the announcement was no more to her aunt than if she had said it rained. She was provoked at herself that she should be so disturbed, yes, annoyed, at his proximity. She wished he had not come not today, at any rate. She looked about for something to do, and began to rearrange this and that trifle in the sitting-room, which she had perfectly arranged once before in the morning, moving about here and there in a rather purposeless manner, until her aunt looked up and for a moment followed her movements till Margaret left the room. In her own chamber she sat by the window and tried to think, but there was no orderly mental process; in vain she tried to run over in her mind the past month and all her reflections and wise resolves. She heard the call of the birds, she inhaled the odor of the new year, she was conscious of all that was gracious and inviting in the fresh scene, but in her sub-consciousness there was only one thought he was there, he was coming. She took up her sewing, but the needle paused in the stitch, and she found herself looking away across the lawn to the hills; she took up a book, but the words had no meaning, read and reread them as she would. He is there, he is coming. And what of it? Why should she be so disturbed? She was uncommitted, she was mistress of her own actions. Had she not been coolly judging his conduct? She despised herself for being so nervous and unsettled. If he was coming, why did he not come? Why was he waiting so long? She arose impatiently and went down-stairs. There was a necessity of doing something.

"Is there anything that you want from town, auntie?"

"Nothing that I know of. Are you going in?"

"No, unless you have an errand. It is such a fine day that it seems a pity to stay indoors."

"Well, I would walk if I were you." But she did not go; she went instead to her room. He might come any moment. She ought not to run away; and yet she wished she were away. He said he was coming on business. Was it not, then, a pretense? She felt humiliated in the idea of waiting for him if the business were not a pretense.

How insensible men are! What a mere subordinate thing to them in life is the love of a woman! Yes, evidently business was more important to him than anything else. He must know that she was waiting; and she blushed to herself at the very possibility that he should think such a thing. She was not waiting. It was lunch-time. She excused herself. In the next moment she was angry that she had not gone down as usual. It was time for him to come. He would certainly come immediately after lunch. She would not see him. She hoped never to see him. She rose in haste, put on her hat, put it on carefully, turning and returning before the glass, selected fresh gloves, and ran down-stairs.

"I'm going, auntie, for a walk to town."

The walk was a long one. She came back tired. It was late in the afternoon. Her aunt was quietly reading. She needed to ask her nothing: Mr. Henderson had not been there. Why had he written to her?

"Oh, the Fairchilds want us to come over to dinner," said Miss Forsythe, without looking up.

"I hope you will go, auntie. I sha'n't mind being alone."

"Why? It's perfectly informal. Mr. Henderson happens to be there."

"I'm too stupid. But you must go. Mr. Henderson, in New York, expressed the greatest desire to make your acquaintance."

Miss Forsythe smiled. "I suppose he has come up on purpose. But, dear, you must go to chaperon me. It would hardly be civil not to go, when you knew Mr. Henderson in New York, and the Fairchilds want to make it agreeable for him."

"Why, auntie, it is just a business visit. I'm too tired to make the effort. It must be this spring weather."

Perhaps it was. It is so unfortunate that the spring, which begets so many desires, brings the languor that defeats their execution. But there is a limit to the responsibility even of spring for a woman's moods. Just as Margaret spoke she saw, through the open window, Henderson coming across the lawn, walking briskly, but evidently not inattentive to the charm of the landscape. It was his springy step, his athletic figure, and, as he came nearer, the joyous anticipation in his face. And it was so sudden, so unexpected the vision so long looked for! There was no time for flight, had she wanted to avoid him; he was on the piazza; he was at the open door. Her hand went quickly to her heart to still the rapid flutter, which might be from pain and might be from joy she could not tell. She had imagined their possible meeting so many times, and it was not at all like this. She ought to receive him coldly, she ought to receive him kindly, she ought to receive him indifferently. But how real he was, how handsome he was! If she could have obeyed the impulse of the moment I am not sure but she would have fled, and cast herself face downward somewhere, and cried a little and thanked God for him. He was in the room. In his manner there was no hesitation, in his expression no uncertainty. His face beamed with pleasure, and there was so much open admiration in his eyes that Margaret, conscious of it to her heart's core, feared that her aunt would notice it. And she met him calmly enough, frankly enough. The quickness with which a woman can pull herself together under such circumstances is testimony to her superior fibre.

"I've been looking across here ever since morning," he said, as soon as the hand-shaking and introduction were over, "and I've only this minute been released." There was no air of apology in this, but a delicate intimation of impatience at the delay. And still, what an unconscious brute a man is!

"I thought perhaps you had returned," said Margaret, "until my aunt was just telling me we were asked to dine with you."

Henderson gave her a quick glance. Was it possible she thought he could go away without seeing her?

"Yes, and I was commissioned to bring you over when you are ready." "I will not keep you waiting long, Mr. Henderson," interposed Miss Forsythe, out of the goodness of her heart. "My niece has been taking a long walk, and this debilitating spring weather "

"Oh, since the sun has gone away, I think I'm quite up to the exertion, since you wish it, auntie," a speech that made Henderson stare again, wholly unable to comprehend the reason of an indirection which he could feel he who had been all day impatient for this moment. There was a little talk about the country and the city at this season, mainly sustained by Miss Forsythe and Henderson, and then he was left alone. "Of course you should go, Margaret," said her aunt, as they went upstairs; "it would not be at all the thing for me to leave you here. And what a fine, manly, engaging fellow Mr. Henderson is!"

"Yes, he acts very much like a man;" and Margaret was gone into her room.

Go? There was not force enough in the commonwealth, without calling out the militia, to keep Margaret from going to the dinner. She stopped a moment in the middle of her chamber to think. She had almost forgotten how he looked his eyes, his smile. Dear me! how the birds were singing outside, and how fresh the world was! And she would not hurry. He could wait. No doubt he would wait now any length of time for her. He was in the house, in the room below, perhaps looking out of the window, perhaps reading, perhaps spying about at her knick-knacks she would like to look in at the door a moment to see what he was doing. Of course he was here to see her, and all the business was a pretext. As she sat a moment upon the edge of her bed reflecting what to put on, she had a little pang that she had been doing him injustice in her thought. But it was only for an instant. He was here. She was not in the least flurried. Indeed, her mental processes were never clearer than when she settled upon her simple toilet, made as it was in every detail with the sure instinct of a woman who dresses for her lover. Heavens! what a miserable day it had been, what a rebellious day! He ought to be punished for it somehow. Perhaps the rose she put in her hair was part of the punishment. But he should not see how happy she was; she would be civil, and just a little reserved; it was so like a man to make a woman wait all day and then think he could smooth it all over simply by appearing.

But somehow in Henderson's presence these little theories of conduct did not apply. He was too natural, direct, unaffected, his pleasure in being with her was so evident! He seemed to brush aside the little defenses and subterfuges. There was this about him that appeared to her admirable, and in contrast with her own hesitating indirection, that whatever he wanted money, or position, or the love of woman he went straight to his object with unconsciousness that failure was possible. Even in walking across the grounds in the soft sunset light, and chatting easily, their relations seemed established on a most natural basis, and Margaret found herself giving way to the simple enjoyment of the hour. She was not only happy, but her spirits rose to inexpressible gayety, which ran into the humor of badinage and a sort of spiritual elation, in which all things seemed possible. Perhaps she recognized in herself, what Henderson saw in her. And with it all there was an access of tenderness for her aunt, the dear thing whose gentle life appeared so colorless.

I had never seen Margaret so radiant as at the dinner; her high spirits infected the table, and the listening and the talking were of the best that the company could give. I remembered it afterwards, not from anything special that was said, but from its flow of high animal spirits, and the electric responsive mood everyone was in; no topic carried too far, and the chance seriousness setting off the sparkling comments on affairs. Henderson's talk had the notable flavor of direct contact with life, and very little of the speculative and reflective tone of Morgan's, who was always generalizing and theorizing about it. He had just come from the West, and his off-hand sketches of men had a special cynicism, not in the least condemnatory, mere good-natured acceptance, and in contrast to Morgan's moralizing and rather pitying cynicism. It struck me that he did not believe in his fellows as much as Morgan did; but I fancied that Margaret only saw in his attitude a tolerant knowledge of the world.

"Are the people on the border as bad as they are represented?" she asked.

"Certainly not much worse than they represent themselves," he replied; "I suppose the difference is that men feel less restraint there."

"It is something more than that," added Morgan. "There is a sort of drift-wood of adventure and devil-may-care-ism that civilization throws in advance of itself; but that isn't so bad as the slag it manufactures in the cities."

"I remember you said, Mr. Morgan, that men go West to get rid of their past," said Margaret.

"As New Yorkers go to Europe to get rid of their future?" Henderson inquired, catching the phrase.

"Yes" Morgan turned to Margaret "doubtless there is a satisfaction sometimes in placing the width of a continent between a man and what he has done. I've thought that one of the most popular verses in the Psalter, on the border, must be the one that says you will know if I quote it right 'Look how wide also the East is from the West; so far hath He set our sins from us.'"

"That is dreadful," exclaimed Margaret. "To think of you spending your time in the service picking out passages to fit other people!"

"It sounds as if you had manufactured it," was Henderson's comment.

"No; that quiet Mr. Lyon pointed it out to me when we were talking about Montana. He had been there."

"By-the-way, Mr. Henderson," my wife asked, "do you know what has become of Mr. Lyon?"

"I believe he is about to go home."

"I fancied Miss Eschelle might have something to say about that," Morgan remarked.

"Perhaps, if she were asked. But Mr. Lyon appeared rather indifferent to American attractions."

Margaret looked quickly at Henderson as he said this, and then ventured, a little slyly, "She seemed to appreciate his goodness."

"Yes; Miss Eschelle has an eye for goodness."

This was said without change of countenance, but it convinced the listener that Carmen was understood.

"And yet," said Margaret, with a little air of temerity, "you seem to be very good friends."

"Oh, she is very charitable; she sees, I suppose, what is good in me; and I'll spare you the trouble of remarking that she must necessarily be very sharp-sighted."

"And I'm not going to destroy your illusion by telling you her real opinion of you," Margaret retorted.

Henderson begged to know what it was, but Margaret evaded the question by new raillery. What did she care at the moment what Carmen thought of Henderson? What did either of them care what they were saying, so long as there was some personal flavor in the talk! Was it not enough to talk to each other, to see each other?

As we sat afterwards upon the piazza with our cigars, inhaling the odor of the apple blossoms, and yielding ourselves, according to our age, to the influence of the mild night, Margaret was in the high spirits which accompany the expectation of bliss, without the sobering effect of its responsibility. Love itself is very serious, but the overture is full of freakish gayety. And it was all gayety that night. We all constituted ourselves a guard of honor to Miss Forsythe and Margaret when they went to their cottage, and there was a merry leave-taking in the moonlight. To be sure, Margaret walked with Henderson, and they lagged a little behind, but I had no reason to suppose that they were speaking of the stars, or that they raised the ordinary question of their being inhabited. I doubt if they saw the stars at all. How one remembers little trifles, that recur like the gay bird notes of the opening scenes that are repeated in the tragedy of the opera! I can see Margaret now, on some bantering pretext, running back, after we had said good-night, to give Henderson the blush-rose she had worn in her hair. How charming the girl was in this freakish action!

"Do you think he is good enough for her?" asked my wife, when we were alone.

"Who is good enough for whom?" I said, a yawn revealing my want of sentiment.

"Don't be stupid. You are not so blind as you pretend."

"Well, if I am not so blind as I pretend, though I did not pretend to be blind, I suppose that is mainly her concern."

"But I wish she had cared for Lyon."

"Perhaps Lyon did not care for her," I suggested.

"You never see anything. Lyon was a noble fellow."

"I didn't deny that. But how was I to know about Lyon, my dear? I never heard you say that you were glad he wasn't your husband."

"Don't be silly. I think Henderson has very serious intentions."

"I hope he isn't frivolous," I said.

"Well, you are. It isn't a joking matter and you pretend to be so fond of Margaret!"

"So that is another thing I pretend? What do you want me to do? Which one do you want me to make my enemy by telling him or her that the other isn't good enough?"

"I don't want you to do anything, except to be reasonable, and sympathize."

"Oh, I sympathize all round. I assure you I've no doubt you are quite right." And in this way I crawled out of the discussion, as usual.

What a pretty simile it is, comparing life to a river, because rivers are so different! There are the calm streams that flow eagerly from the youthful sources, join a kindred flood, and go placidly to the sea, only broadening and deepening and getting very muddy at times, but without a rapid or a fall. There are others that flow carelessly in the upper sunshine, begin to ripple and dance, then run swiftly, and rush into rapids in which there is no escape (though friends stand weeping and imploring on the banks) from the awful plunge of the cataract. Then there is the tumult and the seething, the exciting race and rage through the canon, the whirlpools and the passions of love and revelations of character, and finally, let us hope, the happy emergence into the lake of a serene life. And the more interesting rivers are those that have tumults and experiences.

I knew well enough before the next day was over that it was too late for the rescue of Margaret or Henderson. They were in the rapids, and would have rejected any friendly rope thrown to draw them ashore. And notwithstanding the doubts of my wife, I confess that I had so much sympathy with the genuineness of it that I enjoyed this shock of two strong natures rushing to their fate. Was it too sudden? Do two living streams hesitate when they come together? When they join they join, and mingle and reconcile themselves afterwards. It is only canals that flow languidly in parallel lines, and meet, if they meet at all, by the orderly contrivance of a lock.

In the morning the two were off for a stroll. There is a hill from which a most extensive prospect is had of the city, the teeming valley, with a score of villages and innumerable white spires, of forests and meadows and broken mountain ranges. It was a view that Margaret the night before had promised to show Henderson, that he might see what to her was the loveliest landscape in the world. Whether they saw the view I do not know. But I know the rock from which it is best seen, and could fancy Margaret sitting there, with her face turned towards it and her hands folded in her lap, and Henderson sitting, half turned away from it, looking in her face. There is an apple orchard just below. It was in bloom, and all the invitation of spring was in the air. That he saw all the glorious prospect reflected in her mobile face I do not doubt all the nobility and tenderness of it. If I knew the faltering talk in that hour of growing confidence and expectation, I would not repeat it. Henderson lunched at the Forsythe's, and after lunch he had some talk with Miss Forsythe. It must have been of an exciting nature to her, for, immediately after, that good woman came over in a great flutter, and was closeted with my wife, who at the end of the interview had an air of mysterious importance. It was evidently a woman's day, and my advice was not wanted, even if my presence was tolerated. All I heard my wife say through the opening door, as the consultation ended, was, "I hope she knows her own mind fully before anything is decided."

As to the objects of this anxiety, they were upon the veranda of the cottage, quite unconscious of the necessity of digging into their own minds. He was seated, and she was leaning against the railing on which the honeysuckle climbed, pulling a flower in pieces.

"It is such a short time I have known you," she was saying, as if in apology for her own feeling.

"Yes, in one way;" and he leaned forward, and broke his sentence with a little laugh. "I think I must have known you in some pre-existent state."

"Perhaps. And yet, in another way, it seems long a whole month, you know." And the girl laughed a little in her turn.

"It was the longest month I ever knew, after you left the city."

"Was it? I oughtn't to have said that first. But do you know, Mr. Henderson, you seem totally different from any other man I ever knew."

That this was a profound and original discovery there could be no doubt, from the conviction with which it was announced. "I felt from the first that I could trust you."

"I wish" and there was genuine feeling in the tone "I were worthier of such a generous trust."

There was a wistful look in her face timidity, self-depreciation, worship as Henderson rose and stood near her, and she looked up while he took the broken flower from her hand. There was but one answer to this, and in spite of the open piazza and the all-observant, all-revealing day, it might have been given; but at the moment Miss Forsythe was seen hurrying towards them through the shrubbery. She came straight to where they stood, with an air of New England directness and determination. One hand she gave to Henderson, the other to Margaret. She essayed to speak, but tears were in her eyes, and her lips trembled; the words would not come. She regarded them for an instant with all the overflowing affection of a quarter of a century of repression, and then quickly turned and went in. In a moment they followed her. Heaven go with them!

After Henderson had made his hasty adieus at our house and gone, before the sun was down, Margaret came over. She came swiftly into the room, gave me a kiss as I rose to greet her, with a delightful impersonality, as if she owed a debt somewhere and must pay it at once we men who are so much left out of these affairs have occasionally to thank Heaven for a merciful moment seized my wife, and dragged her to her room.

"I couldn't wait another moment," she said, as she threw herself on my wife's bosom in a passion of tears. "I am so happy! he is so noble, and I love him so!" And she sobbed as if it were the greatest calamity in the world. And then, after a little, in reply to a question for women are never more practical than in such a crisis: "Oh, no not for a long, long, long time. Not before autumn."

And the girl looked, through her glad tears, as if she expected to be admired for this heroism. And I have no doubt she was.

XII

Well, that was another success. The world is round, and like a ball seems swinging in the air, and swinging very pleasantly, thought Henderson, as he stepped on board the train that evening. The world is truly what you make it, and Henderson was determined to make it agreeable. His philosophy was concise, and might be hung up, as a motto: Get all you can, and don't fret about what you cannot get.

He went into the smoking compartment, and sat musing by the window for some time before he lit his cigar, feeling a glow of happiness that was new in his experience. The country was charming at twilight, but he was little conscious of that. What he saw distinctly was Margaret's face, trustful and wistful, looking up into his as she bade him goodby. What he was vividly conscious of was being followed, enveloped, by a woman's love.

"You will write, dear, the moment you get there, will you not? I am so afraid of accidents," she had said.

"Why, I will telegraph, sweet," he had replied, quite gayly.

"Will you? Telegraph? I never had that sort of a message." It seemed a very wonderful thing that he should use the public wire for this purpose, and she looked at him with new admiration.

"Are you timid about the train?" he asked.

"No. I never think of it. I never thought of it for myself; but this is different."

"Oh, I see." He put his arm round her and looked down into her eyes. This was a humorous suggestion to him, who spent half his time on the trains. "I think

I'll take out an accident policy."

"Don't say that. But you men are so reckless. Promise you won't stand on the platform, and won't get off while the train is in motion, and all the rest of the directions," she said, laughing a little with him; "and you will be careful?"

"I'll take such care of myself as I never did before, I promise. I never felt of so much consequence in my life."

"You'll think me silly. But you know, don't you, dear?" She put a hand on each shoulder, and pushing him back, studied his face. "You are all the world. And only to think, day before yesterday, I didn't think of the trains at all."

To have one look like that from a woman! To carry it with him! Henderson still forgot to light his cigar.

"Hello, Rodney!"

"Ah, Hollowell! I thought you were in Kansas City."

The new-comer was a man of middle age, thick set, with rounded shoulders, deep chest, heavy neck, iron-gray hair close cut, gray whiskers cropped so as to show his strong jaw, blue eyes that expressed at once resolution and good-nature.

"Well, how's things? Been up to fix the Legislature?"

"No; Perkins is attending to that," said Henderson, rather indifferently, like a man awakened out of a pleasant dream. "Don't seem to need much fixing. The public are fond of parallels."

Hollowell laughed. "I guess that's so till they get 'em."

"Or don't get them," Henderson added. And then both laughed.

"It looks as if it would go through this time. Bemis says the C. D.'s badly scared. They'll have to come down lively."

"I shouldn't wonder. By-the-way, look in tomorrow. I've got something to show you."

Henderson lit his cigar, and they both puffed in silence for some moments.

"By-the-way, did I ever show you this?" Hollowell took from his breast-pocket a handsome morocco case, and handed it to his companion. "I never travel without that. It's better than an accident policy."

Henderson unfolded the case, and saw seven photographs a showy-looking handsome woman in lace and jewels, and six children, handsome like their mother, the whole group with the photographic look of prosperity.

Henderson looked at it as if it had been a mirror of his own destiny, and expressed his admiration.

"Yes, it's hard to beat," Hollowell confessed, with a soft look in his face. "It's not for sale. Seven figures wouldn't touch it." He looked at it lovingly before he put it up, and then added: "Well, there's a figure for each, Rodney, and a big nest-egg for the old woman besides. There's nothing like it, old man. You'd better come in." And he put his hand affectionately on Henderson's knee.

Jeremiah Hollowell commonly known as Jerry was a remarkable man. Thirty years ago he had come to the city from Maine as a "hand" on a coast schooner, obtained employment in a railroad yard, then as a freight conductor, gone West, become a contractor, in which position a lucky hit set him on the road of the unscrupulous accumulation of property. He was now a railway magnate, the president of a system, a manipulator of dexterity and courage. All this would not have come about if his big head had not been packed with common-sense brains, and he had not had uncommon will and force of character. Success had developed the best side of him, the family side; and the worst side of him a brutal determination to increase his big fortune. He was not hampered by any scruples in business, but he had the good-sense to deal squarely with his friends when he had distinctly agreed to do so.

Henderson did not respond to the matrimonial suggestion; it was not possible for him to vulgarize his own affair by hinting it to such a man as Hollowell; but they soon fell into serious talk about schemes in which they were both interested. This talk so absorbed Henderson that after they had reached the city he had walked some blocks towards his lodging before he recalled his promise about the message. On his table he found a note from Carmen bidding him to dinner informally an invitation which he had no difficulty in declining on account of a previous engagement. And then he went to his club, and passed a cheerful evening. Why not? There was nothing melancholy about the young fellows in the smoking-room, who liked a good story and the latest gossip, and were attracted to the society of Henderson, who was open-handed and full of animal spirits, and above all had a reputation for success, and for being on the inside of affairs. There is nowhere else so much wisdom and such understanding of life as in a city club of young fellows, who have their experience still, for the most part, before them. Henderson was that night in great "force" as the phrase is. His companions thought he had made a lucky turn, and he did not tell them that he had won the love of the finest girl in the world, who was at that moment thinking of him as fondly as he was thinking of her but this was the subconsciousness of his gayety. Late at night he wrote her a long letter an honest letter of love and admiration, which warmed into the tenderness of devotion as it went on; a letter that she never parted with all her life long; but he left a description of the loneliness of his evening without her to her imagination.

It was for Margaret also a happy evening, but not a calm one, and not gay. She was swept away by a flood of emotions. She wanted to be alone, to think it over, every item of the short visit, every look, every tone. Was it all true? The great change made her tremble: of the future she dared scarcely think. She was restless, but not restless as before; she could not be calm in such a great happiness. And then the wonder of it, that he should choose her of all others he who knew the world so well, and must have known so many women. She followed him on his journey, thinking what he was doing now, and now, and now. She would have given the world to see him just for a moment, to look in his eyes and be sure again, to have him say that little word once more: there was a kind of pain in her heart, the separation was so cruel; it had been over two hours now. More than once in the evening she ran down to the sitting-room, where her aunt was pretending to be absorbed in a book, to kiss her, to pet her, to smooth her grayish hair and pat her cheek, and get her to talk about her girlhood days. She was so happy that tears were in her eyes half the time. At nine o'clock there was a pull at the bell that threatened to drag the wire out, and an insignificant little urchin appeared with a telegram, which frightened Miss Forsythe, and seemed to Margaret to drop out of heaven. Such an absurd thing to do at night, said the aunt, and then she kissed Margaret, and laughed a little, and declared that things had come to a queer pass when people made love by telegraph. There wasn't any love in the telegram, Margaret said; but she knew better the sending word of his arrival was a marvelous exhibition of thoughtfulness and constancy.

And then she led her aunt on to talk of Mr. Henderson, to give her impression, how he looked, what she really thought of him, and so on, and so on.

There was not much to say, but it could be said over and over again in various ways. It was the one night of the world, and her overwrought feeling sought relief. It would not be so again. She would be more reticent and more coquettish about her lover, but now it was all so new and strange.

That night when the girl went to sleep the telegram was under her pillow, and it seemed to throb with a thousand messages, as if it felt the pulsation of the current that sent it.

The prospective marriage of the budding millionaire Rodney Henderson was a society paper item in less than a week the modern method of publishing the banns. This was accompanied by a patronizing reference to the pretty schoolma'am, who was complimented upon her good-fortune in phrases so neatly turned as to give Henderson the greatest offense, and leave him no remedy, since nothing could have better suited the journal than further notoriety. He could not remember that he had spoken of it to any one except the Eschelles, to whom his relations made the communication a necessity, and he suspected Carmen, without, however, guessing that she was a habitual purveyor of the town gossiper.

"It is a shameful impertinence," she burst out, introducing the subject herself, when he called to see her. "I would horsewhip the editor." Her indignation was so genuine, and she took his side with such warm good comradeship, that his suspicions vanished for a moment.

"What good?" he answered, cooling down at the sight of her rage. "It is true, we are to be married, and she has taught school. I can't drag her name into a row about it. Perhaps she never will see it."

"Oh dear! dear me! what have I done?" the girl cried, with an accent of contrition. "I never thought of that. I was so angry that I cut it out and put it in the letter that was to contain nothing but congratulations, and told her how perfectly outrageous I thought it. How stupid!" and there was a world of trouble in her big dark eyes, while she looked up penitently, as if to ask his forgiveness for a great crime.

"Well, it cannot be helped," Henderson said, with a little touch of sympathy for Carmen's grief. "Those who know her will think it simply malicious, and the others will not think of it a second time."

"But I cannot forgive myself for my stupidity. I'm not sure but I'd rather you'd think me wicked than stupid," she continued, with the smile in her eyes that most men found attractive. "I confess is that very bad? that I feel it more for you than for her. But" (she thought she saw a shade in his face) "I warn you, if you are not very nice, I shall transfer my affections to her."

The girl was in her best mood, with the manner of a confiding, intimate friend. She talked about Margaret, but not too much, and a good deal more about Henderson and his future, not laying too great stress upon the marriage, as if it were, in fact, only an incident in his career, contriving always to make herself appear as a friend, who hadn't many illusions or much romance, to be sure, but who could always be relied on in any mood or any perplexity, and wouldn't be frightened or very severe at any confidences. She posed as a woman who could make allowances, and whose friendship would be no check or hinderance. This was conveyed in manner as much as in words, and put Henderson quite at his ease. He was not above the weakness of liking the comradeship of a woman of whom he was not afraid, a woman to whom he could say anything, a woman who could make allowances. Perhaps he was hardly conscious of this. He knew Carmen better than she thought he knew her, and he couldn't approve of her as a wife; and yet the fact was that she never gave him any moral worries.

"Yes," she said, when the talk drifted that way, "the chrysalis earl has gone. I think that mamma is quite inconsolable. She says she doesn't understand girls, or men, or anything, these days."

"Do you?" asked Henderson, lightly.

"I? No. I'm an agnostic except in religion. Have you got it into your head, my friend, that I ever fancied Mr. Lyon?"

"Not for himself " began Henderson, mischievously.

"That will do." She stopped him. "Or that he ever had any intention "

"I don't see how he could resist such "

"Stuff! See here, Mr. Rodney!" The girl sprang up, seized a plaque from the table, held it aloft in one hand, took half a dozen fascinating, languid steps, advancing and retreating with the grace of a Nautch girl, holding her dress with the other hand so as to allow a free movement. "Do you think I'd ever do that for John the Lyon's head on a charger?"

Then her mood changed to the domestic, as she threw herself into an easy-chair and said: "After all, I'm rather sorry he has gone. He was a man you could trust; that is, if you wanted to trust anybody I wish I had been made good."

When Henderson bade her good-night it was with the renewed impression that she was a very diverting comrade.

"I'm sort of sorry for you," she said, and her eyes were not so serious as to offend, as she gave him her hand, "for when you are married, you know, as the saying is, you'll want some place to spend your evenings." The audacity of the remark was quite obscured in the innocent frankness and sweetness of her manner.

What Henderson had to show Hollowell in his office had been of a nature greatly to interest that able financier. It was a project that would have excited the sympathy of Carmen, but Henderson did not speak of it to her though he had found that she was a safe deposit of daring schemes in general on account of a feeling of loyalty to Margaret, to whom he had never mentioned it in any of his daily letters. The scheme made a great deal of noise, later on, when it came to the light of consummation in legislatures and in courts, both civil and criminal; but its magnitude and success added greatly to Henderson's reputation as a bold and fortunate operator, and gave him that consideration which always attaches to those who command millions of money, and have the nerve to go undaunted through the most trying crises. I am anticipating by saying that it absolutely ruined thousands of innocent people, caused widespread strikes and practical business paralysis over a large region; but those things were regarded as only incidental to a certain sort of development, and did not impair the business standing, and rather helped the social position, of the two or three men who counted their gains by millions in the operation. It furnished occupation and gave good fees to a multitude of lawyers, and was dignified by the anxious consultation of many learned judges. A moralist, if he were poor and pessimistic, might have put the case in a line, and taken that line from the Mosaic decalogue (which was not intended for this new dispensation); but it was involved in such a cloud of legal technicalities, and took on such an aspect of enterprise and development of resources, and what not, that the general public mind was completely befogged about it. I am charitable enough to suppose that if the scheme had failed, the public conscience is so tender that there would have been a question of Henderson's honesty. But it did not fail.

Of this scheme, however, we knew nothing at the time in Brandon. Henderson was never in better spirits, never more agreeable, and it did not need inquiry to convince one that he was never so prosperous. He was often with us, in flying visits, and I can well remember that his coming and the expectation of it gave a kind of elation to the summer that and Margaret's supreme and sunny happiness. Even my wife admitted that it was on both sides a love-match, and could urge nothing against it except the woman's instinct that made her shrink from the point of ever thinking of him as a husband for herself, which seemed to me a perfectly reasonable feeling under all the circumstances.

The summer or what we call summer in the North, which is usually a preparation for warm weather, ending in a preparation for cold weather seemed to me very short but I have noticed that each summer is a little shorter than the preceding one. If Henderson had wanted to gain the confidence of my wife he could not have done so more effectually than he did in making us the confidants of a little plan he had in the city, which was a profound secret to the party most concerned. This was the purchase and furnishing of a house, and we made many clandestine visits with him to town in the early autumn in furtherance of his plan. He was intent on a little surprise, and when I once hinted to him that women liked to have a hand in making the home they were to occupy, he said he thought that my wife knew Margaret's taste and besides, he added, with a smile, "it will be only temporary; I should like her, if she chooses, to build and furnish a house to suit herself." In any one else this would have seemed like assumption, but with Henderson it was only the simple belief in his career.

We were still more surprised when we came to see the temporary home that Henderson had selected, the place where the bride was to alight, and look about her for such a home as would suit her growing idea of expanding fortune and position. It was one of the old-fashioned mansions on Washington Square, built at a time when people attached more importance to room and comfort than to outside display a house that seemed to have traditions of hospitality and of serene family life. It was being thoroughly renovated and furnished, with as little help from the decorative artist and the splendid upholsterer as consisted with some regard to public opinion; in fact the expenditure showed in solid dignity and luxurious ease, and not in the construction of a museum in which one could only move about with the constant fear of destroying something. My wife was given almost carte blanche in the indulgence of her taste, and she confessed her delight in being able for once to deal with a house without the feeling that she was ruining me. Only in the suite designed for Margaret did Henderson seriously interfere, and insist upon a luxury that almost took my wife's breath away. She opposed it on moral grounds. She said that no true woman could stand such pampering of her senses without destruction of her moral fibre. But Henderson had his way, as he always had it. What pleased her most in the house was the conservatory, opening out from the drawing-room a spacious place with a fountain and cool vines and flowering plants, not a tropical hothouse in a stifling atmosphere, in which nothing could live except orchids and flowers born near the equator, but a garden with a temperature adapted to human lungs, where one could sit and enjoy the sunshine, and the odor of flowers, and the clear and not too incessant notes of Mexican birds. But when it was all done, undoubtedly the most agreeable room in the house was that to which least thought had been given, the room to which any odds and ends could be sent, the room to which everybody gravitated when rest and simple enjoyment without restraint were the object Henderson's own library, with its big open fire, and the books and belongings of his bachelor days. Man is usually not credited with much taste or ability to take care of himself in the matter of comfortable living, but it is frequently noticed that when woman has made a dainty paradise of every other portion of the house, the room she most enjoys, that from which it is difficult to keep out the family, is the one that the man is permitted to call his own, in which he retains some of the comforts and can indulge some of the habits of his bachelor days. There is an important truth in this fact with regard to the sexes, but I do not know what it is.

They were married in October, and went at once to their own house. I suppose all other days were but a preparation for this golden autumn day on which we went to church and returned to the wedding-breakfast. I am sure everybody was happy. Miss Forsythe was so happy that tears were in her eyes half the time, and she bustled about with an affectation of cheerfulness that was almost contagious. Poor, dear, gentle lady! I can imagine the sensations of a peach-tree, in an orchard of trees which bud and bloom and by-and-by are weighty with yellow fruit, year after year a peach-tree that blooms, also, but never comes to fruition, only wastes its delicate sweetness on the air, and finally blooms less and less, but feels nevertheless in each returning spring the stir of the sap and the longing for that fuller life, while all the orchard bursts into flower, and the bees swarm about the pink promises, and the fruit sets and slowly matures to lusciousness in the sun of July. I fancy the wedding, which robbed us all, was hardest for her, for it was in one sense a finality of her life. Whereas if Margaret had regrets and deep sorrow she had in wrenching herself from the little neighborhood, though she never could have guessed the vacancy she caused by the withdrawal of her loved presence her own life was only just beginning, and she was sustained by the longing which every human soul has for a new career, by the curiosity and imagination which the traveler feels when he departs for a land which he desires, and yet dreads to see lest his illusions should vanish. Margaret was about to take that journey in the world which Miss Forsythe had dreamed of in her youth, but had never set out on. There are some who say that those are happiest who keep at home and content themselves with reading about the lands of the imagination. But happily the world does not believe this, and indeed would be very unhappy if it could not try and prove all the possibilities of human nature, to suffer as well as to enjoy.

I do not know how we fell into the feeling that this marriage was somehow exceptional and important, since marriages take place every day, and are so common and ordinarily so commonplace, when the first flutter is over. Even Morgan said, in his wife's presence, that he thought there had been weddings enough; at least he would interdict those that upset things like this one. For one thing, it brought about the house-keeping union of Mrs. Fletcher and Miss Forsythe in the tatter's cottage a sort of closing up of the ranks that happens on the field during a fatal engagement. As we go on, it becomes more and more difficult to fill up the gaps.

We were very unwilling to feel that Margaret had gone out of our life. "But you cannot," Morgan used to say, "be friends with the rich, and that is what makes the position of the very rich so pitiful, for the rich get so tired of each other."

"But Margaret," my wife urged, "will never be of that sort: money will not change either her habits or her affections."

"Perhaps. You can never trust to inherited poverty. I have no doubt that she will resist the world, if anybody can, but my advice is that if you want to keep along with Margaret, you'd better urge your husband to make money. Experience seems to teach that while they cannot come to us, we may sometimes go to them."

My wife and Mrs. Fletcher were both indignant at this banter, and accused Morgan of want of faith, and even lack of affection for Margaret; in short, of worldly-mindedness himself.

"Perhaps I am rather shop-worn," he confessed. "It's not distrust of Margaret's intentions, but knowledge of the strength of the current on which she has embarked. Henderson will not stop in his career short of some overwhelming disaster or of death."

"I thought you liked him? At any rate, Margaret will make a good use of his money."

"It isn't a question, my dear Mrs. Fairchild, of the use of money, but of the use money makes of you. Yes, I do like Henderson, but I can't give up my philosophy of life for the sake of one good fellow."

"Philosophy of fudge!" exclaimed my wife. And there really was no answer to this.

After six weeks had passed, my wife paid a visit to Margaret. Nothing could exceed the affectionate cordiality of her welcome. Margaret was overjoyed to see her, to show the house, to have her know her husband better, to take her into her new life. She was hardly yet over the naive surprises of her lovely surroundings. Or if it is too mach to say that her surprise had lasted six weeks for it is marvelous how soon women adapt themselves to new conditions if they are agreeable she was in a glow of wonder at her husband's goodness, at his love, which had procured all this happiness for her.

"You have no idea," she said, "how thoughtful he is about everything and he makes so little of it all. I am to thank you, he tells me always, for whatever pleases my taste in the house, and indeed I think I should have known you had been here if he had not told me. There are so many little touches that remind me of home. I am glad of that, for it is the more likely to make you feel that it is your home also."

She clung to this idea in the whirl of the new life. In the first days she dwelt much on this theme; indeed it was hardly second in her talk to her worship I can call it nothing less of her husband. She liked to talk of Brandon and the dear life there and the dearer friends this much talk about it showed that it was another life, already of the past, and beginning to be distant in the mind. My wife had a feeling that Margaret, thus early, was conscious of a drift, of a widening space, and was making an effort to pull the two parts of her life together, that there should be no break, as one carried away to sea by a resistless tide grasps the straining rope that still maintains his slender connection with the shore.

But it was all so different: the luxurious house, the carriage at call, the box at the opera, the social duties inevitable with her own acquaintances and the friends of her husband. She spoke of this in moments of confidence, and when she was tired, with a consciousness that it was a different life, but in no tone of regret, and I fancy that the French blood in her veins, which had so long run decorously in Puritan channels, leaped at its return into new gayety. Years ago Margaret had thought that she might some time be a missionary, at least that she should like to devote her life to useful labors among the poor and the unfortunate. If conscience ever reminded her of this, conscience was quieted by the suggestion that now she was in a position to be more liberal than she ever expected to be; that is, to give everything except the essential thing herself. Henderson liked a gay house, brightness, dinners, entertainment, and that his wife should be seen and admired. Proof of his love she found in all this, and she entered into it with spirit, and an enjoyment increased by the thought that she was lightening the burden of his business, which she could see pressed more and more. Not that Henderson made any account of his growing occupations, or that any preoccupation was visible except to the eye of love, which is quick to see all moods. These were indeed happy days, full of the brightness of an expanding prosperity and unlimited possibilities of the enjoyment of life. It was in obedience to her natural instinct, and not yet a feeling of compensation and propitiation, that enlisted Margaret in the city charities, connection with which was a fashionable self-entertainment with some, and a means of social promotion with others. My wife came home a little weary with so much of the world, but, on the whole, impressed with Margaret's good-fortune. Henderson in his own house was the soul of consideration and hospitality, and Margaret was blooming in the beauty that shines in satisfied desire.

XIII

It is so painful to shrink, and so delightful to grow! Every one knows the renovation of feeling often mistaken for a moral renewal when the worn dress of the day is exchanged for the fresh evening toilet. The expansiveness of prosperity has a like effect, though the moralist is always piping about the beneficent uses of adversity. The moralist is, of course, right, time enough given; but what does the tree, putting out its tender green leaves to the wooing of the south wind, care for the moralist? How charming the world is when you go with it, and not against it!

It was better than Margaret had thought. When she came to Washington in the winter season the beautiful city seemed to welcome her and respond to the gayety of her spirit. It was so open, cheerful, hospitable, in the appearance of its smooth, broad avenues and pretty little parks, with the bronze statues which all looked noble in the moonlight; it was such a combination and piquant contrast of shabby ease and stately elegance negro cabins and stone mansions, picket-fences and sheds, and flower-banked terraces before rows of residences which bespoke wealth and refinement. The very aspect of the street population was novel; compared to New York, the city was as silent as a country village, and the passers, who have the fashion of walking in the middle of the street upon the asphalt as freely as upon the sidewalks, had a sort of busy leisureliness, the natural air of thousands of officials hived in offices for a few hours and then left in irresponsible idleness. But what most distinguished the town, after all, in Margaret's first glimpse of it, was the swarming negro population pervading every part of it the slouching plantation negro, the smart mulatto girl with gay raiment and mincing step, the old-time auntie, the brisk waiter-boy with uncertain eye, the washerwoman, the hawkers and fruiterers, the loafing strollers of both sexes carrying everywhere color, abandon, a certain picturesqueness and irresponsibility and good-nature, and a sense of moral relaxation in a too strict and duty-ridden world.

In the morning, when Margaret looked from the windows of the hotel, the sky was gray and yielding, and all the outlines of the looming buildings were softened in the hazy air. The dome of the Capitol seemed to float like a bubble, and to be as unsubstantial as the genii edifices in the Arabian tale. The Monument, the slim white shaft as tall as the Great Pyramid, was still more a dream creation, not really made of hard marble, but of something as soft as vapor, almost melting into the sky, and yet distinct, unwavering, its point piercing the upper air, threatening every instant to dissolve, as if it were truly the baseless fabric of a vision light, unreal, ghost-like, spotless, pure as an unsullied thought; it might vanish in a breath; and yet, no; it is solid: in the mist of doubt, in the assault of storms, smitten by the sun, beaten by the tempests, it stands there, springing, graceful, immovable emblem, let us say, of the purity and permanence of the republic.

"You never half told me, Rodney, how beautiful it all is!" Margaret exclaimed, in a glow of delight.

"Yes," said Henderson, "the Monument is behaving very well this morning. I never saw it before look so little like a factory chimney."

"That is, you never looked at it with my eyes before, cynic. But it is all so lovely, everywhere."

"Of course it is, dear." They were standing together at the window, and his arm was where it should have been. "What did you expect? There are concentrated here the taste and virtue of sixty millions of people."

"But you always said the Washington hotels were so bad. These apartments are charming."

"Yes" and he drew her closer to him "there is no denying that. But presently I shall have to explain to you an odd phenomenon. Virginia, you know, used to be famous for its good living, and Maryland was simply unapproachable for good cooking. It was expected when the District was made out of these two that the result would be something quite extraordinary in the places of public entertainment. But, by a process which nobody can explain, in the union the art of cooking in hotels got mislaid."

"Well," she said, with winning illogicality, "you've got me."

"If you could only eat the breakfasts for me, as you can see the Monument for me!"

"Dear, I could eat the Monument for you, if it would do you any good." And neither of them was ashamed of this nonsense, for both knew that married people indulge in it when they are happy.

Although Henderson came to Washington on business, this was Margaret's wedding journey. There is no other city in the world where a wedding journey can better be combined with such business as is transacted here, for in both is a certain element of mystery. Washington is gracious to a bride, if she is pretty and agreeable devotion to governing, or to legislation, or to diplomacy, does not render a man insensible to feminine attractions; and if in addition to beauty a woman has the reputation of wealth, she is as nearly irresistible here as anywhere. To Margaret, who was able to return the hospitality she received, and whose equipage was almost as much admired as her toilets, all doors were open a very natural thing, surely, in a good-natured, give-and-take world. The colonel Margaret had laughed till she cried when first she heard her husband saluted by this title in Washington by his New Hampshire acquaintances, but he explained to her that he had justly won it years ago by undergoing the hardship of receptions as a member of the Governor's staff the colonel had brought on his horses and carriages, not at all by way of ostentation, but simply out of regard to what was due her as his wife, and because a carriage at call is a constant necessity in this city, whose dignity is equal to the square of its distances, and because there is something incongruous in sending a bride about in a herdic. Margaret's unworldly simplicity had received a little shock when she first saw her servants in livery, but she was not slow to see the propriety and even necessity of it in a republican society, since elegance cannot be a patchwork, but must be harmonious, and there is no harmony between a stylish turnout noble horses nobly caparisoned and a coachman and footman on the box dressed according to their own vulgar taste. Given a certain position, one's sense of fitness and taste mast be maintained. And there is so much kindliness and consideration in human nature Margaret's gorgeous coachman and footman never by a look revealed their knowledge that she was new to the situation, and I dare say that their respectful demeanor contributed to raise her in her own esteem as one of the select and favored in this prosperous world. The most self-poised and genuine are not insensible to the tribute of this personal consideration. My lady giving orders to her respectful servitors, and driving down the avenue in her luxurious turnout, is not at all the same person in feeling that she would be if dragged about in a dissolute-looking hack whose driver has the air of the stable. We take kindly to this transformation, and perhaps it is only the vulgar in soul who become snobbish in it. Little by little, under this genial consideration, Margaret advanced in the pleasant path of worldliness; and we heard, by the newspapers and otherwise indeed, Mr. and Mrs. Morgan were there for a couple of weeks in the winter that she was never more sweet and gracious and lovely than in this first season at the capital. I don't know that the town was raving, as they said, about her beauty and wit there is nothing like the wit of a handsome woman and amiability and unostentatious little charities, but she was a great favorite. We used to talk about it by the fire in Brandon, where everything reminded us of the girl we loved, and rejoice in her good-fortune and happiness, and get rather heavy-hearted in thinking that she had gone away from us into such splendor.

"I wish you were here," she wrote to my wife. "I am sure you would enjoy it. There are so many distinguished people and brilliant people though the distinguished are not always brilliant nor the brilliant distinguished and everybody is so kind and hospitable, and Rodney is such a favorite. We go everywhere, literally, and all the time. You must not scold, but I haven't opened a book, except my prayerbook, in six weeks it is such a whirl. And it is so amusing. I didn't know there were so many kinds of people and so many sorts of provincialism in the world. The other night, at the British Minister's, a French attache, who complimented my awful French I told him that I inherited all but the vocabulary and the accent said that if specimens of the different kinds of women evolved in all out-of-the-way places who come to Washington could be exhibited, nobody would doubt any more that America is an interesting country. Wasn't it an impudent speech? I tried to tell him, in French, how grateful American women are for any little attention from foreigners who have centuries of politeness behind them. Ah me! I sometimes long for one of the old-fashioned talks before your smoldering logs! What we talk about here, Heaven only knows. I sometimes tell Rodney at night it is usually morning that I feel like an extinct piece of fireworks. But next day it is all delightful again; and, dear friend, I don't know but that I like being fireworks."

Among the men who came oftenest to see Henderson was Jerry Hollowell. It seemed to Margaret an odd sort of companionship; it could not be any similarity of tastes that drew them together, and she could not understand the nature of the business transacted in their mysterious conferences. Social life had few attractions for Hollowell, for his family were in the West; he appeared to have no relations with any branch of government; he wanted no office, though his influence was much sought by those who did want it.

"You spend a good deal of time here, Mr. Hollowell," Margaret said one day when he called in Henderson's absence.

"Yes, ma'am, considerable. Things need a good deal of fixing up. Washington is a curious place. It's a sort of exchange for the whole country: you can see everybody here, and it is a good place to arrange matters."

"With Congress, do you mean?" Margaret had heard much of the corruption of Congress.

"No, not Congress particularly. Congressmen are just about like other people. It's all nonsense, this talk about buying Congressmen. You cannot buy them any more than you can buy other people, but you can sort of work together with some of them. We don't want anything of Congress, except to be let alone. If we are doing something to develop the trade in the Southwest, build it up, some member who thinks he is smart will just as likely as not try to put in a block somewhere, or investigate, or something, in order to show his independence, and then he has to be seen, and shown that he is going against the interests of his constituents. It is just as it is everywhere: men have to be shown what their real interest is. No; most Congressmen are poor, and they stay poor. It is a good deal easier to deal with those among them who are rich and have some idea about the prosperity of the country. It is just so in the departments. You've got to watch things, if you expect them to go smooth. You've got to get acquainted with the men. Most men are reasonable when you get well acquainted with them. I tell your husband that people are about as reasonable in Washington as you'll find them anywhere."

"Washington is certainly very pleasant."

"Yes, that's so; it is pleasant. Where most everybody wants something, they are bound to be accommodating. That's my idea. I reckon you don't find Jerry Hollowell trying to pull a cat by its tail," he added, dropping into his native manner.

"Well, I must go and hunt up the old man. Glad to have made your acquaintance, Mrs. Henderson." And then, with a sly look, "If I knew you better, ma'am, I should take the liberty of congratulating you that Henderson has come round so handsomely."

"Come round?" asked Margaret, in amused wonder.

"Well, I took the liberty of giving him a hint that he wasn't cut-out for a single man. I showed him that," and he lugged out his photograph-case from a mass of papers in his breast-pocket and handed it to her.

"Ah, I see," said Margaret, studying the photographs with a peculiar smile.

"Oh, Henderson knows a good thing when he sees it," said Hollowell, complacently.

It was not easy to be offended with Hollowell's kind-hearted boorishness, and after he had gone, Margaret sat a long time reflecting upon this new specimen of man in her experience. She was getting many new ideas in these days, the moral lines were not as clearly drawn as she had thought; it was impossible to ticket men off into good and bad. In Hollowell she had a glimpse of a world low-toned and vulgar; she had heard that he was absolutely unscrupulous, and she had supposed that he would appear to be a very wicked man. But he seemed to be good-hearted and tolerant and friendly. How fond he was of his family, and how charitable about Congress! And she wondered if the world was generally on Hollowell's level. She met many men more cultivated than he, gentlemen in manner and in the first social position, who took, after all, about his tone in regard to the world, very agreeable people usually, easy to get on with, not exacting, or professing much faith in anybody, and mildly cynical only bitterly cynical when they failed to get what they wanted, and felt the good things of life slipping away from them. It was to take her some time to learn that some of the most agreeable people are those who have succeeded by the most questionable means; and when she came to this knowledge, what would be her power of judgment as to these means?

"Mr. Hollowell has been here," she said, when Henderson returned.

"Old Jerry? He is a character."

"Do you trust him?"

"It never occurred to me. Yes, I suppose so, as far as his interests go. He isn't a bad sort of fellow very long-headed."

"Dear," said Margaret, with hesitation, "I wish you didn't have anything to do with such men."

"Why, dearest?"

"Oh, I don't know. You needn't laugh. It rather lets one down; and it isn't like you."

Henderson laughed aloud now. "But you needn't associate with Hollowell. We men cannot pick our companions in business and politics. It needs all sorts to keep the world going."

"Then I'd rather let it stop," Margaret said.

"And sell out at auction?" he cried, with a look of amusement.

"But aren't Mr. Morgan and Mr. Fairchild business men?"

"Yes of the old-fashioned sort. The fact is, Margaret, you've got a sort of preserve up in Brandon, and you fancy that the world is divided into sheep and goats. It's a great mistake. There is no such division. Every man almost is both a sheep and a goat."

"I don't believe it, Rodney. You are neither." She came close to him, and taking the collar of his coat in each hand, gave him a little shake, and looking up into his face with quizzical affection, asked, "What is your business here?"

Henderson stooped down and kissed her forehead, and tenderly lifted the locks of her brown hair. "You wouldn't understand, sweet, if I told you."

"You might try."

"Well, there's a man here from Fort Worth who wants us to buy a piece of railroad, and extend it, and join it with Hollowell's system, and open up a lot of new country."

"And isn't it a good piece of road?"

"Yes; that's the trouble. The owners want to keep it to themselves, and prevent the general development. But we shall get it."

"It isn't anything like wrecking, is it, dear?"

"Do you think we would want to wreck our own property?"

"But what has Congress to do with it?"

"Oh, there's a land grant. But some of the members who were not in the Congress that voted it say that it is forfeited."

In this fashion the explanation went on. Margaret loved to hear her husband talk, and to watch the changing expression of his face, and he explained about this business until she thought he was the sweetest fellow in the world.

The Morgans had arrived at the same hotel, and Margaret went about with them in the daytime, while Henderson was occupied. It was like a breath of home to be with them, and their presence, reviving that old life, gave a new zest to the society spectacle, to the innocent round of entertainments, which more and more absorbed her. Besides, it was very interesting to have Mr. Morgan's point of view of Washington, and to see the shifting panorama through his experience. He had been very much in the city in former years, but he came less and less now, not because it was less beautiful or attractive in a way, but because it had lost for him a certain charm it once had.

"I am not sure," he said, as they were driving one day, "that it is not now the handsomest capital in the world; at any rate, it is on its way to be that. No other has public buildings more imposing, or streets and avenues so attractive in their interrupted regularity, so many stately vistas ending in objects refreshing to the eye a bit of park, banks of flowers, a statue or a monument that is decorative, at least in the distance. As the years go on we shall have finer historical groups, triumphal arches and columns that will give it more and more an air of distinction, the sort of splendor with which the Roman Empire celebrated itself, and, added to this, the libraries and museums and galleries that are the chief attractions of European cities. Oh, we have only just begun the city is so accessible in all directions, and lends itself to all sorts of magnificence and beauty."

"I declare," said Mrs. Morgan to Margaret, "I didn't know that he could be so eloquent. Page, you ought to be in Congress."

"In order to snuff myself out? Congress is not so important a feature as it used to be. Washington is getting to have a character of its own; it seems as if it wouldn't be much without its official life, yet the process is going on here that is so marked all over the country the divorce of social and political life. I used to think, fifteen years ago, that Washington was a standing contradiction to the old aphorism that a democracy cannot make society there was no more agreeable society in the world than that in Washington even ten years ago: society selected itself somehow without any marked class distinction, and it was delightfully simple and accessible."

"And what has changed it?" Margaret asked.

"Money, which changes everything and everybody. The whole scale has altered. There is so much more display and expense. I remember when a private carriage in Washington was a rare object. The possession of money didn't help one much socially. What made a person desired in any company was the talent of being agreeable, talent of some sort, not the ability to give a costly dinner or a big ball."

"But there are more literary and scientific people here, everybody says," said Margaret, who was becoming a partisan of the city.

"Yes, and they keep more to themselves withdraw into their studies, or hive in their clubs. They tell me that the delightful informality and freedom of the old life is gone. Ask the old Washington residents whether the coming in of rich people with leisure hasn't demoralized society, or stiffened it, and made it impossible after the old sort. It is as easy here now as anywhere else to get together a very heavy dinner party all very grand, but it isn't amusing. It is more and more like New York."

"But we have been to delightful dinners," Margaret insisted.

"No doubt. There are still houses of the old sort, where wit and good-humor and free hospitality are more conspicuous than expense; but when money selects, there is usually an incongruous lot about the board. An oracular scientist at the club the other night put it rather neatly when he said that a society that exists mainly to pay its debts gets stupid."

"That's as clever," Margaret retorted, "as the remark of an under-secretary at a cabinet reception the other night, that it is one thing to entertain and another to be entertaining. I won't have you slander Washington. I should like to spend all my winters here."

"Dear me!" said Morgan, "I've been praising Washington. I should like to live here also, if I had the millions of Jerry Hollowell. Jerry is going to build a palace out on the Massachusetts Avenue extension bigger than the White House."

"I don't want to hear anything about Hollowell."

"But he is the coming man. He represents the democratic plutocracy that we are coming to."

All Morgan's banter couldn't shake Margaret's enjoyment of the cheerful city. "You like it as well as anybody," she told him. And in truth he and Mrs. Morgan dipped into every gayety that was going. "Of course I do," he said, "for a couple of weeks. I shouldn't like to be obliged to follow it as a steady business. Washington is a good place to take a plunge occasionally. And then you can go home and read King Solomon with appreciation."

Margaret had thought when she came to Washington that she should spend a good deal of time at the Capitol, listening to the eloquence of the Senators and Representatives, and that she should study the collections and the Patent-office and explore all the public buildings, in which she had such intense historical interest as a teacher in Brandon. But there was little time for these pleasures, which weighed upon her like duties. She did go to the Capitol once, and tired herself out tramping up and down, and was very proud of it all, and wondered how any legislation was ever accomplished, and was confused by the hustling about, the swinging of doors, the swarms in the lobbies, and the racing of messengers, and concluded unjustly that it was a big hive of whispered conference, and bargaining, and private interviewing. Morgan asked her if she expected that the business of sixty millions of people was going to be done with the order and decorum of a lyceum debating society. In one of the committee-rooms she saw Hollowell, looking at ease, and apparently an indispensable part of the government machine. Her own husband, who had accompanied the party, she lost presently, whisked away somewhere. He was sought in vain afterwards, and at last Margaret came away dazed and stunned by the noise of the wheels of the great republic in motion. She did not try it again, and very little strolling about the departments satisfied her. The west end claimed her the rolling equipages, the drawing-rooms, the dress, the vistas of evening lamps, the gay chatter in a hundred shining houses, the exquisite dinners, the crush of the assemblies, the full flow of the tide of fashion and of enjoyment what is there so good in life? To be young, to be rich, to be pretty, to be loved, to be admired, to compliment and be complimented every Sunday at morning service, kneeling in a fluttering row of the sweetly devout, whose fresh toilets made it good to be there, and who might humbly hope to be forgiven for the things they have left undone, Margaret thanked Heaven for its gifts.

And it went well with Henderson meantime. Surely he was born under a lucky star if it is good-luck for a man to have absolute prosperity and the gratification of all his desires. One reason why Hollowell sought his cooperation was a belief in this luck, and besides Henderson was, he knew, more presentable, and had social access in quarters where influence was desirable, although Hollowell was discovering that with most men delicacy in presenting anything that is for their interest is thrown away. He found no difficulty in getting recruits for his little dinners at Champolion's dinners that were not always given in his name, and where he appeared as a guest, though he footed the bills. Bungling grossness has disappeared from all really able and large transactions, and genius is mainly exercised in the supply of motives for a line of conduct. The public good is one of the motives that looks best in Washington.

Henderson and Hollowell got what they wanted in regard to the Southwest consolidation, and got it in the most gentlemanly way. Nobody was bought, no one was offered a bribe. There were, of course, fees paid for opinions and for professional services, and some able men induced to take a prospective interest in what was demonstrably for the public good. But no vote was given for a consideration at least this was the report of an investigating committee later on. Nothing, of course, goes through Congress of its own weight, except occasionally a resolution of sympathy with the Coreans, and the calendar needs to be watched, and the good offices of friends secured. Skillful wording of a clause, the right moment, and opportune recognition do the business. The main thing is to create a favorable atmosphere and avoid discussion. When the bill was passed, Hollowell did give a dinner on his own invitation, a dinner that was talked of for its refinement as well as its cost. The chief topic of conversation was the development of the Southwest and the extension of our trade relations with Mexico. The little scheme, hatched in Henderson's New York office, in order to transfer certain already created values to the pockets of himself and his friends, appeared to have a national importance. When Henderson rose to propose the health of Jerry Hollowell, neither he nor the man he eulogized as a creator of industries whose republican patriotism was not bound by State lines nor circumscribed by sections was without a sense of the humor of the situation.

And yet in a certain way Mr. Hollowell was conscious that he merited the eulogy. He had come to believe that the enterprises in which he was engaged, that absolutely gave him, it was believed, an income of a million a year, were for the public good. Such vast operations lent him the importance of a public man. If he was a victim of the confusion of mind which mistook his own prosperity for the general benefit, he only shared a wide public opinion which regards the accumulation of enormous fortunes in a few hands as an evidence of national wealth.

Margaret left Washington with regret. She had a desire to linger in the opening of the charming spring there, for the little parks were brilliant with flower beds-tulips, hyacinths, crocuses, violets the magnolias and redbuds in their prodigal splendor attracted the eye a quarter of a mile away, and the slender twigs of the trees began to be suffused with tender green. It was the sentimental time of the year. But Congress had gone, and whatever might be the promise of the season, Henderson had already gathered the fruits that had been forced in the hothouse of the session. He was in high spirits.

"It has all been so delightful, dear!" said Margaret as they rode away in the train, and caught their last sight of the dome. They were in Hollowell's private car, which the good-natured old fellow had put at their disposal. And Margaret had a sense of how delightful and prosperous this world is as seen from a private car.

"Yes," Henderson answered, thinking of various things; "it has been a successful winter. The capital is really attractive. It occurred to me the other day that America has invented a new kind of city, the apotheosis of the village Washington."

They talked of the city, of the acquaintances of the winter, of Hollowell's thoughtfulness in lending them his car, that their bridal trip, as he had said, might have a good finish. Margaret's heart opened to the world. She thought of the friends at Brandon, she thought of the poor old ladies she was accustomed to look after in the city, of the ragged-school that she visited, of the hospital in which she was a manager, of the mission chapel. The next Sunday would be Easter, and she thought of a hundred ways in which she could make it brighter for so many of the unfortunates. Her heart was opened to the world, and looking across to Henderson, who was deep in the morning paper, she said, with a wife's unblushing effrontery, "Dearest, how handsome you are!"

The home life took itself up again easily and smoothly in Washington Square. Did there ever come a moment of reflection as to the nature of this prosperity which was altogether so absorbing and agreeable? If it came, did it give any doubts and raise any of the old questions that used to be discussed at Brandon? Wasn't it the use that people made of money, after all, that was the real test? She did not like Hollowell, but on acquaintance he was not the monster that he had appeared to her in the newspapers. She was perplexed now and then by her husband's business, but did it differ from that of other men she had known, except that it was on a larger scale? And how much good could be done with money!

On Easter morning, when Margaret returned from early service, to which she had gone alone, she found upon her dressing-table a note addressed to "My Wife," and in it a check for a large sum to her order, and a card, on which was written, "For Margaret's Easter Charities." Flushed with pleasure, she ran to meet her husband on the landing as he was descending to breakfast, threw her arms about his neck, and, with tears in her eyes, cried, "Dearest, how good you are!"

It is such a good and prosperous generation.

XIV

Our lives are largely made up of the things we do not have. In May, the time of the apple blossoms just a year from the swift wooing of Margaret Miss Forsythe received a letter from John Lyon. It was in a mourning envelope. The Earl of Chisholm was dead, and John Lyon was Earl of Chisholm. The information was briefly conveyed, but with an air of profound sorrow. The letter spoke of the change that this loss brought to his own life, and the new duties laid upon him, which would confine him more closely to England. It also contained congratulations which circumstances had delayed upon Mrs. Henderson's marriage, and a simple wish for her happiness. The letter was longer than it need have been for these purposes; it seemed to love to dwell upon the little visit to Brandon and the circle of friends there, and it was pervaded by a tone, almost affectionate, towards Miss Forsythe, which touched her very deeply. She said it was such a manly letter.

America, the earl said, interested him more and more. In all history, he wrote, there never had been such an opportunity for studying the formation of society, for watching the working out of political problems; the elements meeting were so new, and the conditions so original, that historical precedents were of little service as guides. He acknowledged an almost irresistible impulse to come back, and he announced his intention of another visit as soon as circumstances permitted.

I had noticed this in English travelers of intelligence before. Crude as the country is, and uninteresting according to certain established standards, it seems to have a "drawing" quality, a certain unexplained fascination. Morgan says that it is the social unconventionality that attracts, and that the American women are the loadstone. He declares. that when an Englishman secures and carries home with him an American wife, his curiosity about the country is sated. But this is generalizing on narrow premises.

There was certainly in Lyon's letter a longing to see the country again, but the impression it made upon me when I read it due partly to its tone towards Miss

Forsythe, almost a family tone was that the earldom was an empty thing without the love of Margaret Debree. Life is so brief at the best, and has so little in it when the one thing that the heart desires is denied. That the earl should wish to come to America again without hope or expectation was, however, quite human nature. If a man has found a diamond and lost it, he is likely to go again and again and wander about the field where he found it, not perhaps in any defined hope of finding another, but because there is a melancholy satisfaction in seeing the spot again. It was some such feeling that impelled the earl to wish to see again Miss Forsythe, and perhaps to talk of Margaret, but he certainly had no thought that there were two Margaret Debrees in America.

To her aunt's letter conveying the intelligence of Mr. Lyon's loss, Margaret replied with a civil message of condolence. The news had already reached the Eschelles, and Carmen, Margaret said, had written to the new earl a most pious note, which contained no allusion to his change of fortune, except an expression of sympathy with his now enlarged opportunity for carrying on his philanthropic plans a most unworldly note. "I used to think," she had said, when confiding what she had done to Margaret, "that you would make a perfect missionary countess, but you have done better, my dear, and taken up a much more difficult work among us fashionable sinners. Do you know," she went on, "that I feel a great deal less worldly than I used to?"

Margaret wrote a most amusing account of this interview, and added that Carmen was really very good-hearted, and not half as worldly-minded as she pretended to be; an opinion with which Miss Forsythe did not at all agree. She had spent a fortnight with Margaret after Easter, and she came back in a dubious frame of mind. Margaret's growing intimacy with Carmen was one of the sources of her uneasiness. They appeared to be more and more companionable, although Margaret's clear perception of character made her estimate of Carmen very nearly correct. But the fact remained that she found her company interesting. Whether the girl tried to astonish the country aunt, or whether she was so thoroughly a child of her day as to lack certain moral perceptions, I do not know, but her candid conversation greatly shocked Miss Forsythe.

"Margaret," she said one day, in one of her apparent bursts of confidence, "seems to have had such a different start in life from mine. Sometimes, Miss Forsythe, she puzzles me. I never saw anybody so much in love as she is with Mr. Henderson; she doesn't simply love him, she is in love with him. I don't wonder she is fond of him any woman might be that but, do you know, she actually believes in him."

"Why shouldn't she believe in him?" exclaimed Miss Forsythe, in astonishment.

"Oh, of course, in a way," the girl went on. "I like Mr. Henderson I like him very much but I don't believe in him. It isn't the way now to believe in anybody very much. We don't do it, and I think we get along just as well and better. Don't you think it's nicer not to have any deceptions?"

Miss Forsythe was too much stunned to make any reply. It seemed to her that the bottom had fallen out of society.

"Do you think Mr. Henderson believes in people?" the girl persisted.

"If he does not he isn't much of a man. If people don't believe in each other, society is going to pieces. I am astonished at such a tone from a woman."

"Oh, it isn't any tone in me, my dear Miss Forsythe," Carmen continued, sweetly. "Society is a great deal pleasanter when you are not anxious and don't expect too much."

Miss Forsythe told Margaret that she thought Miss Eschelle was a dangerous woman. Margaret did not defend her, but she did not join, either, in condemning her; she appeared to have accepted her as a part of her world. And there were other things that Margaret seemed to have accepted without that vigorous protest which she used to raise at whatever crossed her conscience. To her aunt she was never more affectionate, never more solicitous about her comfort and her pleasure, and it was almost enough to see Margaret happy, radiant, expanding day by day in the prosperity that was illimitable, only there was to her a note of unreality in all the whirl and hurry of the busy life. She liked to escape to her room with a book, and be out of it all, and the two weeks away from her country life seemed long to her. She couldn't reconcile Margaret's love of the world, her tolerance of Carmen, and other men and women whose lives seemed to be based on Carmen's philosophy, with her devotion to the church services, to the city missions, and the dozens of charities that absorb so much of the time of the leaders of society.

"You are too young, dear, to be so good and devout," was Carmen's comment on the situation.

To Miss Forsythe's wonder, Margaret did not resent this impertinence, but only said that no accumulation of years was likely to bring Carmen into either of these dangers. And the reply was no more satisfactory to Miss Forsythe than the remark that provoked it.

That she had had a delightful visit, that Margaret was more lovely than ever, that Henderson was a delightful host, was the report of Miss Forsythe when she returned to us. In a confidential talk with my wife she confessed, however, that she couldn't tell whither Margaret was going.

One of the worries of modern life is the perplexity where to spend the summer. The restless spirit of change affects those who dwell in the country, as well as those who live in the city. No matter how charming the residence is, one can stay in it only a part of the year. He actually needs a house in town, a villa by the sea, and a cottage in the hills. When these are secured each one an establishment more luxurious year by year then the family is ready to travel about, and is in a greater perplexity than before whether to spend the summer in Europe or in America, the novelties of which are beginning to excite the imagination. This nomadism, which is nothing less than society on wheels, cannot be satirized as a whim of fashion; it has a serious cause in the discovery of the disease called nervous prostration, which demands for its cure constant change of scene, without any occupation. Henderson recognized it, but he said that personally he had no time to indulge in it. His summer was to be a very busy one. It was impossible to take Margaret with him on his sudden and tedious journeys from one end of the country to the other, but she needed a change. It was therefore arranged that after a visit to Brandon she should pass the warm months with the Arbusers in their summer home at Lenox, with a month the right month in the Eschelle villa at Newport; and he hoped never to be long absent from one place or the other.

Margaret came to Brandon at the beginning of June, just at the season when the region was at its loveliest, and just when its society was making preparations to get away from it to the sea, or the mountains, or to any place that was not home. I could never understand why a people who have been grumbling about snow and frost for six months, and longing for genial weather, should flee from it as soon as it comes. I had made the discovery, quite by chance and it was so novel that I might have taken out a patent on it that if one has a comfortable home in our northern latitude, he cannot do better than to stay in it when the hum of the mosquito is heard in the land, and the mercury is racing up and down the scale between fifty and ninety. This opinion, however, did not extend beyond our little neighborhood, and we may be said to have had the summer to ourselves.

I fancied that the neighborhood had not changed, but the coming of Margaret showed me that this was a delusion. No one can keep in the same place in life simply by standing still, and the events of the past two years had wrought a subtle change in our quiet. Nothing had been changed to the eye, yet something had been taken away, or something had been added, a door had been opened into the world. Margaret had come home, yet I fancied it was not the home to her that she had been thinking about. Had she changed?

She was more beautiful. She had the air I should hesitate to call it that of the fine lady of assured position, something the manner of that greater world in which the possession of wealth has supreme importance, but it was scarcely a change of manner so much as of ideas about life and of the things valuable in it gradually showing itself. Her delight at being again with her old friends was perfectly genuine, and she had never appeared more unselfish or more affectionate. If there was a subtle difference, it might very well be in us, though I found it impossible to conceive of her in her former role of teacher and simple maiden, with her heart in the little concerns of our daily life. And why should she be expected to go back to that stage? Must we not all live our lives? Miss Forsythe's solicitude about Margaret was mingled with a curious deference, as to one who had a larger experience of life than her own. The girl of a year ago was now the married woman, and was invested with something of the dignity that Miss Forsythe in her pure imagination attached to that position. Without yielding any of her opinions, this idea somehow changed her relations to Margaret; a little, I thought, to the amusement of Mrs. Fletcher and the other ladies, to whom marriage took on a less mysterious aspect. It arose doubtless from a renewed sense of the incompleteness of her single life, long as it had been, and enriched as it was by observation.

In that June there were vexatious strikes in various parts of the country, formidable combinations of laboring-men, demonstrations of trades-unions, and the exhibition of a spirit that sharply called attention to the unequal distribution of wealth. The discontent was attributed in some quarters to the exhibition of extreme luxury and reckless living by those who had been fortunate. It was even said that the strikes, unreasonable and futile as they were, and most injurious to those who indulged in them, were indirectly caused by the railway manipulation, in the attempt not only to crush out competition, but to exact excessive revenues on fictitious values. Resistance to this could be shown to be blind, and the strikers technically in the wrong, yet the impression gained ground that there was something monstrously wrong in the way great fortunes were accumulated, in total disregard of individual rights, and in a materialistic spirit that did not take into account ordinary humanity. For it was not alone the laboring class that was discontented, but all over the country those who lived upon small invested savings, widows and minors, found their income imperiled by the trickery of rival operators and speculators in railways and securities, who treated the little private accumulations as mere counters in the games they were playing. The loss of dividends to them was poorly compensated by reflections upon the development of the country, and the advantage to trade of great consolidations, which inured to the benefit of half a dozen insolent men.

In discussing these things in our little parliament we were not altogether unprejudiced, it must be confessed. For, to say nothing of interests of Mr. Morgan and my own, which seemed in some danger of disappearing for the "public good," Mrs. Fletcher's little fortune was nearly all invested in that sound "rock-bed" railway in the Southwest that Mr. Jerry Hollowell had recently taken under his paternal care. She was assured, indeed, that dividends were only reserved pending some sort of reorganization, which would ultimately be of great benefit to all the parties concerned; but this was much like telling a hungry man that if he would possess his appetite in patience, he would very likely have a splendid dinner next year. Women are not constituted to understand this sort of reasoning. It is needless to say that in our general talks on the situation these personalities were not referred to, for although Margaret was silent, it was plain to see that she was uneasy.

Morgan liked to raise questions of casuistry, such as that whether money dishonestly come by could be accepted for good purposes.

"I had this question referred to me the other day," he said. "A gambler not a petty cheater in cards, but a man who has a splendid establishment in which he has amassed a fortune, a man known for his liberality and good-fellowship and his interest in politics offered the president of a leading college a hundred thousand dollars to endow a professorship. Ought the president to take the money, knowing how it was made?"

"Wouldn't the money do good as much good as any other hundred thousand dollars?" asked Margaret.

"Perhaps. But the professorship was to bear his name, and what would be the moral effect of that?"

"Did you recommend the president to take the money, if he could get it without using the gambler's name?"

"I am not saying yet what I advised. I am trying to get your views on a general principle."

"But wouldn't it be a sneaking thing to take a man's money, and refuse him the credit of his generosity?"

"But was it generosity? Was not his object, probably, to get a reputation which his whole life belied, and to get it by obliterating the distinction between right and wrong?"

"But isn't it a compromising distinction," my wife asked, "to take his money without his name? The president knows that it is money fraudulently got, that really belongs to somebody else; and the gambler would feel that if the president takes it, he cannot think very disapprovingly of the manner in which it was acquired. I think it would be more honest and straightforward to take his name with the money."

"The public effect of connecting the gambler's name with the college would be debasing," said Morgan; "but, on the contrary, is every charity or educational institution bound to scrutinize the source of every benefaction? Isn't it better that money, however acquired, should be used for a good purpose than a bad one?"

"That is a question," I said, "that is a vital one in our present situation, and the sophistry of it puzzles the public. What would you say to this case? A man notoriously dishonest, but within the law, and very rich, offered a princely endowment to a college very much in need of it. The sum would have enabled it to do a great work in education. But it was intimated that the man would expect, after a while, to be made one of the trustees. His object, of course, was social position."

"I suppose, of course," Margaret replied, "that the college couldn't afford that. It would look like bribery."

"Wouldn't he be satisfied with an LL.D.?" Morgan asked.

"I don't see," my wife said, "any difference between the two cases stated and that of the stock gambler, whose unscrupulous operations have ruined thousands of people, who founds a theological seminary with the gains of his slippery transactions. By accepting his seminary the public condones his conduct. Another man, with the same shaky reputation, endows a college. Do you think that religion and education are benefited in the long-run by this? It seems to me that the public is gradually losing its power of discrimination between the value of honesty and dishonesty. Real respect is gone when the public sees that a man is able to buy it."

This was a hot speech for my wife to make. For a moment Margaret flamed up under it with her old-time indignation. I could see it in her eyes, and then she turned red and confused, and at length said:

"But wouldn't you have rich men do good with their money?"

"Yes, dear, but I would not have them think they can blot out by their liberality the condemnation of the means by which many of them make money. That is what they are doing, and the public is getting used to it."

"Well," said Margaret, with some warmth, "I don't know that they are any worse than the stingy saints who have made their money by saving, and act as if they expected to carry it with them."

"Saints or sinners, it does not make much difference to me," now put in Mrs. Fletcher, who was evidently considering the question from a practical point of view, "what a man professes, if he founds a hospital for indigent women out of the dividends that I never received."

Morgan laughed. "Don't you think, Mrs. Fletcher, that it is a good sign of the times, that so many people who make money rapidly are disposed to use it philanthropically?"

"It may be for them, but it does not console me much just now."

"But you don't make allowance enough for the rich. Perhaps they are under a necessity of doing something. I was reading this morning in the diary of old John Ward of Stratford-on-Avon this sentence: 'It was a saying of Navisson, a lawyer, that no man could be valiant unless he hazarded his body, nor rich unless he hazarded his soul.'"

"Was Navisson a modern lawyer?" I asked.

"No; the diary is dated 1648-1679."

"I thought so."

There was a little laugh at this, and the talk drifted off into a consideration of the kind of conscience that enables a professional man to espouse a cause he knows to be wrong as zealously as one he knows to be right; a talk that I should not have remembered at all, except for Margaret's earnestness in insisting that she did not see how a lawyer could take up the dishonest side.

Before Margaret went to Lenox, Henderson spent a few days with us. He brought with him the abounding cheerfulness, and the air of a prosperous, smiling world, that attended him in all circumstances. And how happy Margaret was! They went over every foot of the ground on which their brief courtship had taken place, and Heaven knows what joy there was to her in reviving all the tenderness and all the fear of it! Busy as Henderson was, pursued by hourly telegrams and letters, we could not but be gratified that his attention to her was that of a lover. How could it be otherwise, when all the promise of the girl was realized in the bloom and the exquisite susceptibility of the woman? Among other things, she dragged him down to her mission in the city, to which he went in a laughing and bantering mood. When he had gone away, Margaret ran over to my wife, bringing in her hand a slip of paper.

"See that!" she cried, her eyes dancing with pleasure. It was a check for a thousand dollars. "That will refurnish the mission from top to bottom," she said, "and run it for a year."

"How generous he is!" cried my wife. Margaret did not reply, but she looked at the check, and there were tears in her eyes.

XV

The Arbuser cottage at Lenox was really a magnificent villa. Richardson had built it. At a distance it had the appearance of a mediaeval structure, with its low doorways, picturesque gables, and steep roofs, and in its situation on a gentle swell of green turf backed by native forest-trees it imparted to the landscape an ancestral tone which is much valued in these days. But near to, it was seen to be mediaevalism adapted to the sunny hospitality of our summer climate, with generous verandas and projecting balconies shaded by gay awnings, and within spacious, open to the breezes, and from its broad windows offering views of lawns and flower-beds and ornamental trees, of a great sweep of pastures and forests and miniature lakes, with graceful and reposeful hills on the horizon.

It was, in short, the modern idea of country simplicity. The passion for country life, which has been in decadence for nearly half a century, has again become the fashion. Nature, which, left to itself, is a little ragged, not to say monotonous and tiresome, is discovered to be a valuable ally for aid in passing the time when art is able to make portions of it exclusive. What the Arbusers wanted was a simple home in the country, and in obtaining it they were indulging a sentiment of returning to the primitive life of their father, who had come to the city from a hill farm, and had been too busy all his life to recur to the tastes of his boyhood. At least that was the theory of his daughters; but the old gentleman had a horror of his early life, and could scarcely be dragged away from the city even in the summer. He would no doubt have been astonished at the lofty and substantial stone stables, the long range of greenhouses, and at a farm which produced nothing except lawns and flower-beds, ornamental fields of clover, avenues of trees, lawn-tennis grounds, and a few Alderneys tethered to feed among the trees, where their beauty would heighten the rural and domestic aspect of the scene. The Arbusers liked to come to this place as early as possible to escape the society exactions of the city. That was another theory of theirs. All their set in the city met there for the same purpose.

Margaret was welcomed with open arms.

"We have been counting the days," said the elder of the sisters. "Your luggage has come, your rooms are all ready, and your coachman, who has been here some days, says that the horses need exercise. Everybody is here, and we need you for a hundred things."

"You are very kind. It is so charming here. I knew it would be, but I couldn't bear to shorten my visit in Brandon."

"Your aunt must miss you very much. Is she well?"

"Perfectly."

"Wouldn't she have come with you? I've a mind to telegraph."

"I think not. She is wedded to quiet, and goes away from her little neighborhood with reluctance."

"So Brandon was a little dull?" said Miss Arbuser, with a shrewd guess at the truth.

"Oh no," quickly replied Margaret, shrinking a little from what was in her own mind; "it was restful and delightful; but you know that we New England people take life rather seriously, and inquire into the reason of things, and want an object in life."

"A very good thing to have," answered this sweet woman of the world, whose object was to go along pleasantly and enjoy it.

"But to have it all the time!" Margaret suggested, lightly, as she ran up-stairs. But even in this suggestion she was conscious of a twinge of disloyalty to her former self. Deep down in her heart, coming to the atmosphere of Lenox was a relief from questionings that a little disturbed her at her old home, and she was indignant at herself that it should be so, and then indignant at the suggestions that put her out of humor with herself. Was it a sin, she said, to be happy and prosperous?

On her dressing-table was a letter from her husband. He was detained in the city by a matter of importance. He scratched only a line, to catch the mail, during a business interview. It was really only a business interview, and had no sort of relation to Lenox or the summer gayety there.

Henderson was in his private office. The clerks in the outer offices, in the neglige of summer costumes, winked to each other as they saw old Jerry Hollowell enter and make his way to the inner room unannounced. Something was in the wind.

"Well, old man," said Uncle Jerry, in the cheeriest manner, coming in, depositing his hat on the table, and taking a seat opposite Henderson, "we seem to have stirred up the animals."

"Only a little flurry," replied Henderson, laying down his pen and folding a note he had just finished; "they'll come to reason."

"They've got to." Mr. Hollowell drew out a big bandanna and mopped his heated face. "I've just got a letter from Jorkins. There's the certificates that make up the two-thirds-more than we need, anyway. No flaw about that, is there?"

"No. I'll put these with the balance in the safe. It's all right, if Jorkins has been discreet. It may make a newspaper scandal if they get hold of his operations."

"Oh, Jorkins is close. But he is a little overworked. I don't know but it would do him good to have a little nervous prostration and go abroad for a while."

"I guess it would do Jorkins good to take a turn in Europe for a year or so."

"Well, you write to him. Give him a sort of commission to see the English bondholders, and explain the situation. They will appreciate that half a loaf is better than no bread. What bothers me is the way the American bondholders take it. They kick."

"Let 'em kick. The public don't care for a few soreheads and impracticables in an operation that is going to open up the whole Southwest. I've an appointment with one of them this morning. He ought to be here now."

At the moment Henderson's private secretary entered and laid on the table the card of Mr. John Hopper, who was invited to come in at once. Mr. Hopper was a man of fifty, with iron-gray hair, a heavy mustache, and a smooth-shaven chin that showed resolution. In dress and manner his appearance was that of the shrewd city capitalist quiet and determined, who is neither to be deceived nor bullied. With a courteous greeting to both the men, whom he knew well, he took a seat and stated his business.

"I have called to see you, Mr. Henderson, about the bonds of the A. and B., and I am glad to find Mr. Hollowell here also."

"What amount do you represent, Mr. Hopper?" asked Henderson.

"With my own and my friends', altogether, rising a million. What do you propose?"

"You got our circular?"

"Yes, and we don't accept the terms."

"I'm sorry. It is the best that we could do."

"That is, the best you would do!"

"Pardon me, Mr. Hopper, the best we could do under the circumstances. We gave you your option, to scale down on a fair estimate of the earnings of the short line (the A. and B.), or to surrender your local bonds and take new ones covering the whole consolidation, or, as is of course in your discretion, to hold on and take the chances."

"Which your operations have practically destroyed."

"Not at all, Mr. Hopper. We offer you a much better security on the whole system instead of a local road."

"And you mean to tell me, Mr. Henderson, that it is for our advantage to exchange a seven per cent. bond on a road that has always paid its interest promptly, for a four and a half on a system that is manipulated nobody knows how? I tell you, gentlemen, that it looks to outsiders as if there was crookedness somewhere."

"That is a rather rough charge, Mr. Hopper," said Henderson, with a smile.

"But we are to understand that if we do not accept your terms, it's a freeze-out?"

"You are to understand that we want to make the best arrangement possible for all parties in interest."

"How some of those interests were acquired may be a question for the courts," replied Mr. Hopper, resolutely. "When we put our money in good seven per cent. bonds, we propose to inquire into the right of anybody to demand that we shall exchange them for four and a half per cents. on other security."

"Perfectly right, Mr. Hopper," said Henderson, with imperturbable good-humor; "the transfer books are open to your inspection."

"Well, we prefer to hold on to our bonds."

"And wait for your interest," interposed Hollowell.

Mr. Hopper turned to the speaker. "And while we are waiting we propose to inquire what has become of the surplus of the A. and B. The bondholders had the first claim on the entire property."

"And we propose to protect it. See here, Mr. Hopper," continued Uncle Jerry, with a most benevolent expression, "I needn't tell you that investments fluctuate the Lord knows mine do! The A. and B. was a good road. I know that. But it was going to be paralleled. We'd got to parallel it to make our Southwest connections. If we had, you'd have waited till the Gulf of Mexico freezes over before you got any coupons paid. Instead of that, we took it into our system, and it's being put on a permanent basis. It's a little inconvenient for holders, and they have got to stand a little shrinkage, but in the long-run it will be better for everybody. The little road couldn't stand alone, and the day of big interest is about over."

"That explanation may satisfy you, Mr. Hollowell, but it don't give us our money, and I notify you that we shall carry the matter into the courts. Good-morning."

When Mr. Hopper had gone, the two developers looked at each other a moment seriously.

"Hopper 'll fight," Hollowell said at last.

"And we have got the surplus to fight him with," replied Henderson.

"That's so," and Uncle Jerry chuckled to himself. "The rats that are on the inside of the crib are a good deal better off than the rats on the outside."

"The reporter of The Planet wants five minutes," announced the secretary, opening the door. Henderson told him to let him in.

The reporter was a spruce young gentleman, in a loud summer suit, with a rose in his button-hole, and the air of assurance which befits the commissioner of the public curiosity.

"I am sent by The Planet," said the young man, "to show you this and ask you if you have anything to say to it."

"What is it?" asked Henderson.

"It's about the A. and B."

"Very well. There is the president, Mr. Hollowell. Show it to him."

The reporter produced a long printed slip and handed it to Uncle Jerry, who took it and began to read. As his eye ran down the column he was apparently more and more interested, and he let it be shown on his face that he was surprised, and even a little astonished. When he had finished, he said:

"Well, my young friend, how did you get hold of this?"

"Oh, we have a way," said the reporter, twirling his straw hat by the elastic, and looking more knowing than old Jerry himself.

"So I see," replied Jerry, with an admiring smile; "there is nothing that you newspaper folks don't find out. It beats the devil!"

"Is it true, sir?" said the young gentleman, elated with this recognition of his own shrewdness.

"It is so true that there is no fun in it. I don't see how the devil you got hold of it."

"Have you any explanations?"

"No, I guess not," said Uncle Jerry, musingly. "If it is to come out, I'd rather The Planet would have it than any, other paper. It's got some sense. No; print it. It'll be a big beat for your paper. While you are about it I s'pose you'll print it anyway?" (the reporter nodded) "you might as well have the whole story."

"Certainly. We'd like to have it right. What is wrong about it?"

"Oh, nothing but some details. You have got it substantially. There's a word or two and a date you are out on, naturally enough, and there are two or three little things that would be exactly true if they were differently stated."

"Would you mind telling me what they are?"

"No," said Jerry, with a little reluctance; "might as well have it all out eh, Henderson?"

And the old man took his pencil and changed some dates and a name or two, and gave to some of the sentences a turn that seemed to the reporter only another way of saying the same thing.

"There, that is all I know. Give my respects to Mr. Goss."

When the commissioner had withdrawn, Uncle Jerry gave vent to a long whistle. Then he rose suddenly and called to the secretary, "Tell that reporter to come back." The reporter reappeared.

"I was just thinking, and you can tell Mr. Goss, that now you have got onto this thing, you might as well keep the lead on it. The public is interested in what we are doing in the Southwest, and if you, or some other bright fellow who has got eyes in his head, will go down there, he will see something that will astonish him. I'm going tomorrow in my private car, and if you could go along, I assure you a good time. I want you to see for yourself, and I guess you would. Don't take my word. I can't give you any passes, and I know you don't want any, but you can just get into my private car and no expense to anybody, and see all there is to be seen. Ask Goss, and let me know tonight."

The young fellow went off feeling several inches higher than when he came in. Such is the power of a good address, and such is the omnipotence of the great organ. Mr. Jerry Hollowell sat down and began to fan himself. It was very hot in the office.

"Seems to me it's lunch-time. Great Scott! what a lot of time I used to waste fighting the newspapers! That thing would have played the devil as it stood. It will be comparatively harmless now. It will make a little talk, but there is nothing to get hold of. Queer, about the difference of a word or two. Come, old man, I'm thirsty."

"Uncle Jerry," said Henderson, taking his arm as they went out, "you ought to be President of the United States."

"The salary is too small," said Uncle Jerry.

Of all this there was nothing to write to Margaret, who was passing her time agreeably in the Berkshire hills, a little impatient for her husband's arrival, postponed from day to day, and full of sympathy for him, condemned to the hot city and the harassment of a business the magnitude of which gave him the obligations and the character of a public man. Henderson sent her instead a column from The Planet devoted to a description of his private library. Mr. Goss, the editor, who was college bred, had been round to talk with Henderson about the Southwest trip, and the conversation drifting into other matters, Henderson had taken from his desk and shown him a rare old book which he had picked up the day before in a second-hand shop. This led to further talk about Henderson's hobby, and the editor had asked permission to send a reporter down to make a note of Henderson's collection. It would make a good midsummer item, "The Stock-Broker in Literature," "The Private Tastes of a Millionaire," etc. The column got condensed into a portable paragraph, and went the rounds of the press, and changed the opinions of a good many people about the great operator he wasn't altogether devoted to vulgar moneymaking. Uncle Jerry himself read the column with appreciation of its value. "It diverts the public mind," he said. He himself had recently diverted the public mind by the gift of a bell to the Norembega Theological (colored) Institute, and the paragraph announcing the fact conveyed the impression that while Uncle Jerry was a canny old customer, his heart was on the right side. "There are worse men than Uncle Jerry who are not worth a cent," was one of the humorous paragraphs tacked on to the item.

Margaret was not alone in finding the social atmosphere of Lenox as congenial as its natural beauties. Mrs. Laflamme declared that it was the perfection of existence for a couple of months, one in early summer and another in the golden autumn with its pathetic note of the falling curtain dropping upon the dream of youth. Mrs. Laflamme was not a sentimental person, but she was capable of drifting for a moment into a poetic mood a great charm in a woman of her vivacity and air of the world. Margaret remembered her very distinctly, although she had only exchanged a word with her at the memorable dinner in New York when Henderson had revealed her feelings to herself. Mrs. Laflamme had the immense advantage it seemed so to her after five years of widowhood of being a widow on the sunny side of thirty-five. If she had lost some illusions she had gained a great deal of knowledge, and she had no feverish anxiety about what life would bring her. Although she would not put it in this way to herself, she could look about her deliberately, enjoying the prospect, and please herself. Her position had two advantages experience and opportunity. A young woman unmarried, she said, always has the uneasy sense of the possibility well, it is impossible to escape slang, and she said it with the merriest laugh the possibility of being left. A day or two after Margaret's arrival she had driven around to call in her dog-cart, looking as fresh as a daisy in her sunhat. She held the reins, but her seat was shared by Mr. Fox McNaughton, the most useful man in the village, indispensable indeed; a bachelor, with no intentions, no occupation, no ambition (except to lead the german), who could mix a salad, brew a punch, organize a picnic, and chaperon anything in petticoats with entire propriety, without regard to age. And he had a position of social authority. This eminence Mr. Fox McNaughton had attained by always doing the correct thing. The obligation of society to such men is never enough acknowledged. While they are trusted and used, and worked to death, one is apt to hear them spoken of in a deprecatory tone.

"You hold the reins a moment, please. No, I don't want any help," she said, as she jumped down with an elastic spring, and introduced him to Margaret. "I've got Mr. McNaughton in training, and am thinking of bringing him out."

She walked in with Margaret, chatting about the view and the house and the divine weather.

"And your husband has not come yet?"

"He may come any day. I think business might suspend in the summer."

"So do I. But then, what would become of Lenox? It is rather hard on the men, only I dare say they like it. Don't you think Mr. Henderson would like a place here?"

"He cannot help being pleased with Lenox."

"I'm sure he would if you are. I have hardly seen him since that evening at the Stotts'. Can I tell you? I almost had five minutes of envy that evening. You won't mind it in such an old woman?"

"I should rather trust your heart than your age, Mrs. Laflamme," said Margaret, with a laugh.

"Yes, my heart is as old as my face. But I had a feeling, seeing you walk away that evening into the conservatory. I knew what was coming. I think I have discovered a great secret, Mrs. Henderson to be able to live over again in other people. By-the-way, what has become of that quiet Englishman, Mr. Lyon?"

"He has come into his title. He is the Earl of Chisholm."

"Dear me, how stupid in us not to have taken a sense of that! And the Eschelles do you know anything of the Eschelles?"

"Yes; they are at their house in Newport."

"Do you think there was anything between Miss Eschelle and Mr. Lyon? I saw her afterwards several times."

"Not that I ever heard. Miss Eschelle says that she is thoroughly American in her tastes."

"Then her tastes are not quite conformed to her style. That girl might be anything Queen of Spain, or coryphee in the opera ballet. She is clever as clever. One always expects to hear of her as the heroine of an adventure."

"Didn't you say you knew her in Europe?"

"No. We heard of her and her mother everywhere. She was very independent. She had the sort of reputation to excite curiosity. But I noticed that the men in New York were a little afraid of her. She is a woman who likes to drive very near the edge."

Mrs. Laflamme rose. "I must not keep Mr. McNaughton waiting for any more of my gossip. We expect you and the Misses Arbuser this afternoon. I warn you it will be dull. I should like to hear of some summer resort where the men are over sixteen and under sixty."

Mrs. Laflamme liked to drive near the edge as much as Carmen did, and this piquancy was undeniably an attraction in her case. But there was this difference between the two: there was a confidence that Mrs. Laflamme would never drive over the edge, whereas no one could tell what sheer Carmen might not suddenly take. A woman's reputation is almost as much affected by the expectation of what she may do as by anything she has done. It was Fox McNaughton who set up the dictum that a woman may do almost anything if it is known that she draws a line somewhere.

The lawn party was not at all dull to Margaret. In the first place, she received a great deal of attention. Henderson's name was becoming very well known, and it was natural that the splendor of his advancing fortune should be reflected in the person of his young wife, whose loveliness was enhanced by her simple enjoyment of the passing hour. Then the toilets of the women were so fresh and charming, the colors grouped so prettily on the greensward, the figures of the slender girls playing at tennis or lounging on the benches under the trees, recalled scenes from the classic poets. It was all so rich and refined. Nor did she miss the men of military age, whose absence Mrs. Laflamme had deplored, for she thought of her husband. And, besides, she found even the college boys (who are always spoken of as men) amusing, and the elderly gentlemen upon whom watering-place society throws much responsibility gallant, facetious, complimentary, and active in whatever was afoot. Their boyishness, indeed, contrasted with the gravity of the undergraduates, who took themselves very seriously, were civil to the young ladies, confidential with the married women, and had generally a certain reserve and dignity which belong to persons upon whom such heavy responsibility rests.

There were, to be sure, men who looked bored, and women who were listless, missing the stimulus of any personal interest; but the scene was so animated, the weather so propitious, that, on the whole, a person must be very cynical not to find the occasion delightful.

There was a young novelist present whose first story, "The Girl I Left Behind Me," had made a hit the last season. It was thought to take a profound hold upon life, because it was a book that could not be read aloud in a mixed company. Margaret was very much interested in him, although Mr. Summers Bass was not her idea of an imaginative writer. He was a stout young gentleman, with very black hair and small black eyes, to which it was difficult to give a melancholy cast even by an habitual frown. Mr. Bass dressed himself scrupulously in the fashion, was very exact in his pronunciation, careful about his manner, and had the air of a little weariness, of the responsibility of one looking at life. It was only at rare moments that his face expressed intensity of feeling.

"It is a very pretty scene. I suppose, Mr. Bass, that you are making studies," said Margaret, by way of opening a conversation.

"No; hardly that. One must always observe. It gets to be a habit. The thing is to see reality under appearances."

"Then you would call yourself a realist?"

Mr. Bass smiled. "That is a slang term, Mrs. Henderson. What you want is nature, color, passion to pierce the artificialities."

"But you must describe appearance."

"Certainly, to an extent form, action, talk as it is, even trivialities especially the trivialities, for life is made up of the trivial."

"But suppose that does not interest me?"

"Pardon me, Mrs. Henderson, that is because you are used to the conventional, the selected. Nature is always interesting."

"I do not find it so."

"No? Nature has been covered up; it has been idealized. Look yonder," and Mr. Bass pointed across the lawn. "See that young woman upon whom the sunlight falls standing waiting her turn. See the quivering of the eyelids, the heaving of the chest, the opening lips; note the curve of her waist from the shoulder, and the line rounding into the fall of the folds of the Austrian cashmere. I try to saturate myself with that form, to impress myself with her every attitude and gesture, her color, her movement, and then I shall imagine the form under the influence of passion. Every detail will tell. I do not find unimportant the tie of her shoe. The picture will be life."

"But suppose, Mr. Bass, when you come to speak with her, you find that she has no ideas, and talks slang."

"All the better. It shows what we are, what our society is. And besides, Mrs. Henderson, nearly everybody has the capacity of being wicked; that is to say, of expressing emotion."

"You take a gloomy view, Mr. Bass."

"I take no view, Mrs. Henderson. My ambition is to record. It will not help matters by pretending that people are better than they are."

"Well, Mr. Bass, you may be quite right, but I am not going to let you spoil my enjoyment of this lovely scene," said Margaret, moving away. Mr. Bass watched her until she disappeared, and then entered in his notebook a phrase for future use, "The prosperous propriety of a pretty plutocrat." He was gathering materials for his forthcoming book, "The Last Sigh of the Prude."

The whole world knows how delightful Lenox is. It even has a club where the men can take refuge from the exactions of society, as in the city. The town is old enough to have "histories"; there is a romance attached to nearly every estate, a tragedy of beauty, and money, and disappointment; great writers have lived here, families whose names were connected with our early politics and diplomacy; there is a tradition of a society of wit and letters, of women whose charms were enhanced by a spice of adventure, of men whose social brilliancy ended in misanthropy. All this gave a background of distinction to the present gayety, luxury, and adaptation of the unsurpassed loveliness of nature to the refined fashion of the age.

Here, if anywhere, one could be above worry, above the passion of envy; for did not every new "improvement" and every new refinement in living add to the importance of every member of this favored community? For Margaret it was all a pageant of beauty. The Misses Arbuser talked about the quality of the air, the variety of the scenery, the exhilaration of the drives, the freedom from noise and dust, the country quiet. There were the morning calls, the intellectual life of the reading clubs, the tennis parties, the afternoon teas, combined with charming drives from one elegant place to another; the siestas, the idle swinging in hammocks, with the latest magazine from which to get a topic for dinner, the mild excitement of a tete-a-tete which might discover congenial tastes or run on into an interesting attachment. Half the charm of life, says a philosopher, is in these personal experiments.

When Henderson came, as he did several times for a few days, Margaret's happiness was complete. She basked in the sun of his easy enjoyment of life. She liked to take him about with her, and see the welcome in all companies of a man so handsome, so natural and cordial, as her husband. Especially aid she like the consideration in which he was evidently held at the club, where the members gathered about him to listen to his racy talk and catch points about the market. She liked to think that he was not a woman's man. He gave her his version of some recent transactions that had been commented on in the newspapers, and she was indignant over the insinuations about him. It was the price, he said, that everybody had to pay for success. Why shouldn't he, she reflected, make money? Everybody would if they could, and no one knew how generous he was. If she had been told that the family of Jerry Hollowell thought of him in the same way, she would have said that there was a world-wide difference in the two men. Insensibly she was losing the old standards she used to apply to success. Here in Lenox, in this prosperous, agreeable world, there was nothing to remind her of them.

In her enjoyment of this existence without care, I do not suppose it occurred to her to examine if her ideals had been lowered. Sometimes Henderson had a cynical, mocking tone about the world, which she reproved with a caress, but he was always tolerant and good-natured. If he had told her that he acted upon the maxim that every man and woman has his and her price she would have been shocked, but she was getting to make allowances that she would not have made before she learned to look at the world through his eyes. She could see that the Brandon circle was over-scrupulous. Her feeling of this would have been confirmed if she had known that when her aunt read the letter announcing a month's visit to the Eschelles in Newport, she laid it down with a sigh.

XVI

Uncle Jerry was sitting on the piazza of the Ocean House, absorbed in the stock reports of a New York journal, answering at random the occasional observations of his wife, who filled up one of the spacious chairs near him a florid woman, with diamonds in her ears, who had the resolute air of enjoying herself. It was an August Newport morning, when there is a salty freshness in the air, but a temperature that discourages exertion. A pony phaeton dashed by containing two ladies. The ponies were cream-colored, with flowing manes and tails, and harness of black and gold; the phaeton had yellow wheels with a black body; the diminutive page with folded arms, on the seat behind, wore a black jacket and yellow breeches. The lady who held the yellow silk reins was a blonde with dark eyes. As they flashed by, the lady on the seat with her bowed, and Mr. Hollowell returned the salute.

"Who's that?" asked Mrs. Hollowell.

"That's Mrs. Henderson."

"And the other one?"

"I don't know her. She knows how to handle the ribbons, though."

"I seen her at the Casino the other night, before you come, with that tandem-driving count. I don't believe he's any more count than you are."

"Oh, he's all right. He's one of the Spanish legation. This is just the place for counts. I shouldn't wonder, Maria, if you'd like to be a countess. We can afford it the Countess Jeremiah, eh?" and Uncle Jerry's eyes twinkled.

"Don't be a goose, Mr. Hollowell," bringing her fat hands round in front of her, so that she could see the sparkle of the diamond rings on them. "She's as pretty as a picture, that girl, but I should think a good wind would blow her away. I shouldn't want to have her drive me round."

"Jorkins has sailed," said Mr. Hollowell, looking up from his paper. "The Planet reporter tried to interview him, but he played sick, said he was just going over and right back for a change. I guess it will be long enough before they get a chance at him again."

"I'm glad he's gone. I hope the papers will mind their own business for a spell."

The house of the Eschelles was on the sea, looking over a vast sweep of lawn to the cliff and the dimpling blue water of the first beach. It was known as the Yellow Villa. Coming from the elegance of Lenox, Margaret was surprised at the magnificence and luxury of this establishment, the great drawing-rooms, the spacious chambers, the wide verandas, the pictures, the flowers, the charming nooks and recessed windows, with handy book-stands, and tables littered with the freshest and most-talked-of issues from the press of Paris, Madrid, and London. Carmen had taken a hint from Henderson's bachelor apartment, which she had visited once with her mother, and though she had no literary taste, further than to dip in here and there to what she found toothsome and exciting in various languages, yet she knew the effect of the atmosphere of books, and she had a standing order at a book-shop for whatever was fresh and likely to come into notice.

And Carmen was a delightful hostess, both because her laziness gave an air of repose to the place, and she had the tact never to appear to make any demands upon her guests, and because she knew when to be piquant and exhibit personal interest, and when to show even a little abandon of vivacity. Society flowed through her house without any obstructions. It was scarcely ever too early and never too late for visitors. Those who were intimate used to lounge in and take up a book, or pass an hour on the veranda, even when none of the family were at home. Men had a habit of dropping in for a five o'clock cup of tea, and where the men went the women needed little urging to follow. At first there had been some reluctance about recognizing the Eschelles fully, and there were still houses that exhibited a certain reserve towards them, but the example of going to this house set by the legations, the members of which enjoyed a chat with Miss Eschelle in the freedom of their own tongues and the freedom of her tongue, went far to break down this barrier. They were spoken of occasionally as "those Eschelles," but almost everybody went there, and perhaps enjoyed it all the more because there had been a shade of doubt about it.

Margaret's coming was a good card for Carmen. The little legend about her French ancestry in Newport, and the romantic marriage in Rochambeau's time, had been elaborated in the local newspaper, and when she appeared the ancestral flavor, coupled with the knowledge of Henderson's accumulating millions, lent an interest and a certain charm to whatever she said and did. The Eschelle house became more attractive than ever before, so much so that Mrs. Eschelle declared that she longed for the quiet of Paris. To her motherly apprehension there was no result in this whirl of gayety, no serious intention discoverable in any of the train that followed Carmen. "You act, child," she said, "as if youth would last forever."

Margaret entered into this life as if she had been born to it. Perhaps she was. Perhaps most people never find the career for which they are fitted, and struggle along at cross-purposes with themselves. We all thought that Margaret's natural bent was for some useful and self-sacrificing work in the world, and never could have imagined that under any circumstances she would develop into a woman of fashion.

"I intend to read a great deal this month," she said to Carmen on her arrival, as she glanced at the litter of books.

"That was my intention," replied Carmen; "now we can read together. I'm taking Spanish lessons of Count Crispo. I've learned two Spanish poems and a Castilian dance."

"Is he married?"

"Not now. He told me, when he was teaching me the steps, that his heart was buried in Seville."

"He seems to be full of sentiment."

"Perhaps that is because his salary is so small. Mamma says, of all things an impecunious count! But he is amusing."

"But what do you care for money?" asked Margaret, by way of testing Carmen's motives.

"Nothing, my dear. But deliver me from a husband who is poor; he would certainly be a tyrant. Besides, if I ever marry, it will be with an American."

"But suppose you fall in love with a poor man?"

"That would be against my principles. Never fall below your ideals that is what I heard a speaker say at the Town and Country Club, and that is my notion. There is no safety for you if you lose your principles."

"That depends upon what they are," said Margaret, in the same bantering tone.

"That sounds like good Mr. Lyon. I suspect he thought I hadn't any. Mamma said I tried to shock him; but he shocked me. Do you think you could live with such a man twenty-four hours, even if he had his crown on?"

"I can imagine a great deal worse husbands than the Earl of Chisholm."

"Well, I haven't any imagination."

There was no reading that day nor the next. In the morning there was a drive with the ponies through town, in the afternoon in the carriage by the sea, with a couple of receptions, the five o'clock tea, with its chatter, and in the evening a dinner party for Margaret. One day sufficed to launch her, and there-after Carmen had only admiration for the unflagging spirit which Margaret displayed. "If you were only unmarried," she said, "what larks we could have!" Margaret looked grave at this, but only for a moment, for she well knew that she could not please her husband better than by enjoying the season to the full. He never criticised her for taking the world as it is; and she confessed to herself that life went very pleasantly in a house where there were never any questions raised about duties. The really serious thought in Carmen's mind was that perhaps after all a woman had no real freedom until she was married. And she began to be interested in Margaret's enjoyment of the world.

It was not, after all, a new world, only newly arranged, like another scene in the same play. The actors, who came and went, were for the most part the acquaintances of the Washington winter, and the callers and diners and opera-goers and charity managers of the city. In these days Margaret was quite at home with the old set: the British Minister, the Belgian, the French, the Spanish, the Mexican, the German, and the Italian, with their families and attaches nothing was wanting, not even the Chinese mandarin, who had rooms at the hotel, going about everywhere in the conscientious discharge of his duties as ambassador to American society, a great favorite on account of his silk apparel, which gave him the appearance of a clumsy woman, and the everlasting, three-thousand-year-old smile on his broad face, punctiliously leaving in every house a big flaring red piece of paper which the ladies pinned up for a decoration; a picture of helpless, childlike enjoyment, and almost independent of the interpreter who followed him about, when he had learned, upon being introduced to a lady, or taking a cup of tea, to say "good-by" as distinctly as an articulating machine; a truly learned man, setting an example of civility and perfect self-possession, but keenly observant of the oddities of the social life to which his missionary government had accredited him. One would like to have heard the comments of the minister and his suite upon our manners; but perhaps they were too polite to make any even in their seclusion. Certain it is that no one ever heard any of the legation express any opinion but the most suave and flattering.

And yet they must have been amazed at the activity of this season of repose, the endurance of American women who rode to the fox meets, were excited spectators of the polo, played lawn-tennis, were incessantly dining and calling, and sat through long dinners served with the formality and dullness and the swarms of liveried attendants of a royal feast. And they could not but admire the young men, who did not care for politics or any business beyond the chances of the stock exchange, but who expended an immense amount of energy in the dangerous polo contests, in riding at fences after the scent-bag, in driving tandems and four-in-hands, and yet had time to dress in the cut and shade demanded by every changing hour.

Formerly the annual chronicle of this summer pageant, in which the same women appeared day after day, and the same things were done over and over again, Margaret used to read with a contempt for the life; but that she enjoyed it, now she was a part of it, shows that the chroniclers for the press were unable to catch the spirit of it, the excitement of the personal encounters that made it new every day. Looking at a ball is quite another thing from dancing.

"Yes, it is lively enough," said Mr. Ponsonby, one afternoon when they had returned from the polo grounds and were seated on the veranda. Mr. Ponsonby was a middle-aged Englishman, whose diplomatic labors at various courts had worn a bald spot on his crown. Carmen had not yet come, and they were waiting for a cup of tea. "And they ride well; but I think I rather prefer the Wild West Show."

"You Englishmen," Margaret retorted, "seem to like the uncivilized. Are you all tired of civilization?"

"Of some kinds. When we get through with the London season, you know, Mrs. Henderson, we like to rough it, as you call it, for some months. But, 'pon my word, I can't see much difference between Washington and Newport."

"We might get up a Wild West Show here, or a prize-fight, for you. Do you know, Mr. Ponsonby, I think it will take full another century for women to really civilize men."

"How so?"

"Get the cruelty and love of brutal sports out of them."

"Then you'd cease to like us. Nothing is so insipid, I fancy, to a woman as a man made in her own image."

"Well, what have you against Newport?"

"Against it? I'm sure nothing could be better than this." And Mr. Ponsonby allowed his adventurous eyes to rest for a moment upon Margaret's trim figure, until he saw a flush in her face. "This prospect," he added, turning to the sea, where a few sails took the slant rays of the sun.

"'Where every prospect pleases,'" quoted Margaret, "'and only man '"

"I beg your pardon, Mrs. Henderson; men are not to be considered. The women in Newport would make the place a paradise even if it were a desert."

"That is another thing I object to in men."

"What's that?"

"Flattery. You don't say such things to each other at the club. What is your objection to Newport?"

"I didn't say I had any. But if you compel me well, the whole thing seems to be a kind of imitation."

"How?"

"Oh, the way things go on the steeple-chasing and fox-hunting, and the carts, and the style of the swell entertainments. Is that ill-natured?"

"Not at all. I like candor, especially English candor. But there is Miss Eschelle."

Carmen drove up with Count Crispo, threw the reins to the groom, and reached the ground with a touch on the shoulder of the count, who had alighted to help her down.

"Carmen," said Margaret, "Mr. Ponsonby says that all Newport is just an imitation."

"Of course it is. We are all imitations, except Count Crispo. I'll bet a cup of tea against a pair of gloves," said Carmen, who had facility in picking up information, "that Mr. Ponsonby wasn't born in England."

Mr. Ponsonby looked redder than usual, and then laughed, and said, "Well, I was only three years old when I left Halifax."

"I knew it!" cried Carmen, clapping her hands. "Now come in and have a cup of English breakfast tea. That's imitation, too."

"The mistake you made," said Margaret, "was not being born in Spain."

"Perhaps it's not irreparable," the count interposed, with an air of gallantry.

"No, no," said Carmen, audaciously; "by this time I should be buried in Seville. No, I should prefer Halifax, for it would have been a pleasure to emigrate from Halifax. Was it not, Mr. Ponsonby?"

"I can't remember. But it is a pleasure to sojourn in any land with Miss Eschelle."

"Thank you. Now you shall have two cups. Come."

The next morning, Mr. Jerry Hollowell, having inquired where Margaret was staying, called to pay his respects, as he phrased it. Carmen, who was with Margaret in the morning-room, received him with her most distinguished manner. "We all know Mr. Hollowell," she said.

"That's not always an advantage," retorted Uncle Jerry, seating himself, and depositing his hat beside his chair. "When do you expect your husband, Mrs. Henderson?"

"Tomorrow. But I don't mean to tell him that you are here not at first."

"No," said Carmen; "we women want Mr. Henderson a little while to ourselves."

"Why, I'm the idlest man in America. I tell Henderson that he ought to take more time for rest. It's no good to drive things. I like quiet."

"And you get it in Newport?" Margaret asked.

"Well, my wife and children get what they call quiet. I guess a month of it would use me up. She says if I had a place here I'd like it. Perhaps so. You are very comfortably fixed, Miss Eschelle."

"It does very well for us, but something more would be expected of Mr. Hollowell. We are just camping-out here. What Newport needs is a real palace, just to show those foreigners who come here and patronize us. Why is it, Mr. Hollowell, that all you millionaires can't think of anything better to do with your money than to put up a big hotel or a great elevator or a business block?"

"I suppose," said Uncle Jerry, blandly, "that is because they are interested in the prosperity of the country, and have simple democratic tastes for themselves. I'm afraid you are not democratic, Miss Eschelle."

"Oh, I'm anxious about the public also. I'm on your side, Mr. Hollowell; but you don't go far enough. You just throw in a college now and then to keep us quiet, but you owe it to the country to show the English that a democrat can have as fine a house as anybody."

"I call that real patriotism. When I get rich, Miss Eschelle, I'll bear it in mind."

"Oh, you never will be rich," said Carmen, sweetly, bound to pursue her whim. "You might come to me for a start to begin the house. I was very lucky last spring in A. and B. bonds."

"How was that? Are you interested in A. and B.?" asked Uncle Jerry, turning around with a lively interest in this gentle little woman.

"Oh, no; we sold out. We sold when we heard what an interest there was in the road. Mamma said it would never do for two capitalists to have their eggs in the same basket."

"What do you mean, Carmen?" asked Margaret, startled. "Why, that is the road Mr. Henderson is in."

"Yes, I know, dear. There were too many in it."

"Isn't it safe?" said Margaret, turning to Hollowell.

"A great deal more solid than it was," he replied. "It is part of a through line. I suppose Miss Eschelle found a better investment."

"One nearer home," she admitted, in the most matter-of-fact way.

"Henderson must have given the girl points," thought Hollowell. He began to feel at home with her. If he had said the truth, it would have been that she was more his kind than Mrs. Henderson, but that he respected the latter more.

"I think we might go in partnership, Miss Eschelle, to mutual advantage but not in building. Your ideas are too large for me there."

"I should be a very unreliable partner, Mr. Hollowell; but I could enlarge your ideas, if I had time."

Hollowell laughed, and said he hadn't a doubt of that. Margaret inquired for Mrs. Hollowell and the children, and she and Carmen appointed an hour for calling at the Ocean House. The talk went to other topics, and after a half-hour ended in mutual good-feeling.

"What a delightful old party!" said Carmen, after he had gone. "I've a mind to adopt him."

In a week Hollowell and Carmen were the best of friends. She called him "Uncle Jerry," and buzzed about him, to his great delight. "The beauty of it is," he said, "you never can tell where she will light."

Everybody knows what Newport is in August, and we need not dwell on it. To Margaret, with its languidly moving pleasures, its well-bred scenery, the luxury that lulled the senses into oblivion of the vulgar struggle and anxiety which ordinarily attend life, it was little less than paradise. To float along with Carmen, going deeper and deeper into the shifting gayety which made the days fly without thought and with no care for tomorrow, began to seem an admirable way of passing life. What could one do fitter, after all, for a world hopelessly full of suffering and poverty and discontent, than to set an example of cheerfulness and enjoyment, and to contribute, as occasion offered, to the less fortunate? Would it help matters to be personally anxious and miserable? To put a large bill in the plate on Sunday, to open her purse wide for the objects of charity and relief daily presented, was indeed a privilege and a pleasure, and a satisfaction to the conscience which occasionally tripped her in her rapid pace.

"I don't believe you have a bit of conscience," said Margaret to Carmen one Sunday, as they walked home from morning service, when Margaret had responded "extravagantly," as Carmen said, to an appeal for the mission among the city pagans.

"I never said I had, dear. It must be the most troublesome thing you can carry around with you. Of course I am interested in the heathen, but charity that is where I agree with Uncle Jerry begins at home, and I don't happen to know a greater heathen than I am."

"If you were as bad as you make yourself out, I wouldn't walk with you another step."

"Well, you ask mother. She was in such a rage one day when I told Mr. Lyon that he'd better look after Ireland than go pottering round among the neglected children. Not that I care anything about the Irish," added this candid person.

"I suppose you wanted to make it pleasant for Mr. Lyon?"

"No; for mother. She can't get over the idea that she is still bringing me up. And Mr. Lyon! Goodness! there was no living with him after his visit to Brandon. Do you know, Margaret, that I think you are just a little bit sly?"

"I don't know what you mean," said Margaret, looking offended.

"Dear, I don't blame you," said the impulsive creature, wheeling short round and coming close to Margaret. "I'd kiss you this minute if we were not in the public road."

When Henderson came, Margaret's world was full; no desire was ungratified. He experienced a little relief when she did not bother him about his business nor inquire into his operations with Hollowell, and he fancied that she was getting to accept the world as Carmen accepted it. There had been moments since his marriage when he feared that Margaret's scruples would interfere with his career, but never a moment when he had doubted that her love for him would be superior to any solicitations from others. Carmen, who knew him like a book, would have said that the model wife for Henderson would be a woman devoted to him and to his interests, and not too scrupulous. A wife is a torment, if you can't feel at ease with her.

"If there were only a French fleet in the harbor, dear," said Margaret one day, "I should feel that I had quite taken up the life of my great-great-grandmother."

They were sailing in Hollowell's yacht, in which Uncle Jerry had brought his family round from New York. He hated the water, but Mrs. Hollowell and the children doted on the sea, he said.

"Wouldn't the torpedo station make up for it?" Henderson asked.

"Hardly. But it shows the change of a hundred years. Only, isn't it odd, this personal dropping back into an old situation? I wonder what she was like?"

"The accounts say she was the belle of Newport. I suppose Newport has a belle once in a hundred years. The time has come round. But I confess I don't miss the French fleet," replied Henderson, with a look of love that thrilled Margaret through and through.

"But you would have been an officer on the fleet, and I should have fallen in love with you. Ah, well, it is better as it is."

And it was better. The days went by without a cloud. Even after Henderson had gone, the prosperity of life filled her heart more and more.

"She might have been like me," Carmen said to herself, "if she had only started right; but it is so hard to get rid of a New England conscience."

When Margaret stayed in her room, one morning, to write a long-postponed letter to her aunt, she discovered that she had very little to write, at least that she wanted to write, to her aunt. She began, however, resolutely with a little account of her life. But it seemed another thing on paper, addressed to the loving eyes at Brandon. There were too much luxury and idleness and triviality in it, too much Carmen and Count Crispo and flirtation and dissipation in it.

She tore it up, and went to the window and looked out upon the sea. She was indignant with the Brandon people that they should care so little about this charming life. She was indignant at herself that she had torn up the letter. What had she done that anybody should criticise her? Why shouldn't she live her life, and not be hampered everlastingly by comparisons?

She sat down again, and took up her pen. Was she changing was she changed? Why was it that she had felt a little relief when her last Brandon visit was at an end, a certain freedom in Lenox and a greater freedom in Newport? The old associations became strong again in her mind, the life in the little neighborhood, the simplicity of it, the high ideals of it, the daily love and tenderness. Her aunt was no doubt wondering now that she did not write, and perhaps grieving that Margaret no more felt at home in Brandon. It was too much. She loved them, she loved them all dearly. She would write that, and speak only generally of her frivolous, happy summer. And she began, but somehow the letter seemed stiff and to lack the old confiding tone.

But why should they disapprove of her? She thought of her husband. If circumstances had altered, was she to blame? Could she always be thinking of what they would think at Brandon? It was an intolerable bondage. They had no right to set themselves up over her. Suppose her aunt didn't like Carmen. She was not responsible for Carmen. What would they have her do? Be unhappy because Henderson was prosperous, and she could indulge her tastes and not have to drudge in school? Suppose she did look at some things differently from what she used to. She knew more of the world. Must you shut yourself up because you found you couldn't trust everybody? What was Mr. Morgan always hitting at? Had he any better opinion of men and women than her husband had? Was he any more charitable than Uncle Jerry? She smiled as she thought of Uncle Jerry and his remark "It's a very decent world if you don't huff it." No; she did like this life, and she was not going to pretend that she didn't. It would be dreadful to lose the love and esteem of her dear old friends, and she cried a little as this possibility came over her. And then she hardened her heart a little at the thought that she could not help it if they chose to misunderstand her and change.

Carmen was calling from the stairs that it was time to dress for the drive. She dashed off a note. It contained messages of love for everybody, but it was the first one in her life written to her aunt not from her heart.

XVII

Shall we never have done with this carping at people who succeed? Are those who start and don't arrive any better than those who do arrive? Did not men always make all the money they had an opportunity to make? Must we always have the old slow-coach merchants and planters thrown up to us? Talk of George Washington and the men of this day! Were things any better because they were on a small scale? Wasn't the thrifty George Washington always adding to his plantations, and squeezing all he could out of his land and his slaves? What are the negro traditions about it? Were they all patriots in the Revolutionary War? Were there no contractors who amassed fortunes then? And how was it in the late war? The public has a great spasm of virtue all of a sudden. But we have got past the day of stage-coaches.

Something like this Henderson was flinging out to Carmen as he paced back and forth in her parlor. It was very unlike him, this outburst, and Carmen knew that he would indulge in it to no one else, not even to Uncle Jerry. She was coiled up in a corner of the sofa, her eyes sparkling with admiration of his indignation and force. I confess that he had been irritated by the comments of the newspapers, and by the prodding of the lawyers in the suit then on trial over the Southwestern consolidation.

"Why, there was old Mansfield saying in his argument that he had had some little experience in life, but he never had known a man to get rich rapidly, barring some piece of luck, except by means that it would make him writhe to have made public. I don't know but that Uncle Jerry was right, that we made a mistake in not retaining him for the corporation."

"Not if you win," said Carmen, softly. "The public won't care for the remark unless you fail."

"And he tried to prejudice the Court by quoting the remark attributed to Uncle Jerry, 'The public be d d' as if, said Mansfield, the public has no rights as against the railroad wreckers. Uncle Jerry laughed, and interrupted: 'That's nonsense, reporters' nonsense. What I said was that if the public thought I was fool enough to make it our enemy, the public might be d -d (begging your honor's pardon).' Then everybody laughed. 'It's the bond holders, who want big dividends, that stand in the way of the development of the country, that's what it is,' said he, as he sat down, to those around him, but loud enough to be heard all over the room. Mansfield asked the protection of the Court against these clap-trap interruptions. The judge said it was altogether irregular, and Uncle Jerry begged pardon. The reporters made this incident the one prominent thing in the case that day."

"What a delightful Uncle Jerry it is!" said Carmen. "You'd better keep an eye on him, Rodney; he'll be giving your money to that theological seminary in Alabama."

"That reminds me," Henderson said, cooling down, "of a paragraph in The Planet, the other day, about the amount of my gifts unknown to the public. I showed it to Uncle Jerry, and he said, 'Yes, I mentioned it to the editor; such things don't do any harm.'"

"I saw it, and wondered who started it," Carmen replied, wrinkling her brows as if she had been a good deal perplexed about it.

"I thought," said Henderson, with a smile, "that it ought to be explained to you."

"No," she said, reflectively; "you are liberal enough, goodness knows too liberal but you are not a flat."

Henderson was in the habit of dropping in at the Eschelles' occasionally, when he wanted to talk freely. He had no need to wear a mask with Carmen. Her moral sense was tolerant and elastic, and feminine sympathy of this sort is a grateful cushion. She admired Henderson, without thinking any too well of the world in general, and she admired him for the qualities that were most conformable to his inclination. It was no case of hero-worship, to be sure, nor for tragedy; but then what a satisfaction it must be to sweet Lady Macbeth, coiled up on her sofa, to feel that the thane of Cawdor has some nerve!

The Hendersons had come back to Washington Square late in the autumn. It is a merciful provision that one has an orderly and well-appointed home to return to from the fatigues of the country. Margaret, at any rate, was a little tired with the multiform excitements of her summer, and experienced a feeling of relief when she crossed her own threshold and entered into the freedom and quiet of her home. She was able to shut the door there even against the solicitations of nature and against the weariness of it also. How quiet it was in the square in those late autumn days, and yet not lifeless by any means! Indeed, it seemed all the more a haven because the roar of the great city environed it, and one could feel, without being disturbed by, the active pulsation of human life. And then, if one has sentiment, is there anywhere that it is more ministered to than in the city at the close of the year? The trees in the little park grow red and yellow and brown, the leaves fall and swirl and drift in windrows by the paths, the flower-beds flame forth in the last dying splendor of their color; the children, chasing each other with hoop and ball about the walks, are more subdued than in the spring-time; the old men, seeking now the benches where the sunshine falls, sit in dreamy reminiscence of the days that are gone; the wandering minstrel of Italy turns the crank of his wailing machine, O! bella, bella, as in the spring, but the notes seem to come from far off and to be full of memory rather than of promise; and at early morning, or when the shadows lengthen at evening, the south wind that stirs the trees has a salt smell, and sends a premonitory shiver of change to the fading foliage. But how bright are the squares and the streets, for all this note of melancholy! Life is to begin again.

But the social season opened languidly. It takes some time to recover from the invigoration of the summer gayety to pick up again the threads and weave them into that brilliant pattern, which scarcely shows all its loveliness of combination and color before the weavers begin to work in the subdued tints of Lent. How delightful it is to see this knitting and unraveling of the social fabric year after year! and how untiring are the senders of the shuttles, the dyers, the hatchelers, the spinners, the ever-busy makers and destroyers of the intricate web we call society! After one campaign, must there not be time given to organize for another? Who has fallen out, who are the new recruits, who are engaged, who will marry, who have separated, who has lost his money? Before we can safely reorganize we must not only examine the hearts but the stock-list. No matter how many brilliant alliances have been arranged, no matter how many husbands and wives have drifted apart in the local whirlpools of the summer's current, the season will be dull if Wall Street is torpid and discouraged. We cannot any of us, you see, live to ourselves alone. Does not the preacher say that? And do we not all look about us in the pews, when he thus moralizes, to see who has prospered? The B's have taken a back seat, the C's have moved up nearer the pulpit. There is a reason for these things, my friends.

I am sorry to say that Margaret was usually obliged to go alone to the little church where she said her prayers; for however restful her life might have been while that season was getting under way, Henderson was involved in the most serious struggle of his life a shameful kind of conspiracy, Margaret told Carmen, against him. I have hinted at his annoyance in the courts. Ever since September he had been pestered with injunctions, threatened with attachments. And now December had come and Congress was in session; in the very first days an investigation had been ordered into the land grants involved in the Southwestern operations. Uncle Jerry was in Washington to explain matters there, and Henderson, with the ablest counsel in the city, was fighting in the courts. The affair made a tremendous stir. Some of the bondholders of the A. and B. happened to be men of prominence, and able to make a noise about their injury. As several millions were involved in this one branch of the case the suit of the bondholders the newspapers treated it with the consideration and dignity it deserved. It was a vast financial operation, some said, scathingly, a "deal," but the magnitude of it prevented it from falling into the reports of petty swindling that appear in the police-court column. It was a public affair, and not to be judged by one's private standard. I know that there were remarks made about Henderson that would have pained Margaret if she had heard them, but I never heard that he lost standing in the street. Still, in justice to the street it must be said that it charitably waits for things to be proven, and that if Henderson had failed, he might have had little more lenient judgment in the street than elsewhere.

In fact, those were very trying days for him-days when he needed all the private sympathy he could get, and to be shielded, in his great fight with the conspiracy, from petty private annoyances. It needed all his courage and good-temper and bonhomie to carry him through. That he went through was evidence not only of his adroitness and ability, but it was proof also that he was a good fellow. If there were people who thought otherwise, I never heard that they turned their backs on him, or failed in that civility which he never laid aside in his intercourse with others.

If a man present a smiling front to the world under extreme trial, is not that all that can be expected of him? Shall he not be excused for showing a little irritation at home when things go badly? Henderson was as good-humored a man as I ever knew, and he loved Margaret, he was proud of her, he trusted her. Since when did the truest love prevent a man from being petulant, even to the extent of wounding those he best loves, especially if the loved one shows scruples when sympathy is needed? The reader knows that the present writer has no great confidence in the principle of Carmen; but if she had been married, and her husband had wrecked an insurance company and appropriated all the surplus belonging to the policy-holders, I don't believe she would have nagged him about it.

And yet Margaret loved Henderson with her whole soul. And in this stage of her progress in the world she showed that she did, though not in the way Carmen would have showed her love, if she had loved, and if she had a soul capable of love.

It may have been inferred from Henderson's exhibition of temper that his case had gone against him. It is true; an injunction had been granted in the lower court, and public opinion went with the decree, and was in a great measure satisfied by it. But this fight had really only just begun; it would go on in the higher courts, with new resources and infinite devices, which the public would be unable to fathom or follow, until by-and-by it would come out that a compromise had been made, and the easy public would not understand that this compromise gave the looters of the railway substantially all they ever expected to get. The morning after the granting of the injunction Henderson had been silent and very much absorbed at breakfast, hardly polite, Margaret thought, and so inattentive to her remarks that she asked him twice whether they should accept the Brandon invitation to Christmas. "Christmas! I don't know. I've got other things to think of than Christmas," he said, scarcely looking at her, and rising abruptly and going away to his library.

When the postman brought Margaret's mail there was a letter in it from her aunt, which she opened leisurely after the other notes had been glanced through, on the principle that a family letter can wait, or from the fancy that some have of keeping the letter likely to be most interesting till the last. But almost the first line enchained her attention, and as she read, her heart beat faster, and her face became scarlet. It was very short, and I am able to print it, because all Margaret's correspondence ultimately came into possession of her aunt:

"BRANDON, December 17th.

"DEAREST MARGARET, You do not say whether you will come for Christmas, but we infer from your silence that you will. You know how pained we shall all be if you do not. Yet I fear the day will not be as pleasant as we could wish. In fact, we are in a good deal of trouble. You know, dear, that poor Mrs. Fletcher had nearly every dollar of her little fortune invested in the A. and B. bonds, and for ten months she has not had a cent of income, and no prospect of any. Indeed, Morgan says that she will be lucky if she ultimately saves half her principal. We try to cheer her up, but she is so cast down and mortified to have to live, as she says, on charity. And it does make rather close house-keeping, though I'm sure I couldn't live alone without her. It does not make so much difference with Mr. Fairchild and Mr. Morgan, for they have plenty of other resources. Mr. Fairchild tells her that she is in very good company, for lots of the bonds are held in Brandon, and she is not the only widow who suffers; but this is poor consolation. We had great hopes, the other day, of the trial, but Morgan says it may be years before any final settlement. I don't believe Mr. Henderson knows. But there, dearest, I won't find fault. We are all well, and eager to see you. Do come.

"Your affectionate aunt,

"GEORGIAN A."

Margaret's hand that held the letter trembled, and the eyes that read these words were hot with indignation; but she controlled herself into an appearance of calmness as she marched away with it straight to the library.

As she entered, Henderson was seated at his desk, with bowed head and perplexed brows, sorting a pile of papers before him, and making notes. He did not look up until she came close to him and stood at the end of his desk. Then, turning his eyes for a moment, and putting out his left hand to her, he said, "Well, what is it, dear?"

"Will you read that?" said Margaret, in a voice that sounded strange in her own ears.

"What?"

"A letter from Aunt Forsythe."

"Family matter. Can't it wait?" said Henderson, going on with his figuring.

"If it can, I cannot," Margaret answered, in a tone that caused him to turn abruptly and look at her. He was so impatient and occupied that even yet he did not comprehend the new expression in her face.

"Don't you see I am busy, child? I have an engagement in twenty minutes in my office."

"You can read it in a moment," said Margaret, still calm.

Henderson took the letter with a gesture of extreme annoyance, ran his eye through it, flung it from him on the table, and turned squarely round in his chair.

"Well, what of it?"

"To ruin poor Mrs. Fletcher and a hundred like her!" cried Margaret, with rising indignation.

"What have I to do with it? Did I make their investments? Do you think I have time to attend to every poor duck? Why don't people look where they put their money?"

"It's a shame, a burning shame!" she cried, regarding him steadily.

"Oh, yes; no doubt. I lost a hundred thousand yesterday; did I whine about it? If I want to buy anything in the market, have I got to look into every tuppenny interest concerned in it? If Mrs. Fletcher or anybody else has any complaint against me, the courts are open. I defy the whole pack!" Henderson thundered out, rising and buttoning his coat "the whole pack!"

"And you have nothing else to say, Rodney?" Margaret persisted, not quailing in the least before his indignation. He had never seen her so before, and he was now too much in a passion to fully heed her.

"Oh, women, women!" he said, taking up his hat, "you have sympathy enough for anybody but your husbands." He pushed past her, and was gone without another word or look.

Margaret turned to follow him. She would have cried "Stop!" but the word stuck in her throat. She was half beside herself with rage for a moment. But he had gone. She heard the outer door close. Shame and grief overcame her. She sat down in the chair he had just occupied. It was infamous the way Mrs. Fletcher was treated. And her husband her husband was so regardless of it. If he was not to blame for it, why didn't he tell her why didn't he explain? And he had gone away without looking at her. He had left her for the first time since they were married without kissing her! She put her head down on the desk and sobbed; it seemed as if her heart would break. Perhaps he was angry, and wouldn't come back, not for ever so long.

How cruel to say that she did not sympathize with her husband! How could he be angry with her for her natural anxiety about her old friend! He was unjust. There must be something wrong in these schemes, these great operations that made so many confiding people suffer. Was everybody grasping and selfish? She got up and walked about the dear room, which recalled to her only the sweetest memories; she wandered aimlessly about the lower part of the house. She was wretchedly unhappy. Was her husband capable of such conduct? Would he cease to love her for what she had done for what she must do? How lovely this home was! Everything spoke of his care, his tenderness, his quickness to anticipate her slightest wish or whim. It had been all created for her. She looked listlessly at the pictures, the painted ceiling, where the loves garlanded with flowers chased each other; she lifted and let drop wearily the rich hangings. He had said that it was all hers. How pretty was this vista through the luxurious rooms down to the green and sunny conservatory. And she shrank instinctively from it all. Was it hers? No; it was his. And was she only a part of it? Was she his? How cold his look as he went away!

What is this love, this divine passion, of which we hear so much? Is it, then, such a discerner of right and wrong? Is it better than anything else? Does it take the place of duty, of conscience? And yet what an unbearable desert, what a den of wild beasts it would be, this world, without love, the passionate, all-surrendering love of the man and the woman!

In the chambers, in her own apartments, into which she dragged her steps, it was worse than below. Everything here was personal. Mrs. Fairchild had said that it was too rich, too luxurious; but her husband would have it so. Nothing was too costly, too good, for the woman he loved. How happy she had been in this boudoir, this room, her very own, with her books, the souvenirs of all her happy life!

It seemed alien now, external, unsympathetic. Here, least of all places, could she escape from herself, from her hateful thoughts. It was a chilly day, and a bright fire crackled on the hearth. The square was almost deserted, though the sun illuminated it, and showed all the delicate tracery of the branches and twigs. It was a December sun. Her easy-chair was drawn to the fire and her book-stand by it, with the novel turned down that she had been reading the night before. She sat down and took up the book. She had lost her interest in the characters. Fiction! What stuff it was compared to the reality of her own life! No, it was impossible. She must do something. She went to her dressing-room and selected a street dress. She took pleasure in putting on the plainest costume she could find, rejecting every ornament, everything but the necessary and the simple. She wanted to get back to herself. Her maid appeared in response to the bell.

"I am going out, Marie."

"Will madame have the carriage?"

"No, I will walk; I need exercise. Tell Jackson not to serve lunch."

Yes, she would walk; for it was his carriage, after all.

It was after mid-day. In the keen air and the bright sunshine the streets were brilliant. Margaret walked on up the avenue. How gay was the city, what a zest of life in the animated scene! The throng increased as she approached Twenty-third Street. In the place where three or four currents meet there was the usual jam of carriages, furniture wagons, carts, cars, and hurried, timid, half-bewildered passengers trying to make their way through it. It was all such a whirl and confusion. A policeman aided Margaret to gain the side of the square. Children were playing there; white-capped maids were pushing about baby-carriages; the sparrows chattered and fought with as much vivacity as if they were natives of the city instead of foreigners in possession. It seemed all so empty and unreal. What was she, one woman with an aching heart, in the midst of it all? What had she done? How could she have acted otherwise? Was he still angry with her? The city was so vast and cruel. On the avenue again there was the same unceasing roar of carts and carriages; business, pleasure, fashion, idleness, the stream always went by. From one and another carriage Margaret received a bow, a cool nod, or a smile of greeting. Perhaps the occupants wondered to see her on foot and alone. What did it matter? How heartless it all was! what an empty pageant! If he was alienated, there was nothing. And yet she was right. For a moment she thought of the Arbusers. She thought of Carmen. She must see somebody. No, she couldn't talk. She couldn't trust herself. She must bear it alone.

And how weary it was, walking, walking, with such a burden! House after house, street after street, closed doors, repellant fronts, staring at her. Suppose she were poor and hungry, a woman wandering forlorn, how stony and pitiless these insolent mansions! And was she not burdened and friendless and forlorn! Tired, she reached at last, and with no purpose, the great white cathedral. The door was open. In all this street of churches and palaces there was no other door open. Perhaps here for a moment she could find shelter from the world, a quiet corner where she could rest and think and pray.

She entered. It was almost empty, but down the vista of the great columns hospitable lights gleamed, and here and there a man or a woman more women than men was kneeling in the great aisle, before a picture, at the side of a confessional, at the steps of the altar. How hushed and calm and sweet it was! She crept into a pew in a side aisle in the shelter of a pillar; and sat down. Presently, in the far apse, an organ began to play, its notes stealing softly out through the great spaces like a benediction. She fancied that the saints, the glorified martyrs in the painted windows illumined by the sunlight, could feel, could hear, were touched by human sympathy in their beatitude. There was peace here at any rate, and perhaps strength. What a dizzy whirl it all was in which she had been borne along! The tones of the organ rose fuller and fuller, and now at the side entrances came pouring in children, the boys on one side, the girls on another-school children with their books and satchels, the poor children of the parish, long lines of girls and of boys, marshaled by priests and nuns, streaming in in frolicsome mood, and filling all the pews of the nave at the front. They had their books out, their singing-books; at a signal they all stood up; a young priest with his baton stepped into the centre aisle; he waved his stick, Margaret heard his sweet tenor voice, and then the whole chorus of children's voices rising and filling all the house with the innocent concord, but always above all the penetrating, soaring notes of the priest-strong, clear, persuading. Was it not almost angelic there at the moment? And how inspired the beautiful face of the singer leading the children!

Ah, me! it is not all of the world worldly, then. I don't know that the singing was very good: it was not classical, I fear; not a voice, maybe, that priest's, not a chorus, probably, that, for the Metropolitan. I hear the organ is played better elsewhere. Song after song, chorus after chorus, repeated, stopped, begun again: it was only drilling the little urchins of the parochial schools little ragamuffins, I dare say, many of them. What was there in this to touch a woman of fashion, sitting there crying in her corner? Was it because they were children's voices, and innocent? Margaret did not care to check her tears. She was thinking of her old home, of her own childhood, nay, of her girlhood it was not so long ago of her ideals then, of her notion of the world and what it would bring her, of the dear, affectionate life, the simple life, the school, the little church, her room in the cottage the chamber where first the realization of love came to her with the odors of May. Was it gone, that life? gone or going out of her heart? And great heavens! if her husband should be cold to her! Was she very worldly? Would he love her if she were as unworldly as she once was? Why should this childish singing raise these contrasts, and put her at odds so with her own life? For a moment I doubt not this dear girl saw herself as we were beginning to see her. Who says that the rich and the prosperous and the successful do not need pity?

Was this a comforting hour, do you think, for Margaret in the cathedral? Did she get any strength, I wonder? When the singing was over and the organ ceased, and the children had filed out, she stole away also, wearily and humbly enough, and took the stage down the avenue. It was near the dinner-hour, and Henderson, if he came, would be at home any moment. It seemed as if she could not wait only to see him!

XVIII

Do you suppose that Henderson had never spoken impatiently and sharply to his wife before, that Margaret had never resented it and replied with spirit, and been hurt and grieved, and that there had never been reconciliations? In writing any biography there are some things that are taken for granted with an intelligent public. Are men always gentle and considerate, and women always even-tempered and consistent, simply by virtue of a few words said to the priest?

But this was a more serious affair. Margaret waited in a tumult of emotion. She felt that she would die if she did not see him soon, and she dreaded his coming. A horrible suspicion had entered her mind that respect for her husband, confidence in him, might be lowered, and a more horrible doubt that she might lose his love. That she could not bear. And was Henderson unconscious of all this? I dare say that in the perplexing excitement of the day he did recall for a moment with a keen thrust of regret the scene of the morning-his wife standing there flushed, wounded, indignant. "I might have turned back, and taken her in my arms, and told her it was all right," he thought. He wished he had done so. But what nonsense it was to think that she could be seriously troubled! Besides, he couldn't have women interfering with him every moment.

How inconsiderate men are! They drop a word or a phrase they do not know how cruel it is or give a look they do not know how cold it is and are gone without a second thought about it; but it sinks into the woman's heart and rankles there. For the instant it is like a mortal blow, it hurts so, and in the brooding spirit it is exaggerated into a hopeless disaster. The wound will heal with a kind word, with kisses. Yes, but never, never without a little scar. But woe to the woman's love when she becomes insensible to these little stabs!

Henderson hurried home, then, more eagerly than usual, with reparation in his heart, but still with no conception of the seriousness of the breach. Margaret heard the key in the door, heard his hasty step in the hall, heard him call, as he always did on entering, "Margaret! where is Margaret?" and she, sitting there in the deep window looking on the square, longed to run to him, as usual also, and be lifted up in his strong arms; but she could not stir. Only when he found her did she rise up with a wistful look and a faint smile. "Have you had a good day, child?" And he kissed her. But her kiss was on her lips only, for her heart was heavy.

"Dinner will be served as soon as you dress," she said. What a greeting was this! Who says that a woman cannot be as cruel as a man? The dinner was not very cheerful, though Margaret did her best not to appear constrained, and Henderson rattled on about the events of the day. It had been a deuce of a day, but it was coming right; he felt sure that the upper court would dissolve the injunction; the best counsel said so; and the criminal proceedings "Had there been criminal proceedings?" asked Margaret, with a stricture at her heart had broken down completely, hadn't a leg to stand on, never had, were only begun to bluff the company. It was a purely malicious prosecution. And Henderson did not think it necessary to tell Margaret that only Uncle Jerry's dexterity had spared both of them the experience of a night in the Ludlow Street jail.

"Come," said Henderson "come into the library. I have something to tell you." He put his arm round her as they walked, and seating himself in his chair by his desk in front of the fire, he tried to draw Margaret to sit on his knee.

"No; I'll sit here, so that I can see you," she said, composed and unyielding.

He took out his pocket-book, selected a slip of paper, and laid it on the table before him. "There, that is a check for seven hundred dollars. I looked in the books. That is the interest for a year on the Fletcher bonds. Might as well make it an even year; it will be that soon."

"Do you mean to say " asked Margaret, leaning forward.

"Yes; to brighten up the Christmas up there a little."

" that you are going to send that to Mrs. Fletcher?" Margaret had risen.

"Oh, no; that wouldn't do. I cannot send it, nor know anything about it. It would raise the well, it would if the other bondholders knew anything about it. But you can change that for your check, and nobody the wiser."

"Oh, Rodney!" She was on his knee now. He was good, after all. Her head was on his shoulder, and she was crying a little. "I've been so unhappy, so unhappy, all day! And I can send that?" She sprang up. "I'll do it this minute I'll run and get my check-book!" But before she reached the door she turned back, and came and stood by him and kissed him again and again, and tumbled up his hair, and looked at him. There is, after all, nothing in the world like a woman.

"Time enough in the morning," said Henderson, detaining her. "I want to tell you all about it."

What he told her was, in fact, the case as it had been presented by his lawyers, and it seemed a very large, a constitutional, kind of case. "Of course," he said, "in the rivalry and competition of business somebody must go to the wall, and in a great scheme of development and reorganization of the transportation of a region as big as an empire some individual interests will suffer. You can't help these changes. I'm sorry for some of them very sorry; but nothing would ever be done if we waited to consider every little interest. And that the men who create these great works, and organize these schemes for the benefit of the whole public, shouldn't make anything by their superior enterprise and courage is all nonsense. The world is not made that way."

The explanation, I am bound to say, was one that half the world considers valid; it was one that squeezed through the courts. And when it was done, and the whole thing had blown over, who cared? There were some bondholders who said that it was rascally, that they had been boldly swindled. In the clubs, long after, you would hear it said that Hollowell and Henderson were awfully sharp, and hard to beat. It is a very bad business, said the Brandon parliament, and it just shows that the whole country is losing its moral sense, its capacity to judge what is right and what is wrong.

I do not say that this explanation, the nature of which I have only indicated, would have satisfied the clear mind of Margaret a year or two before. But it was made by the man she loved, the man who had brought her out into a world that was full of sunlight and prosperity and satisfied desire; and more and more, day by day, she saw the world through his eyes, and accepted his estimate of the motives of people and a low estimate I fear it was. Who would not be rich if he could? Do you mean to tell me that a man who is getting fat dividends out of a stock does not regard more leniently the manner in which that stock is manipulated than one who does not own any of it? I dare say, if Carmen had heard that explanation, and seen Margaret's tearful, happy acceptance of it, she would have shaken her pretty head and said, "They are getting too worldly for me."

In the morning the letter was despatched to Miss Forsythe, enclosing the check for Mrs. Fletcher a joyful note, full of affection. "We cannot come," Margaret wrote. "My husband cannot leave, and he does not want to spare me" the little hypocrite! he had told her that she could easily go for a day "but we shall think of you dear ones all day, and I do hope that now there will not be the least cloud on your Christmas."

It seems a great pity, in view of the scientific organization of society, that there are so many sensibilities unclassified and unprovided for in the otherwise perfect machinery. Why should the beggar to whom you toss a silver dollar from your carriage feel a little grudge against you? Perhaps he wouldn't like to earn the dollar, but if it had been accompanied by a word of sympathy, his sensibility might have been soothed by your recognition of human partnership in the goods of this world. People not paupers are all eager to take what is theirs of right; but anything in the semblance of charity is a bitter pill to swallow until self-respect is a little broken down. Probably the resentment lies in the recognition of the truth that it is much easier to be charitable than to be just. If Margaret had seen the effect produced by her letter she might have thought of this; she might have gone further, and reflected upon what would have been her own state of mind two years earlier if she had received such a letter. Miss Forsythe read it with a very heavy heart. She hesitated about showing it to Mrs. Fletcher, and when she did, and gave her the check, it was with a sense of shame.

"The insolence of the thing!" cried Mrs. Fletcher, as soon as she comprehended it.

"Not insolence," pleaded Miss Forsythe, softly; "it is out of the kindness of her heart. She would be dreadfully wounded to know that you took it so."

"Well," said Mrs. Fletcher, hotly, "I like that kind of sensibility. Does she think I have no feeling? Does she think I would take from her as a charity what her husband knows is mine by right?"

"Perhaps her husband "

"No," Mrs. Fletcher interrupted. "Why didn't he send it, then? why didn't the company send it? They owe it. I'm not a pauper. And all the other bondholders who need the money as much as I do! I'm not saying that if the company sent it I should refuse it because the others had been treated unjustly; but to take it as a favor, like a beggar!"

"Of course you cannot take it from Margaret," said Miss Forsythe sadly.

"How dreadful it is!"

Mrs. Fletcher would have shared her last crust with Miss Forsythe, and if her own fortune were absolutely lost, she would not hesitate to accept the shelter of her present home, using her energies to add to their limited income, serving and being served in all love and trust. But this is different from taking a bounty from the rich.

The check had to go back. Even my wife, who saw no insolence in Margaret's attempt, applauded Mrs. Fletcher's spirit. She told Miss Forsythe that if things did not mend they might get a few little pupils for Mrs. Fletcher from the neighborhood, and Miss Forsythe knew that she was thinking that her own boy might have been one of them if he had lived. Mr. Morgan was a little satirical, as usual. He thought it would be a pity to check Margaret's growing notion that there was no wrong that money could not heal a remark that my wife thought unjust to the girl. Mrs. Fletcher was for re-enclosing the check without a word of comment, but that Miss Forsythe would not do.

"My dearest Margaret," she wrote, "I know the kindness of heart that moved you to do this, and I love you more than ever, and am crying as I think of it. But you must see yourself, when you reflect, that Mrs. Fletcher could not take this from you. Her self-respect would not permit it. Somebody has done a great wrong, and only those who have done it can undo it. I don't know much about such things, my dear, and I don't believe all that the newspapers have been saying, but there would be no need for charity if there had not been dishonesty somewhere. I cannot help thinking that. We do not blame you. And you must not take it to heart that I am compelled to send this back. I understand why you sent it, and you must try to understand why it cannot be kept."

There was more of this sort in the letter. It was full of a kind of sorrowful yearning, as if there was fear that Margaret's love were slipping away and all the old relations were being broken up, but yet it had in it a certain moral condemnation that the New England spinster could not conceal. Softened as it was by affectionate words, and all the loving messages of the season, it was like a slap in the face to Margaret. She read it in the first place with intense mortification, and then with indignation. This was the way her loving spirit was flung back upon her! They did not blame her! They blamed her husband, then. They condemned him. It was his generosity that was spurned.

Is there a particular moment when we choose our path in life, when we take the right or the left? At this instant, when Margaret arose with the crumpled letter in her hand, and marched towards her husband's library, did she choose, or had she been choosing for the two years past, and was this only a publication of her election? Why had she secretly been a little relieved from restraint when her Brandon visit ended in the spring? They were against her husband; they disapproved of him, that was clear. Was it not a wife's duty to stand by her husband? She was indignant with the Brandon scrupulousness; it chafed her.. Was this simply because she loved her husband, or was this indignation a little due also to her liking for the world which so fell in with her inclinations? The motives in life are so mixed that it seems impossible wholly to condemn or wholly to approve. If Margaret's destiny had been united with such a man as John Lyon, what would have been her discernment in such a case as this? It is such a pity that for most people there is only one chance in life.

She laid the letter and the check upon her husband's desk. He read it with a slight frown, which changed to a smile of amusement as he looked up and saw Margaret's excitement.

"Well, it was a miss-go. Those folks up there are too good for this world. You'd better send it to the hospital."

"But you see that they say they do not blame me," Margaret said, with warmth.

"Oh, I can stand it. People usually don't try to hurt my feelings that way. Don't mind it, child. They will come to their senses, and see what nonsense it all is."

Yes, it was nonsense. And how generous and kind at heart her husband was! In his skillful making little of it she was very much comforted, and at the same time drawn into more perfect sympathy with him. She was glad she was not going to Brandon for Christmas; she would not submit herself to its censorship. The note of acknowledgment she wrote to her aunt was short and almost formal. She was very sorry they looked at the matter in that way. She thought she was doing right, and they might blame her or not, but her aunt would see that she could not permit any distinction to be set up between her and her husband, etc.

Was this little note a severance of her present from her old life? I do not suppose she regarded it so. If she had fully realized that it was a step in that direction, would she have penned it with so little regret as she felt? Or did she think that circumstances and not her own choice were responsible for her state of feeling? She was mortified, as has been said, but she wrote with more indignation than pain.

A year ago Carmen would have been the last person to whom Margaret would have spoken about a family affair of this kind. Nor would she have done so now, notwithstanding the intimacy established at Newport, if Carmen had not happened in that day, when Margaret was still hurt and excited, and skillfully and most sympathetically extracted from her the cause of the mood she found her in. But even with all these allowances, that Margaret should confide such a matter to Carmen was the most startling sign of the change that had taken place in her.

"Well," said this wise person, after she had wormed out the whole story, and expressed her profound sympathy, and then fallen into an attitude of deep reflection "well, I wish I could cast my bread upon the waters in that way. What are you going to do with the money?"

"I've sent it to the hospital."

"What extravagance! And did you tell your aunt that?"

"Of course not."

"Why not? I couldn't have resisted such a righteous chance of making her feel bad."

"But I don't want to make her feel bad."

"Just a little? You will never convince people that you are unworldly this way. Even Uncle Jerry wouldn't do that."

"You and Uncle Jerry are very much alike," cried Margaret, laughing in spite of herself "both of you as bad as you can be."

"But, dear, we don't pretend, do we?" asked Carmen, innocently.

To some of us at Brandon, Margaret's letter was scarcely a surprise, though it emphasized a divergence we had been conscious of. But with Miss Forsythe it was far otherwise. The coolness of Margaret's tone filled her with alarm; it was the premonition of a future which she did not dare to face.

There was a passage in the letter which she did not show; not that it was unfeeling, she told my wife afterwards, but that it exhibited a worldly-mindedness that she could not have conceived of in Margaret. She could bear separation from the girl on whom she had bestowed her tenderest affection, that she had schooled herself to expect upon her marriage that, indeed, was only a part of her life of willing self-sacrifice their paths must lie apart, and she could hope to see little of her. But what she could not bear was the separation in spirit, the wrenching apart of sympathy, the loss of her heart, and the thought of her going farther and farther away into that world whose cynical and materialistic view of life made her shudder. I think there are few tragedies in life comparable to this to a sensitive, trusting soul not death itself, with its gracious healing and oblivion and pathos. Family quarrels have something sustaining in them, something of a sense of wrong and even indignation to keep up the spirits. There was no family quarrel here, no indignation, just simple, helpless grief and sense of loss. In one sense it seemed to the gentle spinster that her own life was ended, she had lived so in this girl ever since she came to her a child, in long curls and short frocks, the sweetest, most trustful, mischievous, affectionate thing. These two then never had had any secrets, never any pleasure, never any griefs they did not share. She had seen the child's mind unfold, the girl's grace and intelligence, the woman's character. Oh, Margaret, she cried, to herself, if you only knew what you are to me!

Margaret's little chamber in the cottage was always kept ready for her, much in the condition she had left it. She might come back at any time, and be a girl again. Here were many of the things which she had cherished; indeed everything in the room spoke of the simple days of her maidenhood. It was here that Miss Forsythe sat in her loneliness the morning after she received the letter, by the window with the muslin curtain, looking out through the shrubbery to the blue hills. She must be here; she could stay nowhere else in the house, for here the little Margaret came back to her. Ah, and when she turned, would she hear the quick steps and see the smiling face, and would she put back the tangled hair and lift her up and kiss her? There in that closet still hung articles of her clothing-dresses that had been laid aside when she became a woman kept with the sacred sentiment of New England thrift. How each one, as Miss Forsythe took them down, recalled the girl! In the inner closet was a pile of paper boxes. I do not know what impulse it was that led the heavy-hearted woman to take them down one by one, and indulge her grief in the memories enshrined in them. In one was a little bonnet, a spring bonnet; Margaret had worn it on the Easter Sunday when she took her first communion. The little thing was out of fashion now; the ribbons were all faded, but the spray of moss rose-buds on the side was almost as fresh as ever. How well she remembered it, and the girl's delight in the nodding roses!

When Mrs. Fletcher had called again and again, with no response, and finally opened the door and peeped in, there the spinster sat by the window, the pitiful little bonnet in her hand, and the tears rolling down her cheeks. God help her!

XIX

The medical faculty are of the opinion that a sprain is often worse than a broken limb; a purely scientific, view of the matter, in which the patient usually does not coincide. Well-bred people shrink from the vulgarity of violence, and avoid the publicity of any open rupture in domestic and social relations. And yet, perhaps, a lively quarrel would be less lamentable than the withering away of friendship while appearances are kept up. Nothing, indeed, is more pitiable than the gradual drifting apart of people who have been dear to each other a severance produced by change of views and of principle, and the substitution of indifference for sympathy. This disintegration is certain to take the spring and taste out of life, and commonly to habituate one to a lower view of human nature.

There was no rupture between the Hendersons and the Brandon circle, but there was little intercourse of the kind that had existed before. There was with us a profound sense of loss and sorrow, due partly to the growing knowledge, not pleasing to our vanity, that Margaret could get on very well without us, that we were not necessary to her life. Miss Forsythe recovered promptly her cheerful serenity, but not the elasticity of hope; she was irretrievably hurt; it was as if life was now to be endured. That Margaret herself was apparently unconscious of this, and that it did not affect much her own enjoyment, made it the harder to bear. The absolute truth probably was that she regretted it, and had moments of sentimental unhappiness; but there is great compensation for such loss in the feeling of freedom to pursue a career that is more and more agreeable. And I had to confess, when occasionally I saw Margaret during that winter, that she did not need us. Why should she? Did not the city offer her everything that she desired? And where in the world are beauty, and gayety with a touch of daring, and a magnificent establishment better appreciated? I do not know what criterion newspaper notoriety is of social prestige, but Mrs. Rodney Henderson's movements were as faithfully chronicled as if she had been a visiting princess or an actress of eccentric proclivities. Her name appeared as patroness of all the charities, the balls, the soirees, musical and literary, and if it did not appear in a list of the persons at any entertainment, one might suspect that the affair lacked the cachet of the best society. I suppose the final test of one's importance is to have all the details of one's wardrobe spread before the public. Judged by this, Margaret's career in New York was phenomenal. Even our interested household could not follow her in all the changing splendor of her raiment. In time even Miss Forsythe ceased to read all these details, but she cut them out, deposited them with other relics in a sort of mortuary box of the child and the maiden. I used to wonder if, in the Brandon attitude of mind at this period, there were not just a little envy of such unclouded prosperity. It is so much easier to forgive a failure than a success.

In the spring the Hendersons went abroad. The resolution to go may have been sudden, for Margaret wrote of it briefly, and had not time to run up and say good-by. The newspapers said that the trip was taken on account of Mrs. Henderson's health; that it was because Henderson needed rest from overwork; that he found it convenient to be away for a time, pending the settlement of certain complications. There were ugly stories afloat, but they were put in so many forms, and followed by so many different sorts of denial, and so much importance was attached to every word Henderson uttered, and every step he took, that the general impression of his far-reaching sagacity and Napoleonic command of fortune was immensely raised. Nothing is more significant of our progress than the good-humored deference of the world to this sort of success. It is said that the attraction of gravitation lessens according to the distance from the earth, and there seems to be a region of aerial freedom, if one can attain it, where the moral forces cease to be operative.

They remained in Europe a year, although Mr. Henderson in the interim made two or three hasty trips to this country, always, so far as it was made public, upon errands of great importance, and in connection with names of well-known foreign capitalists and enterprises of dignity. Margaret wrote seldom, but always with evident enjoyment of her experiences, which were mainly social, for wherever they went they commanded the consideration that is accorded to fortune. What most impressed me in these hasty notes was that the woman was so little interested in the persons and places which in the old days she expressed such a lively desire to see. If she saw them at all, it was from a different point of view than that she formerly had. She did indeed express her admiration of some charming literary friends of ours in London, to whom I had written to call on her people in very moderate circumstances, I am ashamed to say but she had not time to see much of them. She and her husband had spent a couple of days at Chisholm delightful days. Of the earl she had literally nothing to say, except that he was very kind, and that his family received them with the most engaging and simple cordiality. "It makes me laugh," she wrote from Chisholm, "when I think what we considered fine at Lenox and Newport. I've got some ideas for our new house." A note came from "John Lyon" to Miss Forsythe, expressing the great pleasure it was to return, even in so poor a way, the hospitality he had received at Brandon. I did not see it, but Miss Forsythe said it was a sad little note.

In Paris Margaret was ill very ill; and this misfortune caused for a time a revival of all the old affection, in sympathy with a disappointment which awoke in our womankind all the tenderness of their natures. She was indeed a little delicate for some time, but all our apprehensions were relieved by the reports from Rome of a succession of gayeties little interfered with by archaeological studies. They returned in June. Of the year abroad there was nothing to chronicle, and there would be nothing to note except that when Margaret passed a day with us on her return, we felt, as never before, that our interests in life were more and more divergent.

How could it be otherwise? There were so many topics of conversation that we had to avoid. Even light remarks on current news, comments that we used to make freely on the conduct of conspicuous persons, now carried condemnation that took a personal color. The doubtful means of making money, the pace of fashionable life, the wasteful prodigality of the time, we instinctively shrank from speaking of before Margaret. Perhaps we did her injustice. She was never more gracious, never more anxious to please. I fancied that there was at times something pathetic in her wistful desire for our affection and esteem. She was always a generous girl, and I have no doubt she felt repelled at the quiet rejection of her well-meant efforts to play the Lady Bountiful. There were moments during her brief visit when her face was very sad, but no doubt her predominant feeling escaped her in regard to the criticism quoted from somebody on Jerry Hollowell's methods and motives. "People are becoming very self-righteous," she said.

My wife said to me that she was reminded of the gentle observation of Carmen Eschelle, "The people I cannot stand are those who pretend they are not wicked." If one does not believe in anybody his cynicism has usually a quality of contemptuous bitterness in it. One brought up as Margaret had been could not very well come to her present view of life without a touch of this quality, but her disposition was so lovely perhaps there is no moral quality in a good temper that change of principle could not much affect it. And then she was never more winning; perhaps her beauty had taken on a more refined quality from her illness abroad; perhaps it was that indefinable knowledge of the world, which is recognized as well in dress as in manner, which increased her attractiveness. This was quite apart from the fact that she was not so sympathetically companionable to us as she once was, and it was this very attractiveness of the worldly sort, I fancied, that pained her aunt, and marked the separateness of their sympathies.

How could it be otherwise than that our interests should diverge? It was a very busy summer with the Hendersons. They were planning the New York house, which had been one of the objects of Henderson's early ambition. The sea-air had been prescribed for Margaret, and Henderson had built a steam-yacht, the equipment and furnishing of which had been a prolific newspaper topic. It was greatly admired by yachtsmen for the beauty of its lines and its speed, and pages were written about its sumptuous and comfortable interior. I never saw it, having little faith in the comfort of any structure that is not immovably reposeful, but from the descriptions it was a boudoir afloat. In it short voyages were made during the summer all along the coast from New York to Maine, and the arrival and departure of the Henderson yacht was one of the telegraphic items we always looked for. Carmen Eschelle was usually of the party on board, sometimes the Misses Arbuser; it was always a gay company, and in whatever harbor it dropped anchor there was a new impetus given to the somewhat languid pleasure of the summer season. We read of the dinners and lunches on board, the entertainments where there were wine and dancing and moonlight, and all that. I always thought of it as a fairy sort of ship, sailing on summer seas, freighted with youth and beauty, and carrying pleasure and good-fortune wherever it went. What more pleasing spectacle than this in a world that has such a bad name for want and misery?

Henderson was master of the situation. The sudden accumulation of millions of money is a mystery to most people. If Henderson had been asked about it he would have said that he had not a dollar which he had not earned by hard work. None worked harder. If simple industry is a virtue, he would have been an example for Sunday-school children. The object of life being to make money, he would have been a perfect example. What an inspiration, indeed, for all poor boys were the names of Hollowell and Henderson, which were as familiar as the name of the President! There was much speculation as to the amount of Henderson's fortune, and many wild estimates of it, but by common consent he was one of the three or four great capitalists. The gauge of this was his power, and the amounts he could command in an emergency. There was a mystery in the very fact that the amount he could command was unknown. I have said that his accumulation was sudden; it was probably so only in appearance. For a dozen years, by operations, various, secret, untiring, he had been laying the foundations for his success, and in the maturing of his schemes it became apparent how vast his transactions had been. For years he had been known as a rising man, and suddenly he became an important man. The telegraph, the newspapers, chronicled his every movement; whatever he said was construed like a Delphic oracle. The smile or the frown of Jay Hawker himself had not a greater effect upon the market. The Southwest operation, which made so much noise in the courts, was merely an incident. In the lives of many successful men there are such incidents, which they do not care to have inquired into, turning-points that one slides over in the subsequent gilded biography, or, as it is called, the nickel-plated biography. The uncomfortable A. and B. bondholders had been settled with and silenced, after a fashion. In the end, Mrs. Fletcher had received from the company nearly the full amount of her investment. I always thought this was due to Margaret, but I made no inquiries. There were many people who had no confidence in Henderson, but generally his popularity was not much affected, and whatever was said of him in private, his social position was almost as unchallenged as his financial. It was a great point in his favor that he was very generous to his family and his friends, and his public charities began to be talked of. Nothing could have been more admirable than a paper which appeared about this time in one of the leading magazines, written by a great capitalist during a strike in his "system," off the uses of wealth and the responsibilities of rich men. It amused Henderson and Uncle Jerry, and Margaret sent it, marked, to her aunt. Uncle Jerry said it was very timely, for at the moment there was a report that Hollowell and Henderson had obtained possession of one of the great steamship lines in connection with their trans-continental system. I thought at the time that I should like to have heard Carmen's comments on the paper.

The continued friendly alliance of Rodney Henderson and Jerry Hollowell was a marvel to the public, which expected to read any morning that the one had sold out the other, or unloaded in a sly deal. The Stock Exchange couldn't understand it; it was so against all experience that it was considered something outside of human nature. But the explanation was simple enough. The two kept a sharp eye on each other, and, as Uncle Jerry would say, never dropped a stitch; but the simple fact was that they were necessary to each other, and there had been no opportunity when the one could handsomely swallow the other. So it was beautiful to see their accord, and the familiar understanding between them.

One day in Henderson's office it was at the time they were arranging the steamship "scoop" while they were waiting for the drafting of some papers, Uncle Jerry suddenly asked:

"By the way, old man, what's all this about a quarter of a million for a colored college down South?"

"Oh, that's Mrs. Henderson's affair. They say it's the most magnificent college building south of Washington. It's big enough. I've seen the plan of it. Henderson Hall, they are going to call it. I suggested Margaret Henderson Hall, but she wouldn't have it."

"What is it for?"

"One end of it is scientific, geological, chemical, electric, biological, and all that; and the other end is theological. Miss Eschelle says it's to reconcile science and religion."

"She's a daisy-that girl. Seems to me, though, that you are educating the colored brother all on top. I suppose, however, it wouldn't have been so philanthropic to build a hall for a white college."

Henderson laughed. "You keep your eye on the religious sentiment of the North, Uncle Jerry. I told Mrs. Henderson that we had gone long on the colored brother a good while. She said this was nothing. We could endow a Henderson University by-and-by in the Southwest, white as alabaster, and I suppose we shall."

"Yes, probably we've got to do something in that region to keep 'em quiet. The public is a curious fish. It wants plenty of bait."

"And something to talk about," continued Henderson. "We are going down next week to dedicate Henderson Hall. I couldn't get out of it."

"Oh, it will pay," said Uncle Jerry, as he turned again to business.

The trip was made in Henderson's private car; in fact, in a special train, vestibuled; a neat baggage car with library and reading-room in one end, a dining-room car, a private car for invited guests, and his own car a luxurious structure, with drawing-room, sleeping-room, bath-room, and office for his telegrapher and type-writer. The whole was a most commodious house of one story on wheels. The cost of it would have built and furnished an industrial school and workshop for a hundred negroes; but this train was, I dare say, a much more inspiring example of what they might attain by the higher education. There were half a dozen in the party besides the Hendersons Carmen, of course; Mr. Ponsonby, the English attache; and Mrs. Laflamme, to matronize three New York young ladies. Margaret and Carmen had never been so far South before.

Is it not agreeable to have sweet charity silver shod? This sumptuous special train caused as much comment as the errand on which it went. Its coming was telegraphed from station to station, and crowds everywhere collected to see it. Brisk reporters boarded it; the newspapers devoted columns to descriptions of it; editorials glorified it as a signal example of the progress of the great republic, or moralized on it as a sign of the luxurious decadence of morals; pointing to Carthage and Rome and Alexandria in withering sarcasm that made those places sink into insignificance as corrupters of the world. There were covert allusions to Cleopatra ensconced in the silken hangings of the boudoir car, and one reporter went so far as to refer to the luxury of Capua and Baiae, to their disparagement. All this, however, was felt to add to the glory of the republic, and it all increased the importance of Henderson. To hear the exclamations, "That's he!" "That's him!" "That's Henderson!" was to Margaret in some degree a realization of her ambition; and Carmen declared that it was for her a sweet thought to be identified with Cleopatra.

So the Catachoobee University had its splendid new building as great a contrast to the shanties from which its pupils came as is the Capitol at Washington to the huts of a third of its population. If the reader is curious he may read in the local newspapers of the time glowing accounts of its "inaugural dedication"; but universities are so common in this country that it has become a little wearisome to read of ceremonies of this sort. Mr. Henderson made a modest reply to the barefaced eulogy on himself, which the president pronounced in the presence of six hundred young men and women of various colors and invited guests a eulogy which no one more thoroughly enjoyed than Carmen. I am sorry to say that she refused to take the affair seriously.

"I felt for you, Mr. Henderson,"; she said, after the exercises were over. "I blushed for you. I almost felt ashamed, after all the president said, that you had given so little."

"You seem, Miss Eschelle," remarked Mr. Ponsonby, "to be enthusiastic about the education and elevation of the colored people."

"Yes, I am; I quite share Mr. Henderson's feeling about it. I'm for the elevation of everything."

"There is a capital chance for you," said Henderson; "the university wants some scholarships."

"And I've half a mind to found one the Eschelle Scholarship of Washing and Clear-starching. You ought to have seen my clothes that came back to the car. Probably they were not done by your students. The things looked as if they had been dragged through the Cat-a-what-do-you-call-it River, and ironed with a pine chip."

"Could you do them any better, with all your cultivation?" asked Margaret.

"I think I could, if I was obliged to. But I couldn't get through that university, with all its ologies and laboratories and Greek and queer bottles and machines. You have neglected my education, Mr. Henderson."

"It is not too late to begin now; you might see if you could pass the examination here. It is part of our plan gradually to elevate the whites," said Henderson.

"Yes, I know; and did you see that some of the scholars had red hair and blue eyes, quite in the present style? And how nice the girls looked," she rattled on; "and what a lot of intelligent faces, and how they kindled up when the president talked about the children of Israel in the wilderness forty years, and

Caesar crossing the Rubicon! And you, sir" she turned to the Englishman "I've heard, were against all this emancipation during the war."

"Bless my soul!" exclaimed Ponsonby, "we never were against emancipation, and wanted the best side to win."

"You had a mighty queer way of showing it, then."

"Well, honestly, Miss Eschelle, do you think the negroes are any better off?"

"You'd better ask them. My opinion is that everybody should do what he likes in this world."

"Then what are you girding Mr. Henderson for about his university?"

"Because these philanthropists, like Mr. Henderson and Uncle Jerry Hollowell, are all building on top; putting on the frosting before the cake rises."

"Haven't you found out, Mr. Ponsonby," Margaret interrupted, "that if there were eight sides to a question, Miss Eschelle would be on every one of them?"

"And right, too. There are eight sides to every question, and generally more. I think the negro question has a hundred. But there is only one side to Henderson Hall. It is a noble institution. I like to think about it, and Uncle Caesar Hollowell crossing the Rubicon in his theological seminary. It is all so beautiful!"

"You are a bad child," said Margaret. "We should have left you at home."

"No, not bad, dear; only confused with such a lot of good deeds in a naughty world."

That this junketing party was deeply interested in the cause of education for whites or blacks, no one would have gathered from the conversation. Margaret felt that Carmen had exactly hit the motives of this sort of philanthropy, and she was both amused and provoked by the girl's mockery. By force of old habit she defended, as well she might, these schools.

"You must have a high standard," she said. "You cannot have good lower schools without good higher schools. And these colleges, which you think above the colored people, will stimulate them and gradually raise the whole mass. You cannot do anything until you educate teachers."

"So I have always heard," replied the incorrigible. "I have always been a philanthropist about the negro till I came down here, and I intend to be again when I go back."

Mrs. Laflamme was not a very eager apostle either, and the young ladies devoted themselves to the picturesque aspects of the population, without any concern for the moral problems. They all declared that they liked the negro. But Margaret was not to be moved from her good-humor by any amount of badgering. She liked Henderson Hall; she was proud of the consideration it brought her husband; she had a comfortable sense of doing something that was demanded by her opportunity. It is so difficult to analyze motives, and in Margaret's case so hard to define the change that had taken place in her. That her heart was not enlisted in this affair, as it would have been a few years before, she herself knew. Insensibly she had come to look at the world, at men and women, through her husband's eyes, to take the worldly view, which is not inconsistent with much good feeling and easy-going charity. She also felt the necessity a necessity totally unknown to such a nature as Carmen's of making compensation, of compounding for her pleasures. Gradually she was learning to play her husband's game in life, and to see no harm in it. What, then, is this thing we call conscience? Is it made of India-rubber? I once knew a clever Southern woman, who said that New England women seemed to her all conscience Southern women all soul and impulse. If it were possible to generalize in this way, we might say that Carmen had neither conscience nor soul, simply very clever reason. Uncle Jerry had no more conscience than Carmen, but he had a great deal of natural affection. Henderson, with an abundance of good-nature, was simply a man of his time, troubled with no scruples that stood in the way of his success. Margaret, with a finer nature than either of them, stifling her scruples in an atmosphere of worldly-mindedness, was likely to go further than either of them. Even such a worldling as Carmen understood this. "I do things," she said to Mrs. Laflamme she made anybody her confidant when the fit was on her "I do things because I don't care. Mrs. Henderson does the same, but she does care."

Margaret would be a sadder woman, but not a better woman, when the time came that she did not care. She had come to the point of accepting Henderson's methods of overreaching the world, and was tempering the result with private liberality. Those were hypocrites who criticised him; those were envious who disparaged him; the sufficient ethics of the world she lived in was to be successful and be agreeable. And it is difficult to condemn a person who goes with the general opinion of his generation. Carmen was under no illusions about Henderson, or the methods and manners of which she was a part. "Why pretend?" she said. "We are all bad together, and I like it. Uncle Jerry is the easiest person to get on with." I remember a delightful, wicked old baroness whom I met in my youth stranded in Geneva on short allowance European resorts are full of such characters. "My dear," she said, "why shouldn't I renege? Why shouldn't men cheat at cards? It's all in the game. Don't we all know we are trying to deceive each other and get the best of each other? I stopped pretending after Waterloo. Fighting for the peace of Europe! Bah! We are all fighting for what we can get."

So the Catachoobee Henderson Hall was dedicated, and Mr. Henderson got great credit out of it.

"It's a noble deed, Mr. Henderson," Carmen remarked, when they were at dinner on the car the day of their departure. "But" in an aside to her host "I advise the lambs in Wall Street to look alive at your next deal."

XX

We can get used to anything. Morgan says that even the New England summer is endurable when you learn to dress warmly enough. We come to endure pain and loss with equanimity; one thing and another drops out of our lives-youth, for instance, and sometimes enthusiasm and still we go on with a good degree of enjoyment. I do not say that Miss Forsythe was quite the same, or that a certain zest of life and spring had not gone out of the little Brandon neighborhood.

As the months and the years went by we saw less and less of Margaret less and less, that is, in the old way. Her rare visits were perfunctory, and gave little satisfaction to any of us; not that she was ungracious or unkindly, but simply because the things we valued in life were not the same. There was no doubt that any of us were welcome at the Hendersons' when they were in the city, genuinely, though in an exterior way, but gradually we almost ceased to keep up an intercourse which was a little effort on both sides. Miss Forsythe came back from her infrequent city visits weary and sad.

Was Margaret content? I suppose so. She was gay; she was admired; she was always on view in that semi-public world in which Henderson moved; she attained a newspaper notoriety which many people envied. If she journeyed anywhere, if she tarried anywhere, if she had a slight illness, the fact was a matter of public concern. We knew where she worshiped; we knew the houses she frequented, the charities she patronized, the fetes she adorned, every new costume that her wearing made the fashion. Was she content? She could perhaps express no desire that an attempt was not made to gratify it. But it seems impossible to get enough things enough money, enough pleasure. They had a magnificent place in Newport; it was not large enough; they were always adding to it awning, a ballroom, some architectural whim or another. Margaret had a fancy for a cottage at Bar Harbor, but they rarely went there. They had an interest in Tuxedo; they belonged to an exclusive club on Jekyl Island. They passed one winter yachting among the islands in the eastern Mediterranean; a part of another sailing from one tropical paradise to another in the West Indies. If there was anything that money could not obtain, it seemed to be a place where they could rest in serene peace with themselves.

I used to wonder whether Margaret was satisfied with her husband's reputation. Perhaps she mistook the newspaper homage, the notoriety, for public respect. She saw his influence and his power. She saw that he was feared, and of course hated, by some the unsuccessful but she saw the terms he was on with his intimates, due to the fact that everybody admitted that whatever Henderson was in "a deal," privately he was a deuced good fellow.

Was this an ideal married life? Henderson's selfishness was fully developed, and I could see that he was growing more and more hard. Would Margaret not have felt it, if she also had not been growing hard, and accustomed to regard the world in his unbelieving way? No, there was sharpness occasionally between them, tiffs and disagreements. He was a great deal away from home, and she plunged into a life of her own, which had all the external signs of enjoyment. I doubt if he was ever very selfish where she was concerned, and love can forgive almost any conduct where there is personal indulgence. I had a glimpse of the real state of things in a roundabout way. Henderson loved his wife and was proud of her, and he was not unkind, but he might have been a brute and tied her up to the bedpost, and she never would have shown by the least sign to the world that she was not the most happy of wives.

When the Earl of Chisholm was in this country it was four years after Margaret's marriage we naturally saw a great deal of him. The young fellow whom we liked so much had become a man, with a graver demeanor, and I thought a trace of permanent sadness in his face; perhaps it was only the responsibility of his position, or, as Morgan said, the modern weight that must press upon an earl who is conscientious. He was still unmarried. The friendship between him and Miss Forsythe, which had been kept alive by occasional correspondence, became more cordial and confidential. In New York he had seen much of Margaret, not at all to his peace of mind in many ways, though the generous fellow would have been less hurt if he had not estimated at its real value the life she was leading. It did not need Margaret's introduction for the earl to be sought for by the novelty and pleasure loving society of the city; but he got, as he confessed, small satisfaction out of the whirl of it, although we knew that he met Mrs. Henderson everywhere, and in a manner assisted in her social triumphs. But he renewed his acquaintance with Miss Eschelle, and it was the prattle of this ingenuous creature that made him more heavy-hearted than anything else.

"How nice it is of you, Mr. Lyon may I call you so, to bring back the old relations? to come here and revive the memory of the dear old days when we were all innocent and happy! Dear me, I used to think I could patronize that little country girl from Brandon! I was so worldly don't you remember? and she was so good. And now she is such a splendid woman, it is difficult for the rest of us to keep pace with her. The nerve she has, and the things she will do! I just envy her. I sometimes think she will drive me into a convent. And don't you think she is more beautiful than ever? Of course her face is a little careworn, but nobody makes up as she does; she was just ravishing the other night. Do you know, I think she takes her husband too seriously."

"I trust she is happy," the earl had said.

"Why shouldn't she be?" Carmen asked in return. "She has everything she wants. They both have a little temper; life would be flat without that; she is a little irritable sometimes; she didn't use to be; and when they don't agree they let each other alone for a little. I think she is as happy as anybody can be who is married. Now you are shocked! Well, I don't know any one who is more in love than she is, and that may be happiness. She is becoming exactly like Mr. Henderson. You couldn't ask anything more than that."

If Margaret were really happy, the earl told Miss Forsythe, he was glad, but it was scarcely the career he would have thought would have suited her.

Meantime, the great house was approaching completion. Henderson's palace, in the upper part of the city, had long been a topic for the correspondents of the country press. It occupied half a square. Many critics were discontented with it because it did not occupy the whole square. Everybody was interested in having it the finest residence on the continent. Why didn't Henderson take the whole block of ground, build his palace on three sides, with the offices and stables on the fourth, throw a glass roof over the vast interior court, plant it with tropical trees and plants, adorn it with flower-beds and fountains, and make a veritable winter-garden, giving the inhabitants a temperate climate all the cold months? He might easily have summer in the centre of the city from November to April. These rich people never know what to do with their money. Such a place would give distinction to the city, and compel foreigners to recognize the high civilization of America. A great deal of fault was found with Henderson privately for his parsimony in such a splendid opportunity.

Nevertheless it was already one of the sights of the town. Strangers were taken to see it, as it rose in its simple grandeur. Local reporters made articles on the progress of the interior whenever they could get an entrance. It was not ornate enough to please, generally, but those who admired the old Louvre liked the simplicity of its lines and the dignity of the elevations. They discovered the domestic note in its quiet character, and said that the architect had avoided the look of an "institution" in such a great mass. He was not afraid of dignified wall space, and there was no nervous anxiety manifested, which would have belittled it with trivial ornamentation.

Perhaps it was not an American structure, although one could find in it all the rare woods and stones of the continent. Great numbers of foreign workmen were employed in its finishing and decoration. One could wander in it from Pompeii to Japan, from India to Versailles, from Greece to the England of the Tudors, from the Alhambra to colonial Salem. It was so cosmopolitan that a representative of almost any nationality, ancient or modern, could have been suited in it with an apartment to his taste, and if the interior lacked unity it did not lack a display of variety that appealed to the imagination. From time to time paragraphs appeared in English, French, and Italian journals, regarding the work of this and that famous artist who was designing a set of furniture or furnishing the drawings of a room, or carving the paneling and statuary, or painting the ceiling of an apartment in the great Palazzo Henderson in New York Washington. The United American Workers (who were half foreigners by birth) passed resolutions denouncing Henderson for employing foreign pauper labor, and organized more than one strike while the house was building. It was very unpatriotic and un-American to have anything done that could not be done by a member of the Union. There was a firm of excellent stone-cutters which offered to make all the statuary needed in the house, and set it up in good shape, and when the offer was declined, it memorialized Congress for protection.

Although Henderson gave what time he could spare to the design and erection of the building, it pleased him to call it Margaret's house, and to see the eagerness with which she entered into its embellishment. There was something humorous in the enlargement of her ideas since the days when she had wondered at the magnificence of the Washington Square home, and modestly protested against its luxury. Her own boudoir was a cheap affair compared with that in the new house.

"Don't you think, dear," she said, puzzling over the drawings, "that it would better be all sandalwood? I hate mosaics. It looks so cheap to have little bits of precious woods stuck about."

"I should think so. But what do you do with the ebony?"

"Oh, the ebony and gold? That is the adjoining sitting-room such a pretty contrast."

"And the teak?"

"It has such a beautiful polish. That is another room. Carmen says that will be our sober room, where we go when we want to repent of things."

"Well, if you have any sandal-wood left over, you can work it into your Boys' Lodging-house, you know."

"Don't be foolish! And then the ballroom, ninety feet long it looks small on the paper. And do you think we'd better have those life-size figures all round, mediaeval statues, with the incandescents? Carmen says she would prefer a row of monks something piquant about that in a ballroom. I don't know that I like the figures, after all; they are too crushing and heavy."

"It would make a good room for the Common Council," Henderson suggested. "Wouldn't it be prettier hung with silken arras figured with a chain of dancing-girls? Dear me, I don't know what to do. Rodney, you must put your mind on it."

"Might line it with gold plate. I'll make arrangements so that you can draw on the Bank of England."

Margaret looked hurt. "But you told me, dear, not to spare anything that we would have the finest house in the city. I'm sure I sha'n't enjoy it unless you want it."

"Oh, I want it," resumed Henderson, good-humoredly. "Go ahead, little wife. We shall pull through."

"Women beat me," Henderson confessed to Uncle Jerry next day. "They are the most economical of beings and the most extravagant. I've got to look round for an extra million somewhere today."

"Yes, there is this good thing about women," Uncle Jerry responded, with a twinkle in his eyes, "they share your riches just as cheerfully as they do your poverty. I tell Maria that if I had the capacity for making money that she has for spending it I could assume the national debt."

To have the finest house in the city, or rather, in the American newspaper phrase, in the Western world, was a comprehensible ambition for Henderson, for it was a visible expression of his wealth and his cultivated taste. But why Margaret should wish to exchange her dainty and luxurious home in Washington Square for the care of a vast establishment big enough for a royal court, my wife could not comprehend. But why not? To be the visible leader in her world, to be able to dispense a hospitality which should surpass anything heretofore seen, to be the mistress and autocrat of an army of servants, with ample room for their evolution, in a palace whose dimensions and splendor should awaken envy and astonishment would this not be an attraction to a woman of imagination and spirit?

Besides, they had outgrown the old house. There was no longer room for the display, scarcely for the storage, of the works of art, the pictures, the curiosities, the books, that unlimited money and the opportunity of foreign travel had collected in all these years. "We must either build or send our things to a warehouse," Henderson had long ago said. Among the obligations of wealth is the obligation of display. People of small means do not allow for the expansion of mind that goes along with the accumulation of property. It was only natural that Margaret, who might have been contented with two rooms and a lean-to as the wife of a country clergyman, should have felt cramped in her old house, which once seemed a world too large for the country girl.

"I don't see how you could do with less room," Carmen said, with an air of profound conviction. They were looking about the house on its last uninhabited day, directing the final disposition of its contents. For Carmen, as well as for Margaret, the decoration and the furnishing of the house had been an occupation. The girl had the whim of playing the part of restrainer and economizer in everything; but Henderson used to say, when Margaret told him of Carmen's suggestions, that a little more of her economy would ruin him.

"Yes," Margaret admitted, "there does not seem to be anything that is not necessary."

"Not a thing. When you think of it, two people require as much space as a dozen; when you go beyond one room, you must go on. Of course you couldn't get on without a reception-room, drawing-rooms, a conservatory, a music-room, a library, a morning-room, a breakfast-room, a small dining-room and a state dining-room, Mr. Henderson's snuggery, with his own library, a billiard-room, a picture-gallery it is full already; you'll have to extend it or sell some pictures your own suite and Mr. Henderson's suite, and the guest-rooms, and I forgot the theatre in the attic. I don't see but you have scrimped to the last degree."

"And yet there is room to move about," Margaret acknowledged, with a gratified smile, as they wandered around. "Dear me, I used to think the Stotts' house was a palace."

It was the height of the season before Lent. There had been one delay and another, but at last all the workmen had been expelled, and Margaret was mistress of her house. Cards for the house-warming had been out for two weeks, and the event was near. She was in her own apartments this pale, wintry afternoon, putting the finishing touches to her toilet. Nothing seemed to suit. The maid found her in a very bad humor. "Remember," she had said to her husband, when he ordered his brougham after breakfast, "sharp seven, we are to dine alone the first time." It lacked two hours yet of dinner-time, but she was dressing for want of other occupation.

Was this then the summit of her ambition? She had indeed looked forward to some such moment as this as one of exultation in the satisfaction of all her wishes. She took up a book of apothegms that lay on the table, and opened by chance to this, "Unhappy are they whose desires are all ratified." It was like a sting. Why should she think at this moment of her girlhood; of the ideals indulged in during that quiet time; of her aunt's cheerful, tender, lonely life; of her rejection of Mr. Lyon? She did not love Mr. Lyon; she was not satisfied then. How narrow that little life in Brandon had been! She threw the book from her. She hated all that restraint and censoriousness. If her aunt could see her in all this splendor, she would probably be sadder than ever. What right had she to sit there and mourn as she knew her aunt did and sigh over her career? What right had they to sit in judgment on her?

She went out from her room, down the great stairway, into the spacious house, pausing in the great hall to see opening vista after vista in the magnificent apartments. It was the first time that she had alone really taken the full meaning of it had possessed it with the eye. It was hers. Wherever she went, all hers. No, she had desires yet. It should be filled with life it should be the most brilliant house in the world. Society should see, should acknowledge the leadership. Yes as she glanced at herself in a drawing-room mirror they should see that Henderson's wife was capable of a success equal to his own, and she would stop the hateful gossip about him. She set her foot firmly as she thought about it; she would crush those people who had sneered at them as parvenu. She strayed into the noble gallery. Some face there touched her, some landscape soothed her. No, she said to herself, I will win them, I do not want hateful strife.

Who knows what is in a woman? how many moods in a quarter of an hour, and which is the characteristic one? Was this the Margaret who had walked with Lyon that Sunday afternoon of the baptism, and had a heart full of pain for the pitiful suffering of the world?

As she sat there she grew calmer. Her thoughts went away in a vision of all the social possibilities of this wonderful house. From vaguely admiring what she looked at, she began to be critical; this and that could be changed to advantage; this shade of hanging was not harmonious; this light did not fall right. She smiled to think that her husband thought it all done. How he would laugh to find that she was already planning to rearrange it! Hadn't she been satisfied for almost twenty-four hours? That was a long time for a woman. Then she thought of the reception; of the guests; of what some of them would wear; how they would look about; what they would say. She was already in that world which was so shining and shifting and attractive. She did not hear Henderson come in until his arm was around her.

"Well, sweet, keeping house alone? I've had a jolly day; lucky as old Mr. Luck."

"Have you?" she cried, springing up. "I'm so glad. Come, see the house."

"You look a little pale," he said, as they strolled out to the conservatory together.

"Just a little tired," she admitted. "Do you know, Rodney, I hated this house at five o'clock positively hated it?"

"Why?"

"Oh, I don't know; I was thinking. But I liked it at half-past six. I love it now. I've got used to it, as if I had always lived here. Isn't it beautiful everywhere? But I'm going to make some changes."

"A hanging garden on the roof?" Henderson asked, with meekness.

"That would be nice. No, not now. But to make over and take off the new look. Everything looks so new."

"Well, we will try to live that down."

And so they wandered on, admiring, bantering, planning. Could Etienne Debree have seen his descendant at this moment he would have been more than ever proud of his share in establishing the great republic, and of his appreciation of the promise of its beauty. What satisfies a woman's heart is luxury, thought Henderson, in an admiring cynical moment.

They had come into his own den and library, and he stood looking at the rows of his favorite collection shining in their new home. For all its newness it had a familiar look. He thought for a moment that he might be in his old bachelor quarters. Suddenly Margaret made a rush at him. She shook the great fellow. She feasted her eyes on him.

"What's got into you to look so splendid? Do you hear, go this instant and dress, and make yourself ten times as fascinating."

XXI

Live not unto yourselves! Can any one deny that this blessed sentiment is extending in modern life? Do we build houses for ourselves or for others? Do we make great entertainments for our own comfort? I do not know that anybody regarded the erection of the Henderson palace as an altruistic performance. The socialistic newspapers said that it was pure ostentation. But had it not been all along in the minds of the builders to ask all the world to see it, to share the delight of it? Is this a selfish spirit? When I stroll in the Park am I not pleased with the equipages, with the display of elegance upon which so much money has been lavished for my enjoyment?

All the world was asked to the Henderson reception. The coming event was the talk of the town. I have now cuttings from the great journals, articles describing the house, more beautifully written than Gibbon's stately periods about the luxury of later Rome. It makes one smile to hear that the day of fine writing is over. Everybody was eager to go; there was some plotting to obtain invitations by those who felt that they could not afford to be omitted from the list that would be printed; by those who did not know the Hendersons, and did not care to know them, but who shared the general curiosity; and everybody vowed that he supposed he must go, but he hated such a crush and jam as it was sure to be. Yet no one would have cared to go if it had not promised to be a crush. I said that all the world was asked, which is our way of saying that a thousand or two had been carefully selected from the million within reach.

Invitations came to Brandon, of course, for old times' sake. The Morgans said that they preferred a private view; Miss Forsythe declared that she hadn't the heart to go; in short, Mr. and Mrs. Fairchild alone went to represent the worldly element.

I am sorry to say that the reader must go to the files of the city press for an account of the night's festivity. The pen that has been used in portraying Margaret's career is entirely inadequate to it. There is a general impression that an American can do anything that he sets his hand to, but it is not true; it is true only that he tries everything. The reporter is born, as the poet is; it cannot be acquired that astonishing, irresponsible command of the English language; that warm, lyrical tone; that color, and bewildering metaphorical brilliancy; that picturesqueness; that use of words as the painter uses pigments, in splashes and blotches which are so effective; that touch of raillery and sarcasm and condescension; that gay enjoyment of reveling in the illimitable; that air of superior knowledge and style; that dash of sentiment; that calm and somewhat haughty judgment.

I am always impressed at such an entertainment with the good-humor of the American people, no matter what may be the annoyance and discomfort.

In all the push and thrust and confusion, amid the rending of trains, the tearing of lace, the general crushing of costumes, there was the merriest persiflage, laughter, and chatter, and men and women entered into and drew out of the fashionable wreck in the highest spirits. For even in such a spacious mansion there were spots where currents met, and rooms where there was a fight for mere breath. It would have been a tame affair without this struggle. And what an epitome of life it all was! There were those who gave themselves up to admiration, who gushed with enthusiasm; there were those who had the weary air of surfeit with splendor of this sort; there were the bustling and volatile, who made facetious remarks, and treated the affair like a Fourth of July; and there were also groups dark and haughty, like the Stotts, who held a little aloof, and coldly admitted that it was most successful; it lacked je ne sais quoi, but it was in much better taste than they had expected. Is there something in the very nature of a crowd to bring out the inherent vulgarity of the best-bred people, so that some have doubted whether the highest civilization will tolerate these crushing and hilarious assemblies?

At any rate, one could enjoy the general effect. There might be vulgar units, and one caught notes of talk that disenchanted, but there were so many women of rare and stately beauty, of exquisite loveliness, of charm in manner and figure so many men of fine presence, with such an air of power and manly prosperity and self-reliance I doubt if any other assembly in the world, undecorated by orders and uniforms, with no blazon of rank, would have a greater air of distinction. Looking over it from a landing in the great stairway that commanded vistas and ranges of the lofty, brilliant apartments, vivified by the throng, which seemed ennobled by the spacious splendor in which it moved, one would be pardoned a feeling of national pride in the spectacle. I drew aside to let a stately train of beauty and of fashion descend, and saw it sweep through the hall, and enter the drawing-rooms, until it was lost in a sea of shifting color. It was like a dream.

And the centre of all this charming plutocratic graciousness and beauty was Margaret Margaret and her handsome husband. Where did the New Hampshire boy learn this simple dignity of bearing, this good-humored cordiality without condescension, this easy air of the man of the world? Was this the railway wrecker, the insurance manipulator, the familiar of Uncle Jerry, the king of the lobby, the pride and the bugaboo of Wall Street? Margaret was regnant. And how charmingly she received her guests! How well I knew that half-imperious toss of the head, and the glance of those level, large gray eyes, softened instantly, on recognition, into the sweetest smile of welcome playing about the dimple and the expressive mouth! What woman would not feel a little thrill of triumph? The world was at her feet. Why was it, I wonder, as I stood there watching the throng which saluted this queenly woman of the world, in an hour of supreme social triumph, while the notes of the distant orchestra came softly on the air, and the overpowering perfume of banks of flowers and tropical plants why was it that I thought of a fair, simple girl, stirred with noble ideals, eager for the intellectual life, tender, sympathetic, courageous? It was Margaret Debree how often I had seen her thus! sitting on her little veranda, swinging her chip hat by the string, glowing from some errand in which her heart had played a much more important part than her purse. I caught the odor of the honeysuckle that climbed on the porch, and I heard the note of the robin that nested there.

"You seem to be in a brown study," said Carmen, who came up, leaning on the arm of the Earl of Chisholm.

"I'm lost in admiration. You must make allowance, Miss Eschelle, for a person from the country."

"Oh, we are all from the country. That is the beauty of it. There is Mr. Hollowell, used to drive a peddler's cart, or something of that sort, up in Maine, talking with Mr. Stott, whose father came in on the towpath of the Erie Canal. You don't dance? The earl has just been giving me a whirl in the ballroom, and I've been trying to make him understand about democracy."

"Yes," the earl rejoined; "Miss Eschelle has been interpreting to me republican simplicity."

"And he cannot point out, Mr. Fairchild, why this is not as good as a reception at St. James. I suppose it's his politeness."

"Indeed, it is all very charming. It must be a great thing to be the architect of your own fortune."

"Yes; we are all self-made," Carmen confessed.

"I am, and I get dreadfully tired of it sometimes. I have to read over the Declaration and look at the map of the Western country at such times. A body has to have something to hold on to."

"Why, this seems pretty substantial," I said, wondering what the girl was driving at.

"Oh, yes; I suppose the world looks solid from a balloon. I heard one man say to another just now, 'How long do you suppose Henderson will last?' Probably we shall all come down by the run together by-and-by."

"You seem to be on a high plane," I suggested.

"I guess it's the influence of the earl. But I am the most misunderstood of women. What I really like is simplicity. Can you have that without the social traditions," she appealed to the earl, "such as you have in England?"

"I really cannot say," the earl replied, laughing. "I fancied there was simplicity in Brandon; perhaps that was traditional."

"Oh, Brandon!" Carmen cried, "see what Brandon does when it gets a chance. I assure your lordship that we used to be very simple people in New York. Come, let us go and tell Mrs. Henderson how delightful it all is. I'm so sorry for her."

As I moved about afterwards with my wife we heard not many comments, a word here and there about Henderson's wonderful success, a remark about Margaret's beauty, some sympathy for her in such a wearisome ordeal the world is full of kindness the house duly admired, and the ordinary compliments paid; the people assembled were, as usual, absorbed in their own affairs. From all we could gather, all those present were used to living in a palace, and took all the splendor quite as a matter of course. Was there no envy? Was there nothing said about the airs of a country school-ma'am, the aplomb of an adventurer? Were there no criticisms afterwards as the guests rolled home in their carriages, surfeited and exhausted? What would you have? Do you expect the millennium to begin in New York?

The newspapers said that it was the most brilliant affair the metropolis had ever seen. I have no doubt it was. And I do not judge, either, by the newspaper estimates of the expense. I take the simple words addressed by the earl to Margaret, when he said good-night, at their full value. She flushed with pleasure at his modest commendation. Perhaps it was to her the seal of her night's triumph.

The house was opened. The world had seen it. The world had gone. If sleep did not come that night to her tired head on the pillow, what wonder? She had a position in the great world. In imagination it opened wider and wider. Could not the infinite possibilities of it fill the hunger of any soul?

The echoes of the Henderson reception continued long in the country press. Items multiplied as to the cost. It was said that the sum expended in flowers alone, which withered in a night, would have endowed a ward in a charity hospital. Some wag said that the price of the supper would have changed the result of the Presidential election. Views of the mansion were given in the illustrated papers, and portraits of Mr. and Mrs. Henderson. In country villages, in remote farmhouses, this great social event was talked of,

Henderson's wealth was the subject of conjecture, Margaret's toilet was an object of interest. It was a shining example of success. Preachers, whose sensational sermons are as widely read as descriptions of great crimes, moralized on Henderson's career and Henderson's palace, and raised up everywhere an envied image of worldly prosperity. When he first arrived in New York, with only fifty cents in his pocket so the story ran-and walked up Broadway and Fifth Avenue, he had nearly been run over at the corner of Twenty-sixth Street by a carriage, the occupants of which, a lady and gentleman, had stared insolently at the country youth. Never mind, said the lad to himself, the day will come when you will cringe to me. And the day did come when the gentleman begged Henderson to spare him in Wall Street, and his wife intrigued for an invitation to Mrs. Henderson's ball. The reader knows there is not a word of truth in this. Alas! said the preacher, if he had only devoted his great talents to the service of the Good and the True! Behold how vain are all the triumphs of this world! see the result of the worship of Mammon! My friends, the age is materialized, a spirit of worldliness is abroad; be vigilant, lest the deceitfulness of riches send your souls to perdition. And the plain country people thanked God for such a warning, and the country girl dreamed of Margaret's career, and the country boy studied the ways of Henderson's success, and resolved that he, too, would seek his fortune in this bad metropolis.

The Hendersons were important people. It was impossible that a knowledge of their importance should not have a reflex influence upon Margaret. Could it be otherwise than that gradually the fineness of her discrimination should be dulled by the almost universal public consent in the methods by which Henderson had achieved his position, and that in time she should come to regard adverse judgment as the result of envy? Henderson himself was under less illusion; the world was about what he had taken it for, only a little worse more gullible, and with less principle. Carmen had mocked at Margaret's belief in Henderson. It is certainly a pitiful outcome that Margaret, with her naturally believing nature, should in the end have had a less clear perception of what was right and wrong than Henderson himself. Yet Henderson would not have shrunk, any more than Carmen would, from any course necessary to his ends, while Margaret would have shrunk from many things; but in absolute worldliness, in devotion to it, the time had come when Henderson felt that his Puritan wife was no restraint upon him. It was this that broke gentle Miss Forsythe's heart when she came fully to realize it.

I said that the world was at Margaret's feet. Was it? How many worlds are there, and does one ever, except by birth (in a republic), conquer them all? Truth to say, there were penetralia in New York society concerning which this successful woman was uneasy in her heart. There were people who had accepted her invitations, to whose houses she had been, who had a dozen ways of making her feel that she was not of them. These people I suppose that if two castaways landed naked on a desert island, one of them would instantly be the ancien regime had spoken of Mrs. Henderson and her ambition to the Earl of Chisholm in a way that pained him. They graciously assumed that he, as one of the elect, would understand them. It was therefore with a heavy heart that he came to say good-by to Margaret before his return.

I cannot imagine anything more uncomfortable for an old lover than a meeting of this sort; but I suppose the honest fellow could not resist the inclination to see Margaret once more. I dare say she had a little flutter of pride in receiving him, in her consciousness of the change in herself into a wider experience of the world. And she may have been a little chagrined that he was not apparently more impressed by her surroundings, nor noticed the change in herself, but met her upon the ground of simple sincerity where they had once stood. What he tried to see, what she felt he was trying to see, was not the beautiful woman about whose charm and hospitality the town talked, but the girl he had loved in the old days.

He talked a little, a very little, about himself and his work in England, and a great deal about what had interested him here on his second visit, the social drift, the politics, the organized charities; and as he talked, Margaret was conscious how little the world in which she lived seemed to interest him; how little importance he attached to it. And she saw, as in a momentary vision of herself, that the things that once absorbed her and stirred her sympathies were now measurably indifferent to her. Book after book which he casually mentioned, as showing the drift of the age, and profoundly affecting modern thought, she knew only by name. "I guess," said Carmen, afterwards, when Margaret spoke of the earl's conversation, "that he is one of those who are trying to live in the spirit what do they call it? care for things of the mind."

"You are doing a noble work," he said, "in your Palace of Industry."

"Yes, it is very well managed," Margaret replied; "but it is uphill work, the poor are so ungrateful for charity."

"Perhaps nobody, Mrs. Henderson, likes to be treated as an object of charity."

"Well, work isn't what they want when we give it, and they'd rather live in the dirt than in clean apartments."

"Many of them don't know any better, and a good many of our poor resent condescension."

"Yes," said Margaret, with warmth; "they are getting to demand things as their right, and they are insolent. The last time I drove down in that quarter I was insulted by their manner. What are you going to do with such people? One big fellow who was leaning against a lamp-post growled, 'You'd better stay in your own palace, miss, and not come prying round here.' And a brazen girl cried out: 'Shut yer mouth, Dick; the lady's got to have some pleasure. Don't yer see, she's a-slummin'?'"

"It's very hard, I know," said the earl; "perhaps we are all on the wrong track."

"Maybe. Mr. Henderson says that the world would get on better if everybody minded his own business."

"I wish it were possible," the earl remarked, with an air of finishing the topic. "I have just been up to Brandon, Mrs. Henderson. I fear that I have seen the dear place for the last time."

"You don't mean that you are tired of America?"

"Not that. I shall never, even in thought, tire of Brandon."

"Yes, they are dear, good people."

"I thought Miss Forsythe what a sweet, brave woman she is! was looking sad and weary."

"Oh, aunt won't do anything, or take an interest in anything. She just stays there. I've tried in vain to get her here. Do you know" and she turned upon the earl a look of the old playfulness "she doesn't quite approve of me."

"Oh," he replied, hesitating a little "I think, Mrs. Henderson, that her heart is bound up in you. It isn't for me to say that you haven't a truer friend in the world."

"Yes, I know. If I'd only " and she stopped, with a petulant look on her fair face "well, it doesn't matter. She is a dear soul."

"I suppose," said the earl, rising, "we shall see you again on the other side?"

"Perhaps," with a smile. Could anything be more commonplace than such a parting? Good-by, I shall see you tomorrow or next year, or in the next world. Hail and farewell! That is the common experience. But, oh, the bitterness of it to many a soul!

It is quite possible that when the Earl of Chisholm said good-by, with an air of finality, Margaret felt that another part of her life was closed. He was not in any way an extraordinary person, he was not a very rich peer, probably with his modesty and conscientiousness, and devotion to the ordinary duties of his station, he would never attain high rank in the government. Yet no one could be long with him without apprehending that his life was on a high plane. It was with a little irritation that Margaret recognized this, and remembered, with a twinge of conscience, that it was upon that plane that her life once traveled. The time had been when the more important thing to her was the world of ideas, of books, of intellectual life, of passionate sympathy with the fortunes of humanity, of deepest interest in all the new thoughts struck out by the leaders who studied the profound problems of life and destiny.

That peace of mind which is found only in the highest activity for the noblest ends she once had, though she thought it then unrest and striving what Carmen, who was under no illusions about Henderson, or Uncle Jerry, or the world of fashion, and had an intuitive perception of cant that is sometimes denied to the children of light, called "taking pleasure in the things of the mind." To do Margaret justice, there entered into her reflections no thought of the title and position of the Earl of Chisholm. They had never been alluring to her. If one could take any satisfaction in this phase of her character, her worldiness was purely American.

"I hardly know which I should prefer," Carmen was saying when they were talking over the ball and the earl's departure, "to be an English countess or the wife of an American millionaire."

"It might depend upon the man," replied Margaret, with a smile.

"The American," continued Carmen, not heeding this suggestion, "has the greater opportunities, and is not hindered by traditions. If you were a countess you would have to act like a countess. If you are an American you can act like anything you can do what you please. That is nicer. Now, an earl must do what an earl has always done. What could you do with such a husband? Mind! Yes, I know, dear, about things of the mind. First, you know, he will be a gentleman socialist (in the magazines), and maybe a Christian socialist, or a Christian scientist, or something of that sort, interested in the Mind Cure."

"I should think that would suit you. Last I knew, you were deep in the Mind Cure."

"So I was. That was last week. Now I'm in the Faith Cure; I've found out about both. The difference is, in the Mind Cure you don't require any faith; in the Faith Cure you don't require any mind. The Faith Cure just suits me."

"So you put your faith in an American millionaire?"

"Yes, I think I should, until an American millionaire put faith in me. That might shake me. It is such a queer world. No, I'm in doubt. If you loved an earl he would stay an earl. If you loved an American millionaire, ten to one he would fail."

Margaret did not escape the responsibility of her success. Who does? My dear Charmian, who wrote the successful novel of last year, do you not already repent your rash act? If you do not write a better novel this year, will not the public flout you and jeer you for a pretender? Did the public overpraise you at first? Its mistaken partiality becomes now your presumption. Last year the press said you were the rival of Hawthorne. This year it is, "that Miss Charmian who set herself up as a second Hawthorne." When the new house was opened, it might be said that socially Mrs. Henderson had "arrived." Had she? When one enters on the path of worldliness is there any resting-place? Is not eternal vigilance the price of position?

Henderson was apparently on good terms with the world. Many envied him, many paid him the sincerest flattery, that of imitation. He was a king in the street, great enterprises sought his aid, all the charities knocked at his door, his word could organize a syndicate or a trust, his nod could smash a "corner." There were fabulous stories about his wealth, about his luck. This also was Margaret's world. Her ambition expanded in it with his. The things he set his heart on she coveted. Alas! there is always another round to the ladder.

Seeing the means by which he gained his ends, and the public condonation of them, would not his cynicism harden into utter unbelief in general virtue and goodness? I don't know that Henderson changed much, accented as his grasping selfishness was on occasion; prosperity had not impaired that indifferent good-fellowship and toleration which had early gained him popularity. His presence was nowhere a rebuke to whatever was going on. He was always accessible, often jocular. The younger members in the club said Henderson was a devilish good fellow, whatever people said. The President of the United States used to send for him and consult him, because he wanted no office; he knew men, and it was a relief to talk with a liberal rich man of so much bonhomie who wanted nothing.

And Margaret, what view of the world did all this give her? Did she come in contact with any one who had not his price, who was not going or wanting to go in the general current? Was it not natural that she should take Henderson's view? Dear me, I am not preaching about her. We did not see much of her in those days, and for one or two years of what I suppose was her greatest enjoyment of her social triumphs. So far as we heard, she was liked, admired, followed, envied. It could not be otherwise, for she did not lose her beauty nor her charm, and she tried to please. Once when I saw her in the city and we fell into talk and the talk was gay enough and unconstrained I was struck with a certain hardness of tone, a little bitterness quite unlike her old self. It is a very hard thing to say, and I did not say it even to my wife, but I had a painful impression that she was valuing people by the money they had, by the social position they had attained.

Was she content in that great world in which she moved? I had heard stories of slights, of stabs, of rebuffs, of spiteful remarks. Had she not come to know how success even in social life is sometimes attained the meannesses, the jealousies, the cringing? Even with all her money at command, did she not know that her position was at the price of incessant effort? Because she had taken a bold step today, she must take a bolder one tomorrow more display, more servants, some new invention of luxury and extravagance. And seeing, as I say, the inside of this life and what it required, and how triumphs and notoriety were gained, was it a wonder that she gradually became in her gayety cynical, in her judgments bitter?

I am not criticising her. What are we, who have had no opportunities, to sit in judgment on her! I believe that it is true that it was at her solicitation that Henderson at last did endow a university in the Southwest. I know that her name was on all the leading charities of the city. I know that of all the patronesses of the charity ball her costume was the most exquisite, and her liberality was most spoken of. I know that in the most fashionable house of worship (the newspapers call it that) she was a constant attendant; that in her modest garb she never missed a Lenten service; and we heard that she performed a novena during this penitential season.

Why protract the story of how Margaret was lost to us? Could this interest any but us we who felt the loss because we still loved her? And why should we presume to set up our standard of what is valuable in life, of what is a successful career? She had not become what we hoped, and little by little all the pleasure of intercourse on both sides, I dare say, disappeared. Could we say that life, after all, had not given her what she most desired? Rather than write on in this strain about her, I would like to read her story as it appeared to the companions whose pleasures were her pleasures, whose successes were her successes her story written by one who appreciated her worldly advantages, and saw all the delight there was in this attractive worldliness.

What comfort there was in it we had in knowing that she was a favorite in the society of which we read such glowing descriptions, and that no one else bore its honors more winningly. It was not an easy life, with all its exactions and incessant movement. It demanded more physical strength than most women possess, and we were not surprised to hear from time to time that she was delicate, and that she went through her season with feverish excitement. But she chose it; it had become necessary to her. Can women stop in such a career, even if they wish to stop?

Yes, she chose it. I, for one, never begrudged her any pleasure she had in life, and I do not know but she was as happy as it is possible for human being to be in a full experiment of worldliness. Who is the judge? But we, I say, who loved her, and knew so well the noble possibilities of her royal nature under circumstances favorable to its development, felt more and more her departure from her own ideals. Her life in its spreading prosperity seemed more and more shallow. I do not say she was heartless, I do not say she was uncharitable, I do not say that in all the externals of worldly and religious observance she was wanting; I do not say that the more she was assimilated to the serenely worldly nature of her husband she did not love him, or that she was unlovely in the worldliness that ingulfed her and bore her onward. I do not know that there is anything singular in her history. But the pain of it to us was in the certainty and it seemed so near that in the decay of her higher life, in the hardening process of a material existence, in the transfer of all her interests to the trivial and sensuous gratifications time, mind, heart, ambition, all fixed on them we should never regain our Margaret. What I saw in a vision of her future was a dead soul a beautiful woman in all the success of envied prosperity, with a dead soul.

XXII

It is difficult not to convey a false impression of Margaret at this time. Habits, manners, outward conduct nay, the superficial kindliness in human intercourse, the exterior graceful qualities, may all remain when the character has subtly changed, when the real aims have changed, when the ideals are lowered. The fair exterior may be only a shell. I can imagine the heart retaining much tenderness and sympathy with suffering when the soul itself has ceased to struggle for the higher life, when the mind has lost, in regard to life, the final discrimination of what is right and wrong.

Perhaps it is fairer to Margaret to consider the general opinion of the world regarding her. No doubt, if we had now known her for the first time, we should have admired her exceedingly, and probably have accounted her thrice happy in filling so well her brilliant position. That her loss of interest in things intellectual, in a wide range of topics of human welfare, which is in the individual soul a sign of warmth and growth, made her less companionable to some is true, but her very absorption in the life of her world made her much more attractive to others. I well remember a dinner one day at the Hendersons', when Mr. Morgan and I happened to be in town, and the gay chat and persiflage of the society people there assembled. Margaret shone in it. The light and daring touch of her raillery Carmen herself might have envied, and the spirit in which she handled the trifles and personal gossip tossed to the surface, like the bubbles on the champagne.

It was such a pretty picture the noble diningroom, the table sparkling with glass and silver and glowing with masses of choicest flowers from the conservatory, the animated convives, and Margaret presiding, radiant in a costume of white and gold.

"After all," Morgan was saying, apropos of the position of women, "men get mighty little out of it in the modern arrangement."

"I've always said, Mr. Morgan," Margaret retorted, "that you came into the world a couple of centuries too late; you ought to have been here in the squaw age."

"Well, men were of some account then. I appeal to Henderson," Morgan persisted, "if he gets more than his board and clothes."

"Oh, my husband has to make his way; he's no time for idling and philosophizing round."

"I should think not. Come, Henderson, speak up; what do you get out of it?"

"Oh," said Henderson, glancing at his wife with an amused expression, "I'm doing very well. I'm very well taken care of, but I often wonder what the fellows did when polygamy was the fashion."

"Polygamy, indeed!" cried Margaret. "So men only dropped the a pluribus unum method on account of the expense?"

"Not at all," replied Henderson. "Women are so much better now than formerly that one wife is quite enough."

"You have got him well in hand, Mrs. Henderson, but " Morgan began.

"But," continued Margaret for him, "you think as things are going that polyandry will have to come in fashion a woman will need more than one husband to support her?"

"And I was born too soon," murmured Carmen.

"Yes, dear, you'll have to be born again. But, Mr. Morgan, you don't seem to understand what civilization is."

"I'm beginning to. I've been thinking this is entirely impersonal that it costs more to keep one fine lady going than it does a college. Just reckon it up." (Margaret was watching him with sparkling eyes.) "The palace in town is for her, the house in the mountains, the house by the sea, are for her, the army of servants is for her, the horses and carriages for all weathers are for her, the opera box is for her, and then the wardrobe why, half Paris lives on what women wear. I say nothing of what would become of the medical profession but for her."

"Have you done?" asked Margaret.

"No, but I'm taking breath."

"Well, why shouldn't we support the working-people of Paris and elsewhere? Do you want us to make our own clothes and starve the sewing-women? Suppose there weren't any balls and fine dresses and what you call luxury. What would the poor do without the rich? Isn't it the highest charity to give them work? Even with it they are ungrateful enough."

"That is too deep for me," said Morgan, evasively. "I suppose they ought to be contented to see us enjoying ourselves. It's all in the way of civilization, I dare say."

"It's just as I thought," said Margaret, more lightly. "You haven't an inkling of what civilization is. See that flower before you. It is the most exquisite thing in this room. See the refinement of its color and form. That was cultivated. The plant came from South Africa. I don't know what expense the gardener has been to about it, what material and care have been necessary to bring it to perfection. You may take it to Mrs. Morgan as an object-lesson. It is a thing of beauty. You cannot put any of your mercantile value on it. Well, that is woman, the consummate flower of civilization. That is what civilization is for."

"I'm sorry for you, old fellow," said Henderson.

"I'm sorry for myself," Carmen said, demurely.

"I admit all that," Morgan replied. "Take Mr. Henderson as a gardener, then."

"Suppose you take somebody else, and let my husband eat his dinner."

"Oh, I don't mind preaching; I've got used to being made to point a moral."

"But he will go on next about the luxury of the age, and the extravagance of women, and goodness knows what," said Margaret.

"No, I'm talking about men," Morgan continued. "Consider Henderson it's entirely impersonal as a gardener. What does he get out of his occupation? He can look at the flower. Perhaps that is enough. He gets a good dinner when he has time for it, an hour at his club now and then, occasionally an evening or half a day off at home, a decent wardrobe "

"Fifty-two suits," interposed Margaret.

"His own brougham "

"And a four-in-hand," added Margaret.

"A pass on the elevated road "

"And a steam-yacht."

"Which he never gets time to sail in; practically all the time on the road, or besieged by a throng in his office, hustled about from morning till night, begged of, interviewed, a telegraphic despatch every five minutes, and "

"And me!" cried Margaret, rising. The guests all clapped their hands.

The Hendersons liked to have their house full, something going on dinners, musicales, readings, little comedies in the theatre; there was continual coming and going, calling, dropping in for a cup of tea, late suppers after the opera; the young fellows of town found no place so agreeable for a half-hour after business as Mrs. Henderson's reception-room. I fancied that life would be dull and hang heavily, especially for Margaret, without this perpetual movement and excitement. Henderson, who certainly had excitement enough without seeking it at home, was pleased that his wife should be a leader in society, as he was in the great enterprises in which his fortune waxed to enormous proportions. About what we call the home life I do not know. Necessarily, as heretofore, Henderson was often absent, and whether Margaret accompanied him or not, a certain pace of life had to be kept up.

I suppose there is no delusion more general than that of retiring upon a fortune as if, when gained, a fortune would let a person retire, or, still more improbable, as if it ever were really attained. It is not at all probable that Henderson had set any limit to that he desired; the wildest speculations about its amount would no doubt fall short of satisfying the love of power which he expected to gratify in immeasurably increasing it. Does not history teach us that to be a great general, or poet, or philanthropist, is not more certain to preserve one's name than to be the richest man, the Croesus, in his age? I could imagine Margaret having a certain growing pride in this distinction, and a glowing ambition to be socially what her husband was financially.

Heaven often plans more mercifully for us than we plan for ourselves. Had not the Hebrew prophets a vision of the punishment by prosperity? Perhaps it applied to an old age, gratified to the end by possession of everything that selfishness covets, and hardened into absolute worldliness. I knew once an old lady whose position and wealth had always made her envied, and presumably happy, who was absolutely to be pitied for a soul empty of all noble feeling.

The sun still shone on Margaret, and life yielded to her its specious sweets. She was still young. If in her great house, in her dazzling career, in the whirl of resplendent prosperity, she had hours of unsatisfied yearning for something unattainable in this direction, the world would not have guessed it. Whenever we heard of her she was the centre and star of whatever for the moment excited the world of fashion. It was indeed, at last, in the zenith of her gay existence that I, became aware of a certain feminine anxiety about her in our neighborhood. She had been, years before, very ill in Paris, and the apprehensions for her safety now were based upon the recollection of her peril then. The days came when the tender-hearted Miss Forsythe went about the house restless, impatient, tearful, waiting for a summons that was sure to come when she was needed. She thought only of her child, as she called her, and all the tenderness of her nature was stirred-these years of cloud and separation and pain were as they had not been. Little Margaret had promised to send for her. She would not obtrude before she was wanted, but Margaret was certain to send. And she was ready for departure the instant the despatch came from Henderson "Margaret wants you to come at once." I went with her.

In calamity, trouble, sorrow, it is wonderful how the ties of blood assert themselves. In this hour I am sure that Margaret longed for no one more than her dear aunt, in whose arms, as a child, she had so often forgotten her griefs. She had been able to live without her nay, for a long time her presence had been something of a restraint and a rebuke, and her feelings had hardened towards her. Why is it that the heart hardens in prosperity?

When we arrived Margaret was very ill. The house itself had a serious air: it was no longer the palace of festivity and gayety, precautions had been taken to secure quiet, the pavement was littered, and within the hushed movements and the sombre looks spoke of apprehension and the absence of the spirit that had been the life and light of the house. Our arrival seemed to be a relief to Henderson. Little was said. I had never before seen him nervous, never before so restless and anxious, probably never before in all his career had he been unnerved with a sense of his own helplessness.

"She has been asking for you this moment," he said, as he accompanied Miss Forsythe to Margaret's apartment.

"Dear, dear aunt, I knew you would come I love you so;" she had tried to raise herself a little in her bed, and was sobbing like a child in her aunt's arms.

"You must have courage, Margaret; it will all be well."

"Yes, but I'm so discouraged; I'm so tired."

The vigil began. The nurses were in waiting. The family physician would not leave the house. He was a man of great repute in his profession. Dr. Seftel's name was well known to me, but I had never met him before; a man past middle life, smooth shaven, thin iron-gray hair, grave, usually taciturn, deliberate in all his movements, as if every gesture were important and significant, but with a kindly face. Knowing that every moment of his waking life was golden, I could not but be impressed with the power that could command his exclusive service for an indefinite time. When he came down, we talked together in Henderson's room.

"It is a question of endurance, of constitution," he said; "many weak women have this quality of persistence; many strong women go to pieces at once; we know little about it. Mrs. Henderson" glancing about him "has everything to live for; that's in her favor. I suppose there are not two other men in the country whose fortune equals Henderson's."

I do not know how it was, probably the patient was not forgotten, but in a moment the grave doctor was asking me if I had seen the last bulletin about the yacht regatta. He took the keenest interest in the contest, and described to me the build and sailing qualities of the different yachts entered, and expressed his opinion as to which would win, and why. From this he passed to the city government and the recent election like a true New Yorker, his chief interest centred in the city politics and not in the national elections. Without the least unbending from his dignity, he told me many anecdotes about city politicians, which would have been amusing if I had not been anxious about other things.

The afternoon passed, and the night, and the day, I cannot tell how. But at evening I knew by the movements in the house that the crisis had come. I was waiting in Henderson's library. An hour passed, when Henderson came hurrying in, pale, excited, but joyous.

"Thank God," he cried, "it is a boy!"

"And Margaret?" I gasped.

"Is doing very well!" He touched a bell, and gave an order to the servant. "We will drink to the dear girl and to the heir of the house."

He was in great spirits. The doctor joined us, but I noticed that he was anxious, and he did not stay long. Henderson was in and out, talking, excited, restless.

But everything was going very well, he thought. At last, as we sat talking, a servant appeared at the door, with a frightened look.

"The baby, sir!"

"What?"

Alas! there had been an heir of the house of Henderson for just two hours; and Margaret was not sustaining herself.

Why go on? Henderson was beside himself; stricken with grief, enraged, I believe, as well, at the thought of his own impotence. Messengers were despatched, a consultation was called. The best skill of the city, at any cost, was at Margaret's bedside. Was there anything, then, that money could not do? How weak we are!

The next day the patient was no better, she was evidently sinking. The news went swiftly round the city. It needed a servant constantly at the door to answer the stream of sympathetic inquirers. Reporters were watching the closed house from the opposite pavement. I undertook to satisfy some of them who gained the steps and came forward, civil enough and note-books in hand, when the door was opened. This intrusion of curiosity seemed so dreadful.

The great house was silent. How vain and empty and pitiful it all seemed as I wandered alone through the gorgeous apartments! What a mockery it all was of the tragedy impending above-stairs the approach on list-shod feet of the great enemy! Let us not be unjust. He would have come just the same if his prey had lain in a farmhouse among the hills, or in a tenement-house in C Street.

A day and a night, and another day and then! It was Miss Forsythe who came down to me, with strained eyes and awe in her face. It needed no words. She put her face upon my shoulder, and sobbed as if her heart were broken.

I could not stay in the house. I went out into the streets, the streets brilliant in the sun of an autumn day, into the town, gay, bustling, crowded, pulsing with vigorous life. How blue the sky was! The sparrows twittered in Madison Square, the idlers sat in the sun, the children chased their hoops about the fountain.

I wandered into the club. The news had preceded me there. More than one member in the reading-room grasped my hand, with just a word of sympathy. Two young fellows, whom I had last seen at the Henderson dinner, were seated at a small table.

"It's rough, Jack" the speaker paused, with a match in his hand "it's rough. I'll be if she was not the finest woman I ever knew."

My wife and I were sitting in the orchestra stalls of the Metropolitan. The opera was Siegfried. At the close of the first act, as we turned to the house, we saw Carmen enter a box, radiant, in white. Henderson followed, and took a seat a little in shadow behind her. There were others in the box. There was a little movement and flutter as they came in and glasses were turned that way.

"Married, and it is only two years," I said.

"It is only a year and eight months," my wife replied.

And the world goes on as cheerfully and prosperously as ever.

www.ingramcontent.com/pod-product-compliance
Lightning Source LLC
Chambersburg PA
CBHW082127180726
48291CB00010B/2758
9781836579663